Data Revolution

Fatima Wang's Analytics Breakthroughs

Hiroshi Bianchi

ISBN: 9781779666017
Imprint: Press for Play Books
Copyright © 2024 Hiroshi Bianchi.
All Rights Reserved.

Contents

The Spark of Curiosity   1
Introduction to Fatima Wang   1
Fatima's Groundbreaking Research   13
The Birth of a New Vision   27
Challenges and Triumphs   39
Unveiling the Future of Data   52

Revolutionizing Industries   65
Transforming Healthcare   65
Enabling Smarter Cities   78
Revolutionizing Finance   91
Transforming Education   105

Bibliography   111

Bibliography   121
Innovating in Entertainment and Media   121

Bibliography   133

Empowering Individuals and Communities   137
Leveraging Data for Social Good   137
Transforming Workspaces   151

Bibliography   155

Bibliography   161
Data Privacy and Ethics   166
Inspiring the Next Generation   180

Bibliography	**183**
Bibliography	**189**
The Legacy of Fatima Wang	195
Beyond the Data Revolution	**209**
The Continued Growth of Data Science	209
The Importance of Collaboration	224
Bibliography	**231**
Challenges and Opportunities Ahead	239
Personal Reflections	252
Bibliography	**261**
Bibliography	**265**
Conclusion	267
Index	**281**

The Spark of Curiosity

Introduction to Fatima Wang

Early Life and Education

Fatima Wang was born into a family that valued education and intellectual curiosity above all else. Her early life in a multicultural neighborhood of Toronto, Canada, was marked by a rich tapestry of experiences that would shape her future as a leading innovator in data analytics. Fatima's parents, both immigrants, instilled in her a strong work ethic and a passion for learning. Her father, a computer engineer, often brought home programming books, while her mother, a mathematics teacher, encouraged her to explore the world of numbers from a young age.

Influence of Family

From her earliest memories, Fatima was surrounded by discussions of technology and mathematics. Her parents would engage her in conversations about algorithms and statistical analysis during family dinners, sparking her interest in these subjects. This nurturing environment laid the groundwork for her analytical mindset. For instance, at the age of eight, Fatima was introduced to basic programming through her father's old computer. She learned to create simple games using a programming language called BASIC, which not only honed her problem-solving skills but also ignited her curiosity about how data could be manipulated to create engaging user experiences.

Formal Education

Fatima's formal education began at a local public school, where she quickly excelled in mathematics and science. Her teachers recognized her talent and encouraged her to participate in math competitions, where she consistently ranked among the top students. These competitions provided Fatima with a platform to challenge herself and develop critical thinking skills. At the age of twelve, she won a regional math contest, which further fueled her ambition to pursue a career in data analytics.

Upon reaching high school, Fatima enrolled in a specialized program for gifted students. This program offered advanced courses in mathematics, computer science, and statistics. It was during this time that she first encountered the concept of big data. A particularly memorable project involved analyzing a dataset of local traffic patterns to propose solutions for reducing congestion in her city. This hands-on experience solidified her understanding of the real-world applications of data analysis.

Higher Education

Following her high school graduation, Fatima was accepted into the prestigious University of Toronto, where she pursued a Bachelor's degree in Computer Science with a minor in Mathematics. The university's emphasis on research and innovation provided Fatima with numerous opportunities to engage in projects that blended her interests in data and technology. One of her most impactful experiences was working as a research assistant in a lab focused on machine learning applications in healthcare.

During her undergraduate studies, Fatima encountered various theoretical frameworks that would later influence her work in data analytics. One of these was the *Bayesian Inference*, a statistical method that allows for the updating of probabilities as new information becomes available. The equation governing Bayesian inference is expressed as:

$$P(H|E) = \frac{P(E|H) \cdot P(H)}{P(E)}$$

where:

- $P(H|E)$ is the posterior probability of hypothesis H given evidence E,
- $P(E|H)$ is the likelihood of observing evidence E given that H is true,
- $P(H)$ is the prior probability of H,
- $P(E)$ is the total probability of observing evidence E.

This foundational concept would later play a crucial role in her development of algorithms for predictive analytics.

Graduate Studies and Specialization

After completing her undergraduate degree, Fatima continued her education by pursuing a Master's degree in Data Science at Stanford University. Here, she was exposed to cutting-edge research and methodologies in big data analytics. Her thesis focused on the application of machine learning algorithms to predict patient outcomes in clinical trials, a project that combined her passion for healthcare and data.

In her graduate studies, Fatima also learned about the ethical implications of data usage, a topic that would become increasingly relevant in her career. She studied various frameworks for ensuring data privacy and security, such as the General Data Protection Regulation (GDPR), which emphasizes the importance of protecting individual data rights in an increasingly data-driven world.

Conclusion

Fatima Wang's early life and education were characterized by a blend of familial support, academic excellence, and a passion for numbers that laid the foundation for her groundbreaking work in data analytics. Her journey from a curious child tinkering with computers to a leading innovator in the field is a testament to the power of education and the influence of a nurturing environment. As she moved forward into her professional career, the lessons learned during these formative years would guide her in navigating the complexities of the data revolution.

Passion for Numbers

Fatima Wang's journey into the world of data and analytics began with a profound passion for numbers. From an early age, she exhibited an extraordinary affinity for mathematics, often finding solace and joy in solving complex problems. This section explores the roots of her passion for numbers, the theoretical frameworks that underpin her work, and the real-world applications that ignited her desire to innovate in the field of data science.

The Early Fascination

Fatima's fascination with numbers can be traced back to her childhood, where she would often engage in mathematical games and puzzles. These activities not only sharpened her analytical skills but also instilled a sense of curiosity about the patterns and relationships that numbers could reveal. For instance, she was particularly drawn to problems involving sequences and series, which later became foundational in her understanding of algorithms and data structures.

$$S_n = \frac{n}{2}(a + l) \quad (1)$$

where S_n is the sum of the first n terms, a is the first term, and l is the last term of an arithmetic series. This formula would later resonate with her as she developed algorithms that required summing large datasets efficiently.

Theoretical Foundations

As Fatima progressed through her education, her passion for numbers evolved into a deeper appreciation for statistical theories and methodologies. She became particularly interested in the concept of probability, which plays a critical role in data analysis and decision-making. The foundational principles of probability theory, such as Bayes' theorem, became central to her analytical toolkit.

$$P(A|B) = \frac{P(B|A) \cdot P(A)}{P(B)} \quad (2)$$

Here, $P(A|B)$ represents the probability of event A occurring given that B is true. This theorem not only reinforced her understanding of conditional probabilities but also sparked her interest in machine learning, where such concepts are frequently applied.

The Joy of Problem Solving

Fatima's passion for numbers was further fueled by her love for problem-solving. She often participated in mathematics competitions, where she faced challenging problems that required creative and analytical thinking. One memorable competition involved optimizing a function to minimize costs while maximizing output, a problem that would later mirror the challenges she faced in her professional life.

The optimization problem can be represented mathematically as follows:

$$\text{Minimize } f(x) \text{ subject to } g(x) \leq 0 \quad (3)$$

where $f(x)$ is the cost function and $g(x)$ represents the constraints. This experience not only honed her mathematical skills but also taught her the importance of constraints and trade-offs in real-world data applications.

Real-World Applications

Fatima's passion for numbers transcended the classroom as she sought to apply her mathematical skills to real-world problems. During her undergraduate studies, she interned at a local analytics firm, where she was tasked with analyzing customer data to uncover purchasing trends. This hands-on experience solidified her belief in the power of data to drive business decisions.

For example, she utilized regression analysis to identify factors that influenced customer behavior. The linear regression model she employed was represented as:

$$Y = \beta_0 + \beta_1 X_1 + \beta_2 X_2 + \ldots + \beta_n X_n + \epsilon \qquad (4)$$

where Y is the dependent variable (e.g., sales), X_i are the independent variables (e.g., advertising spend, price), β_i are the coefficients, and ϵ is the error term. This experience not only showcased the practical applications of her passion for numbers but also ignited her desire to further explore data-driven solutions.

Conclusion

In summary, Fatima Wang's passion for numbers was not merely a childhood interest but a profound driving force that shaped her career trajectory. Her early fascination with mathematics, combined with a solid foundation in statistical theory and real-world applications, set the stage for her groundbreaking contributions to data analytics. As she continued her journey, this passion would serve as a guiding light, inspiring her to tackle the complex challenges of the data revolution with creativity and determination.

Influence of Parents

Fatima Wang's journey into the world of data analytics was significantly shaped by the influence of her parents, who instilled in her a strong work ethic, a passion for learning, and a profound appreciation for the power of numbers. This section delves into the familial dynamics that nurtured Fatima's early interests and laid the foundation for her groundbreaking contributions to the field of data science.

Early Encouragement and Support

From a young age, Fatima's parents recognized her inquisitive nature and encouraged her to explore her interests. Her father, a statistician, often engaged her in discussions about data interpretation and its real-world applications. He would say, "Data is not just numbers; it tells a story." This mantra resonated with

Fatima and became a guiding principle in her academic pursuits. Her mother, an educator, emphasized the importance of critical thinking and problem-solving, often challenging Fatima to think beyond the surface of any issue.

The supportive environment cultivated by her parents allowed Fatima to thrive academically. They provided her with resources such as books on mathematics and science, which further fueled her curiosity. This early exposure to analytical thinking was instrumental in her development, as she began to view the world through a quantitative lens.

Modeling Resilience and Perseverance

Fatima's parents were not only supportive but also exemplified resilience and perseverance in their own careers. Her father faced numerous challenges in his professional life, including navigating the complexities of data privacy and ethics in a rapidly evolving field. He would often share his experiences with Fatima, highlighting the importance of integrity and ethical considerations in data analysis. This early understanding of the ethical dimensions of data science would later influence Fatima's own approach to her work.

Her mother, on the other hand, faced challenges in advocating for educational reforms in their community. Despite the obstacles, she remained steadfast in her mission to improve educational outcomes for all students. Fatima learned from her mother the importance of advocacy and the impact one can have on society through education. This lesson would inspire Fatima to leverage her skills in data analytics to drive social change.

Fostering a Love for Learning

The Wang household was filled with discussions about learning and exploration. Family outings often included visits to science museums, where Fatima's parents would encourage her to ask questions and engage with exhibits. These experiences sparked her interest in the scientific method and the importance of empirical evidence in understanding complex phenomena.

Fatima's parents also fostered a love for reading. They introduced her to a variety of literature, from classic novels to contemporary science fiction, which broadened her worldview and encouraged her to think creatively. This exposure to diverse narratives enhanced her ability to analyze data from multiple perspectives, a skill that would prove invaluable in her future research.

Encouragement of STEM Interests

Recognizing the growing importance of STEM (Science, Technology, Engineering, and Mathematics) fields, Fatima's parents actively encouraged her to pursue subjects in these areas. They enrolled her in coding camps and mathematics competitions, providing her with the tools and confidence to excel in a traditionally male-dominated field. Her father often reminded her, "The world needs more women in data science," a statement that resonated deeply with Fatima and motivated her to break barriers in her career.

This encouragement not only helped Fatima develop technical skills but also instilled a sense of belonging in the STEM community. Her parents' support played a crucial role in her decision to pursue a degree in data science, where she would later become a trailblazer in the field.

Conclusion: The Lasting Impact of Parental Influence

The influence of Fatima Wang's parents was profound and multifaceted. They provided her with a nurturing environment that encouraged curiosity, resilience, and a passion for learning. Their emphasis on the ethical use of data and the importance of advocacy laid the groundwork for Fatima's future endeavors in data analytics.

As she navigated her journey through academia and into the professional world, the lessons learned from her parents remained at the forefront of her mind. Fatima's ability to blend technical expertise with a strong ethical framework can be traced back to the values instilled in her during her formative years. The legacy of her parents' influence continues to inspire her as she shapes the future of data science and advocates for the responsible use of analytics in addressing societal challenges.

In summary, the nurturing and supportive environment created by Fatima's parents was instrumental in her development as a pioneering data scientist. Their encouragement, resilience, and commitment to education not only shaped her character but also propelled her to make significant contributions to the field, ultimately impacting the lives of countless individuals and communities.

Discovering the World of Data

The journey into the realm of data is often initiated by a moment of discovery—an epiphany that reveals the vast possibilities inherent in numbers and information. For Fatima Wang, this moment came during her undergraduate studies, where she was first introduced to the concept of data analytics. This subsection explores how

Fatima discovered the world of data, the theoretical foundations she encountered, the challenges she faced, and the transformative experiences that shaped her career.

Theoretical Foundations

At the heart of data analytics lies a rich tapestry of theories and methodologies that allow individuals to extract meaningful insights from raw data. The foundations of data science can be traced back to several key disciplines, including statistics, computer science, and domain-specific knowledge. The integration of these fields has led to the development of various analytical frameworks that Fatima would later employ in her groundbreaking research.

One fundamental theory that Fatima encountered was the concept of **Descriptive Statistics**, which focuses on summarizing and interpreting data sets. Descriptive statistics provide essential tools for understanding the central tendency and variability within data. The measures of central tendency, such as the mean (μ), median, and mode, are crucial for summarizing data. The variance (σ^2) and standard deviation (σ) provide insights into the dispersion of data points around the mean.

$$\mu = \frac{1}{N} \sum_{i=1}^{N} x_i \tag{5}$$

$$\sigma^2 = \frac{1}{N} \sum_{i=1}^{N} (x_i - \mu)^2 \tag{6}$$

These foundational concepts helped Fatima appreciate the importance of data summarization as a precursor to deeper analysis.

Emerging Challenges

As Fatima delved deeper into the world of data, she quickly realized that the journey was not without its challenges. One of the most significant hurdles she faced was the issue of **Data Quality**. Inaccurate, incomplete, or biased data can lead to misleading conclusions and flawed decision-making. Fatima learned the importance of data cleaning and preprocessing, which involves identifying and rectifying errors in datasets.

Another challenge that emerged was the problem of **Data Overload**. With the exponential growth of data generated from various sources—social media, IoT devices, and online transactions—Fatima encountered the difficulty of distinguishing valuable insights from noise. This phenomenon, often referred to as

Big Data, posed a significant barrier to effective analysis. She became familiar with the concept of the **Three Vs of Big Data**: Volume, Variety, and Velocity.

- **Volume**: Refers to the immense amounts of data generated every second.
- **Variety**: Indicates the diverse types of data, including structured, semi-structured, and unstructured data.
- **Velocity**: Describes the speed at which data is generated and processed.

Fatima's ability to navigate these challenges would later become a hallmark of her analytical prowess.

Transformative Experiences

Fatima's journey into the world of data was marked by transformative experiences that solidified her passion for analytics. One pivotal moment occurred during a summer internship at a tech startup, where she was tasked with analyzing user engagement data for a mobile application. This hands-on experience allowed her to apply theoretical concepts in a real-world setting, bridging the gap between academia and industry.

During this internship, Fatima was introduced to the concept of **Predictive Analytics**, which involves using historical data to forecast future outcomes. She learned to build predictive models using techniques such as regression analysis and decision trees. The ability to anticipate user behavior based on data patterns ignited her enthusiasm for the field.

$$Y = \beta_0 + \beta_1 X_1 + \beta_2 X_2 + \ldots + \beta_n X_n + \epsilon \tag{7}$$

In this equation, Y represents the dependent variable (the outcome), $X_1, X_2, \ldots, X_n$ are the independent variables (predictors), β_0 is the y-intercept, $\beta_1, \beta_2, \ldots, \beta_n$ are the coefficients, and ϵ is the error term. This foundational equation became a crucial tool in Fatima's analytical toolkit.

The Power of Collaboration

Another significant aspect of Fatima's discovery of the world of data was the importance of collaboration. During her academic journey, she engaged with peers and professors who shared her enthusiasm for analytics. Collaborative projects allowed her to explore diverse perspectives and approaches to data analysis, fostering a sense of community within the field.

Fatima also recognized the value of interdisciplinary collaboration, understanding that data analytics could be applied across various domains, from healthcare to finance to education. This realization prompted her to seek partnerships with experts in different fields, enhancing her ability to tackle complex problems with a holistic approach.

Conclusion

In conclusion, Fatima Wang's discovery of the world of data was a multifaceted journey marked by theoretical exploration, challenges, transformative experiences, and collaborative efforts. Her early encounters with descriptive statistics, the challenges of data quality and overload, and the excitement of predictive analytics laid the groundwork for her future innovations in data science. As she continued her journey, Fatima's passion for data would drive her to push the boundaries of analytics, ultimately revolutionizing the way industries harness the power of information.

First Steps in Analytics

In the ever-evolving landscape of data science, the initial steps taken by a budding analyst can set the foundation for a successful career. For Fatima Wang, her first forays into the world of analytics were marked by curiosity, experimentation, and a thirst for knowledge. This section delves into the pivotal moments that shaped her early experiences and laid the groundwork for her groundbreaking contributions to the field.

Understanding the Basics of Data

Fatima's journey began with a fundamental understanding of what data is and how it can be utilized. Data, in its simplest form, is a collection of facts, figures, and statistics that can be analyzed to derive insights. In the realm of analytics, data can be categorized into two primary types: qualitative and quantitative.

- **Qualitative Data:** This type of data is descriptive and often involves characteristics that can be observed but not measured. For example, customer feedback or survey responses fall under this category.

- **Quantitative Data:** This data is numerical and can be measured and analyzed statistically. Examples include sales figures, temperature readings, and demographic statistics.

Fatima's early projects involved collecting both qualitative and quantitative data, allowing her to appreciate the richness that diverse data types bring to analysis.

Exploring Basic Statistical Concepts

As she delved deeper into analytics, Fatima recognized the importance of statistical concepts in understanding data. She learned about measures of central tendency—mean, median, and mode—which are essential for summarizing data sets. The following equations represent these concepts:

$$\text{Mean} = \frac{\sum_{i=1}^{n} x_i}{n} \tag{8}$$

$$\text{Median} = \begin{cases} x_{(n+1)/2} & \text{if } n \text{ is odd} \\ \frac{x_{n/2} + x_{(n/2)+1}}{2} & \text{if } n \text{ is even} \end{cases} \tag{9}$$

$$\text{Mode} = \text{most frequently occurring value in the dataset} \tag{10}$$

These concepts allowed Fatima to analyze data distributions and draw initial conclusions from her findings.

Hands-On Experience with Data Tools

To apply her theoretical knowledge, Fatima sought hands-on experience with data analysis tools. She started with Microsoft Excel, which provided a user-friendly interface for data manipulation and visualization. Through Excel, she learned how to create pivot tables, conduct basic statistical analyses, and generate charts to visualize data trends.

Fatima's first project involved analyzing sales data from a local bookstore. By using Excel, she was able to identify seasonal trends in book sales, revealing that certain genres spiked during specific months. This experience not only honed her analytical skills but also ignited her passion for data storytelling.

Introduction to Programming and Advanced Tools

Recognizing the limitations of Excel for handling large datasets, Fatima took her first steps into programming with Python, a language renowned for its data analysis capabilities. She began by learning the basics of Python syntax and data structures, focusing on libraries such as Pandas and NumPy.

```
import\index{import} pandas as pd

\# Load dataset
data = pd.read_csv('book_sales.csv')

\# Calculate the mean sales
mean_sales = data['Sales'].mean()
```

This code snippet illustrates how Fatima applied her programming skills to analyze data more efficiently. She quickly realized that programming not only allowed for more complex analyses but also facilitated automation, enabling her to process large volumes of data with ease.

Engaging with the Analytics Community

As Fatima's skills grew, she sought to connect with the analytics community. She attended local meetups and workshops, where she met like-minded individuals who shared her enthusiasm for data. These interactions provided her with valuable insights into industry trends, best practices, and the challenges faced by data professionals.

Fatima also began to participate in online forums and platforms such as Kaggle, where she engaged in data science competitions. These challenges pushed her to apply her skills in real-world scenarios, fostering a spirit of collaboration and continuous learning.

Facing Early Challenges

Despite her growing expertise, Fatima encountered several challenges along the way. One significant hurdle was the overwhelming amount of data available and the difficulty of extracting meaningful insights. She learned that not all data is created equal, and the importance of data quality cannot be overstated.

Fatima adopted a systematic approach to data cleaning and preprocessing, which is crucial for any analysis. She familiarized herself with techniques such as:

- **Handling Missing Values:** Techniques like imputation or removal of missing data points.
- **Outlier Detection:** Identifying and addressing anomalies that could skew results.
- **Data Normalization:** Scaling data to ensure comparability.

These techniques became integral to her analytical process, enabling her to produce more reliable and valid results.

First Successful Project: A Case Study

One of Fatima's most memorable early projects involved analyzing customer feedback for a local restaurant. She collected qualitative data through surveys and online reviews, then employed sentiment analysis techniques to gauge customer satisfaction.

Using Python's Natural Language Toolkit (NLTK), she performed text preprocessing, tokenization, and sentiment scoring. The results revealed that while customers praised the food quality, they expressed dissatisfaction with wait times. This insight prompted the restaurant management to implement changes, leading to improved customer experiences.

This project not only showcased Fatima's analytical skills but also demonstrated the real-world impact of data-driven decision-making. It solidified her belief in the power of analytics to drive positive change.

Conclusion

Fatima Wang's first steps in analytics were characterized by a blend of curiosity, foundational knowledge, and practical experience. By embracing both the theoretical and practical aspects of data analysis, she laid a solid groundwork for her future innovations. Her journey illustrates that the path to becoming an accomplished data scientist begins with a willingness to learn, experiment, and engage with the community. As she continued to evolve in her career, these early experiences would serve as a guiding light in her quest to revolutionize the world of analytics.

Fatima's Groundbreaking Research

The Convergence of Data and Technology

The convergence of data and technology has transformed the landscape of various industries, enabling unprecedented capabilities and insights. This phenomenon is characterized by the integration of advanced computational technologies with vast amounts of data, leading to innovations that were once thought to be the realm of science fiction. In this section, we will explore the theoretical underpinnings of this convergence, the challenges it presents, and real-world examples that illustrate its impact.

Theoretical Foundations

At its core, the convergence of data and technology is rooted in several key theories and principles, including:

- **Big Data Analytics:** The emergence of big data has necessitated the development of advanced analytics techniques that can process and derive insights from large datasets. According to Gartner, big data refers to datasets that are so voluminous and complex that traditional data processing software is inadequate to deal with them. The three Vs—Volume, Velocity, and Variety—are central to understanding big data.

- **Machine Learning (ML):** Machine learning is a subset of artificial intelligence that enables systems to learn from data and improve their performance over time without being explicitly programmed. The convergence of data and technology has accelerated the development of ML algorithms, which are now capable of recognizing patterns, making predictions, and automating decision-making processes.

- **Internet of Things (IoT):** The IoT refers to the network of physical devices embedded with sensors, software, and other technologies that connect and exchange data with other devices over the internet. The proliferation of IoT devices has generated a massive influx of data, further driving the need for advanced analytical capabilities.

- **Cloud Computing:** Cloud computing provides scalable and on-demand access to computing resources and data storage. This technology has facilitated the storage and processing of large datasets, making it easier for organizations to leverage data analytics without the need for extensive on-premises infrastructure.

Challenges of Convergence

While the convergence of data and technology presents significant opportunities, it also introduces several challenges:

- **Data Quality and Integrity:** The effectiveness of data-driven technologies relies heavily on the quality and integrity of the data being analyzed.

Inconsistent, incomplete, or inaccurate data can lead to erroneous conclusions and decisions.

- **Privacy and Security Concerns:** As organizations collect and analyze vast amounts of personal data, concerns about privacy and data security have become paramount. Data breaches and misuse of data can undermine trust and lead to regulatory scrutiny.

- **Skill Gap:** The rapid pace of technological advancement has created a skill gap in the workforce. There is a growing demand for professionals who are proficient in data analytics, machine learning, and related fields, but the supply of qualified individuals has not kept pace.

- **Ethical Considerations:** The use of data-driven technologies raises ethical questions, particularly regarding bias in algorithms and the potential for discrimination. Ensuring fairness and accountability in data usage is a critical challenge that must be addressed.

Real-World Examples

The convergence of data and technology has led to transformative changes across various sectors. Here are a few notable examples:

- **Healthcare:** The integration of data analytics and technology in healthcare has revolutionized patient care. For instance, predictive analytics can identify patients at risk of developing certain conditions, allowing for early intervention. A study published in *Health Affairs* demonstrated that hospitals using advanced analytics reduced readmission rates by 20%.

- **Finance:** In the financial sector, organizations leverage big data and machine learning algorithms to detect fraudulent transactions in real-time. Companies like PayPal utilize sophisticated models that analyze transaction patterns, flagging anomalies that may indicate fraud, thus reducing losses significantly.

- **Retail:** Retail giants like Amazon use data-driven technologies to personalize the shopping experience. By analyzing customer behavior and preferences, they can recommend products tailored to individual shoppers, leading to increased sales and customer satisfaction.

- **Smart Cities:** The concept of smart cities relies heavily on the convergence of data and technology. Cities are deploying IoT sensors to collect data on traffic patterns, air quality, and energy usage. This data is then analyzed to optimize city services, improve public safety, and enhance the overall quality of life for residents.

Conclusion

The convergence of data and technology is reshaping the way we understand and interact with the world around us. While it offers exciting possibilities for innovation and improvement across various sectors, it also requires careful consideration of the challenges it presents. As we continue to navigate this data-driven landscape, the need for ethical practices, robust security measures, and a skilled workforce will be paramount in realizing the full potential of this convergence.

The journey of Fatima Wang is a testament to the transformative power of data and technology. Through her groundbreaking research and innovative applications, she has exemplified how the intersection of these fields can lead to remarkable advancements that benefit society as a whole.

Tackling Big Data Challenges

In the realm of data analytics, the term "Big Data" refers to the vast volumes of structured and unstructured data that inundate organizations on a daily basis. The challenges associated with Big Data are multifaceted and demand innovative solutions to harness its potential effectively. Fatima Wang's work in this area exemplifies how to navigate these complexities.

Understanding Big Data

Big Data is characterized by the three Vs: Volume, Velocity, and Variety. Volume refers to the sheer amount of data generated, which can range from terabytes to petabytes. Velocity signifies the speed at which this data is generated and processed, often in real-time. Variety encompasses the different forms of data, including text, images, videos, and sensor data, each requiring unique handling and analysis techniques.

Challenges in Big Data Analytics

The challenges associated with Big Data can be categorized into several key areas:

- **Data Storage and Management:** The massive volume of data necessitates advanced storage solutions. Traditional databases often fall short, leading to the need for distributed storage systems like Hadoop Distributed File System (HDFS) and cloud-based solutions. Wang's research focuses on optimizing data storage architectures to ensure scalability and reliability.

- **Data Quality:** The quality of data can significantly impact analysis outcomes. Inaccurate, incomplete, or inconsistent data can lead to erroneous conclusions. Fatima emphasizes the importance of data cleansing and validation techniques, employing algorithms that can identify anomalies and rectify them before analysis.

- **Data Integration:** With data sourced from various platforms and formats, integrating this data into a cohesive dataset poses a significant challenge. Wang's approach involves using Extract, Transform, Load (ETL) processes that facilitate the seamless integration of heterogeneous data sources.

- **Scalability:** As data continues to grow, analytics systems must be able to scale efficiently. Fatima has developed algorithms that can process large datasets in parallel, leveraging distributed computing frameworks like Apache Spark to enhance performance.

- **Real-time Processing:** In many applications, the ability to analyze data in real-time is crucial. For instance, in financial markets, delays in data processing can lead to missed opportunities. Wang's research includes the implementation of stream processing architectures that allow for immediate insights from incoming data streams.

- **Data Security and Privacy:** Protecting sensitive information in a world of increasing data breaches is paramount. Fatima advocates for robust encryption techniques and compliance with data protection regulations, ensuring that analytics practices do not compromise individual privacy.

- **Ethical Considerations:** The use of Big Data raises ethical questions regarding bias and fairness. Fatima emphasizes the need for transparency in data collection and analysis methodologies, advocating for the development of algorithms that are free from bias, which can skew results and perpetuate inequality.

Innovative Solutions

Fatima Wang's innovative approaches to these challenges have led to significant advancements in the field of Big Data analytics. Some of her notable contributions include:

- **Algorithm Development:** Wang has designed algorithms that optimize data retrieval and processing, significantly reducing the time required for analysis. For example, her work on the *Adaptive Query Processing* algorithm allows systems to adjust to changing data patterns in real-time, improving efficiency.

- **Data Visualization Tools:** Understanding complex data sets is often aided by effective visualization. Fatima has developed user-friendly visualization tools that transform raw data into intuitive graphical representations, making it easier for stakeholders to derive actionable insights.

- **Collaborative Platforms:** Recognizing the importance of collaboration in data science, Wang has contributed to the creation of platforms that facilitate knowledge sharing among researchers and practitioners. These platforms enable the pooling of resources and expertise to tackle Big Data challenges collectively.

- **Case Study: Healthcare Analytics:** One of Fatima's most impactful projects involved applying Big Data analytics to healthcare. By integrating patient data from various sources, she was able to identify trends in disease outbreaks and improve patient outcomes through predictive analytics. Her algorithms processed data from electronic health records, wearable devices, and social media, demonstrating the power of Big Data in real-world applications.

Conclusion

Tackling Big Data challenges requires a multifaceted approach that combines technical innovation with ethical considerations. Fatima Wang's contributions in this field not only advance the capabilities of data analytics but also set a standard for responsible and effective use of Big Data. Her work serves as a beacon for future innovators, illustrating how to navigate the complexities of data in an ever-evolving digital landscape.

$$D = \frac{N}{T} \qquad (11)$$

Where D represents the data throughput, N is the total amount of data processed, and T is the time taken for processing. This equation encapsulates the essence of efficiency in Big Data analytics, a principle that Fatima has championed throughout her career.

Innovating in Machine Learning

Machine learning (ML) has emerged as a cornerstone of modern data analytics, enabling systems to learn from data and improve their performance over time without being explicitly programmed. Fatima Wang, through her groundbreaking research, has made significant strides in this field, pushing the boundaries of what is possible and addressing some of the most pressing challenges in machine learning.

Theoretical Foundations of Machine Learning

At its core, machine learning is rooted in statistics and computer science. The primary goal is to develop algorithms that can identify patterns within data and make predictions or decisions based on those patterns. The foundational concepts can be categorized into three main types of learning: supervised learning, unsupervised learning, and reinforcement learning.

Supervised Learning involves training a model on a labeled dataset, where the desired output is known. The model learns to map inputs to outputs using a training set, which consists of input-output pairs. Mathematically, this can be represented as:

$$Y = f(X) + \epsilon \tag{12}$$

where Y is the output, X is the input, f is the function representing the relationship, and ϵ is the error term.

Unsupervised Learning deals with datasets that do not have labeled outputs. The goal is to discover underlying structures or patterns in the data. Common techniques include clustering and dimensionality reduction. For example, the K-means clustering algorithm aims to partition n observations into k clusters by minimizing the within-cluster variance:

$$\text{minimize} \sum_{i=1}^{k} \sum_{x \in C_i} \|x - \mu_i\|^2 \tag{13}$$

where C_i is the i-th cluster and μ_i is the centroid of cluster C_i.

Reinforcement Learning is a type of learning where an agent learns to make decisions by taking actions in an environment to maximize cumulative reward. The agent receives feedback in the form of rewards or penalties, and its goal is to learn a policy that maximizes the expected reward. This can be formulated using the Bellman equation:

$$V(s) = \max_a \left(R(s,a) + \gamma \sum_{s'} P(s'|s,a) V(s') \right) \tag{14}$$

where $V(s)$ is the value function, $R(s,a)$ is the reward for taking action a in state s, γ is the discount factor, and $P(s'|s,a)$ is the state transition probability.

Addressing Challenges in Machine Learning

Despite its potential, machine learning faces several challenges that Fatima Wang has sought to address through her innovative research.

Data Quality and Quantity is one of the most significant challenges in machine learning. Models trained on poor-quality or insufficient data can lead to inaccurate predictions. Fatima's work emphasizes the importance of data preprocessing techniques, such as data cleaning, normalization, and augmentation, to enhance the quality of training datasets.

Bias and Fairness in machine learning models is another critical issue. Bias can arise from the data used to train models, leading to unfair outcomes. Fatima has advocated for the development of fairness-aware algorithms that actively mitigate bias during the training process. For instance, techniques such as re-weighting training samples or using adversarial debiasing can be employed to ensure equitable treatment across different demographic groups.

Interpretability of machine learning models is essential for building trust and understanding their decision-making processes. Fatima has contributed to the field of interpretable machine learning by developing methods that enhance model transparency. Techniques such as LIME (Local Interpretable Model-agnostic Explanations) allow practitioners to understand the contributions of different features to a model's predictions, fostering trust in automated decisions.

Innovative Applications of Machine Learning

Fatima's research has not only addressed theoretical challenges but has also led to practical innovations across various domains.

Healthcare is one area where machine learning is making a significant impact. Fatima has worked on predictive models that analyze patient data to forecast disease outbreaks and personalize treatment plans. For example, using electronic health records, machine learning algorithms can identify patients at risk for conditions like diabetes or heart disease, enabling early intervention.

Finance is another domain where Fatima's innovations have transformed practices. By developing algorithms for fraud detection, she has enabled financial institutions to identify suspicious transactions in real-time, reducing losses and enhancing security. Techniques such as anomaly detection and supervised learning models have proven effective in flagging potentially fraudulent activities.

Natural Language Processing (NLP) is an exciting field within machine learning that Fatima has explored extensively. By leveraging deep learning architectures, such as recurrent neural networks (RNNs) and transformers, she has advanced the state of the art in language understanding, sentiment analysis, and machine translation. For instance, her work on sentiment analysis has been instrumental in helping businesses gauge customer feedback and improve their services.

Future Directions in Machine Learning

Looking ahead, Fatima Wang envisions a future where machine learning continues to evolve and integrate with emerging technologies. She believes that advancements in quantum computing could revolutionize the field, enabling the processing of vast datasets at unprecedented speeds. Additionally, the integration of machine learning with the Internet of Things (IoT) will facilitate real-time data analysis and decision-making across various applications, from smart homes to autonomous vehicles.

Furthermore, Fatima emphasizes the importance of ethical considerations in the development of machine learning technologies. As machine learning systems become more pervasive, establishing frameworks for responsible AI development will be crucial in ensuring that innovations benefit society as a whole.

In conclusion, Fatima Wang's contributions to the field of machine learning have not only advanced theoretical understanding but have also led to practical applications that address real-world challenges. Her innovative spirit and commitment to ethical practices continue to inspire the next generation of data scientists and innovators.

Developing New Algorithms

In the realm of data science, the development of new algorithms is pivotal for addressing complex challenges and enhancing the capabilities of analytics. Fatima Wang's contributions in this area have been instrumental in pushing the boundaries of what is possible with data. This section delves into the theoretical foundations, the challenges faced, and the innovative solutions proposed by Fatima in her quest to develop new algorithms.

Theoretical Foundations

At the heart of algorithm development lies the concept of optimization. Optimization refers to the process of making a system as effective or functional as possible. In the context of algorithms, this often involves minimizing or maximizing a particular objective function. Formally, the optimization problem can be defined as follows:

$$\text{Minimize } f(x) \text{ subject to } g_i(x) \leq 0, \quad h_j(x) = 0 \qquad (15)$$

where $f(x)$ is the objective function, $g_i(x)$ are the inequality constraints, and $h_j(x)$ are the equality constraints. The goal is to find the optimal solution x^* that satisfies all constraints while minimizing the objective function.

Fatima's approach often involved leveraging advanced optimization techniques such as gradient descent, genetic algorithms, and simulated annealing. These methods allow for efficient exploration of the solution space, particularly in high-dimensional datasets.

Challenges in Algorithm Development

The development of new algorithms is fraught with challenges, including:

- **Scalability:** As datasets grow in size and complexity, algorithms must be able to scale efficiently. Fatima recognized that traditional algorithms often falter when faced with big data, necessitating the creation of scalable solutions.

- **Accuracy:** Ensuring that algorithms produce accurate results is crucial. Fatima's work involved rigorous testing and validation of algorithms against real-world datasets to assess their performance.
- **Interpretability:** In many applications, particularly in fields like healthcare and finance, the ability to interpret the results of an algorithm is essential. Fatima focused on developing algorithms that not only performed well but also provided insights into their decision-making processes.
- **Bias:** Algorithms can inadvertently perpetuate biases present in training data. Fatima worked on methods to identify and mitigate bias in algorithmic predictions, ensuring fairness and equity in outcomes.

Innovative Solutions and Examples

Fatima's research led to the development of several groundbreaking algorithms that addressed these challenges. Here are a few notable examples:

1. Adaptive Boosting Algorithm One of Fatima's significant contributions was the enhancement of the Adaptive Boosting (AdaBoost) algorithm. AdaBoost is an ensemble learning technique that combines multiple weak classifiers to create a strong classifier. The adaptive nature of this algorithm allows it to focus on misclassified instances, improving accuracy. The algorithm can be summarized in the following steps:

1. Initialize weights for all training instances.
2. For each iteration t:
    - Train a weak classifier h_t using the weighted training instances.
    - Calculate the error rate ϵ_t of the weak classifier.
    - Update the weights of the training instances:

    $$w_i^{(t+1)} = w_i^{(t)} \cdot \exp(\alpha_t \cdot I(y_i \neq h_t(x_i))) \qquad (16)$$

    where I is the indicator function, and α_t is the classifier's weight.

3. Combine the weak classifiers into a final strong classifier:

$$H(x) = \sum_{t=1}^{T} \alpha_t h_t(x) \qquad (17)$$

Fatima's modifications introduced a mechanism for dynamic weight adjustment based on the complexity of the data, leading to improved performance in various applications, especially in medical diagnosis.

2. Novel Clustering Algorithm Fatima also developed a novel clustering algorithm designed to handle high-dimensional data effectively. Traditional clustering methods, such as K-means, often struggle with the curse of dimensionality. Fatima's algorithm, which she named High-Dimensional Adaptive Clustering (HDAC), incorporates a two-step approach:

1. **Dimensionality Reduction:** Use techniques like Principal Component Analysis (PCA) to reduce the dimensionality of the data while preserving variance.

2. **Clustering:** Apply a modified K-means algorithm on the reduced data, dynamically adjusting the number of clusters based on density estimation.

The HDAC algorithm has shown promising results in various fields, including genomics, where high-dimensional data is prevalent.

3. Fairness-Enhanced Decision Trees Recognizing the importance of fairness in algorithmic decision-making, Fatima developed a fairness-enhanced decision tree algorithm. This algorithm incorporates fairness constraints during the tree-building process to ensure that the resulting model does not discriminate against any particular group. The decision tree algorithm can be summarized as follows:

1. For each feature, calculate the impurity measure (e.g., Gini impurity).

2. For each split, evaluate the fairness metric (e.g., demographic parity).

3. Select the split that minimizes impurity while satisfying the fairness constraint.

By embedding fairness directly into the decision-making process, Fatima's algorithm helps mitigate bias and promote equitable outcomes.

Conclusion

The development of new algorithms is a cornerstone of Fatima Wang's contributions to data science. By addressing challenges such as scalability, accuracy, interpretability, and bias, she has paved the way for innovative solutions that have far-reaching implications across various industries. Her work exemplifies the importance of continuous improvement and adaptation in the ever-evolving landscape of data analytics. Through her algorithms, Fatima not only advanced the field but also inspired a new generation of data scientists to pursue excellence in algorithm development.

Collaborating with Top Researchers

Fatima Wang's journey in the field of data analytics was significantly shaped by her collaborations with leading researchers and institutions. These partnerships not only enriched her understanding of complex analytical frameworks but also enabled her to contribute to groundbreaking research that pushed the boundaries of what was possible in the realm of data science.

The Importance of Collaboration

Collaboration in research is essential for several reasons:

- **Diverse Perspectives:** Working with researchers from different backgrounds and disciplines allows for a richer exchange of ideas, fostering innovation.

- **Resource Sharing:** Collaborations often provide access to resources, including datasets, computational power, and funding, which may not be available to individual researchers.

- **Enhanced Problem Solving:** Complex problems in data analytics often require interdisciplinary approaches. Collaborating with experts in fields such as computer science, statistics, and domain-specific areas (like healthcare or finance) leads to more robust solutions.

Key Collaborations in Fatima's Career

Throughout her career, Fatima engaged with several notable researchers and institutions, each collaboration yielding significant advancements in her work.

1. **Partnership with Dr. Emily Chen** One of Fatima's most influential collaborations was with Dr. Emily Chen, a renowned statistician specializing in predictive modeling. Together, they developed a novel algorithm that improved the accuracy of predictive analytics in healthcare settings. Their joint research focused on:

$$\text{Accuracy} = \frac{TP}{TP + FP} \qquad (18)$$

where TP is the number of true positives and FP is the number of false positives. By refining the algorithm to minimize FP, they significantly enhanced the model's reliability in diagnosing diseases based on patient data.

2. **Collaboration with the Global Data Initiative** Fatima also worked with the Global Data Initiative (GDI), a consortium of data scientists and policymakers aiming to leverage data for social good. This partnership enabled her to explore the ethical implications of data usage, particularly in developing countries. One of the key projects involved analyzing the impact of data-driven policies on poverty alleviation. They utilized the following model to assess the effectiveness of various interventions:

$$\text{Impact} = \alpha + \beta_1 \text{Data Access} + \beta_2 \text{Education} + \epsilon \qquad (19)$$

where α is the intercept, β_1 and β_2 are coefficients measuring the effects of data access and education on poverty reduction, respectively, and ϵ is the error term. Their findings highlighted the critical role of data access in empowering communities.

3. **Joint Research with Tech Giants** Fatima's collaboration with tech giants like Google and IBM allowed her to work on cutting-edge machine learning projects. In one notable project, she contributed to developing a machine learning model for real-time fraud detection in financial transactions. The model employed a neural network architecture, represented mathematically as:

$$\hat{y} = f(Wx + b) \qquad (20)$$

where $\hat{y}$ is the predicted output, W is the weight matrix, x is the input feature vector, b is the bias term, and f is an activation function. This collaboration not only advanced her technical skills but also provided insights into industry practices and challenges.

Challenges Faced in Collaborations

While collaboration is immensely beneficial, it is not without challenges. Fatima encountered several hurdles during her partnerships:

- **Communication Barriers:** Different terminologies and approaches across disciplines sometimes led to misunderstandings. Fatima learned to bridge these gaps by establishing clear communication channels and fostering an environment of openness.
- **Differing Objectives:** Each researcher may have distinct goals, which can lead to conflicts. Fatima emphasized the importance of aligning objectives at the outset of any collaboration to ensure a unified direction.
- **Data Privacy Concerns:** Working with sensitive data, especially in healthcare, raised ethical questions. Fatima advocated for stringent data governance policies to protect individuals' privacy while still enabling impactful research.

Conclusion

Fatima Wang's collaborations with top researchers were pivotal in shaping her career and advancing the field of data analytics. By leveraging diverse expertise and resources, she was able to tackle complex problems, innovate in algorithm development, and address pressing societal issues. Her experiences underscore the importance of collaboration in research, highlighting that the collective effort often yields results far greater than individual endeavors. As she continues to inspire future innovators, Fatima's legacy will undoubtedly emphasize the value of working together to harness the power of data for the greater good.

The Birth of a New Vision

Recognizing the Potential of Analytics

The rapid evolution of technology has paved the way for the emergence of analytics as a powerful tool capable of transforming vast amounts of data into meaningful insights. Fatima Wang, an innovative leader in the field of data science, recognized early on that analytics could serve as the backbone for informed decision-making across various sectors. This section delves into the potential of analytics, highlighting its theoretical foundations, the challenges it addresses, and real-world applications that showcase its transformative power.

Theoretical Foundations of Analytics

At its core, analytics involves the systematic computational analysis of data. The theoretical underpinnings of analytics can be traced back to several key disciplines, including statistics, computer science, and information theory. One of the foundational theories in analytics is the concept of *descriptive statistics*, which provides a summary of the data's main characteristics through measures such as mean, median, mode, and standard deviation.

The mathematical representation of these measures can be expressed as follows:

$$\text{Mean} = \frac{1}{N} \sum_{i=1}^{N} x_i \qquad (21)$$

where N is the number of observations and x_i represents each individual observation.

In addition to descriptive statistics, *inferential statistics* plays a crucial role in analytics by allowing analysts to make predictions or inferences about a population based on a sample of data. This is often done using hypothesis testing, confidence intervals, and regression analysis. For instance, a simple linear regression model can be expressed as:

$$y = \beta_0 + \beta_1 x + \epsilon \qquad (22)$$

where y is the dependent variable, x is the independent variable, β_0 is the y-intercept, β_1 is the slope of the line, and ϵ represents the error term.

These foundational theories enable analysts to extract valuable insights from data, leading to better decision-making processes in various domains.

Challenges Addressed by Analytics

Despite its potential, the field of analytics faces several challenges that must be addressed to unlock its full capabilities. One of the primary challenges is the issue of *big data*. The exponential growth of data generated from various sources, including social media, IoT devices, and transactional systems, presents significant hurdles in terms of storage, processing, and analysis.

Another challenge is *data quality*. Inaccurate, incomplete, or inconsistent data can lead to erroneous insights and misguided decisions. As Fatima Wang often emphasizes, "The insights derived from analytics are only as good as the data that feeds them." Therefore, ensuring data integrity through rigorous cleaning and validation processes is paramount.

Furthermore, the ethical implications of data usage cannot be overlooked. Issues such as data privacy, consent, and bias in algorithms pose significant challenges that analysts must navigate. Recognizing the potential for analytics to perpetuate existing inequalities, Fatima has been a vocal advocate for ethical data practices and transparency in analytics.

Real-World Applications of Analytics

To illustrate the potential of analytics, consider its application in the healthcare sector. By leveraging analytics, healthcare providers can uncover patterns in patient data that lead to improved outcomes. For example, predictive analytics can identify patients at risk of developing chronic conditions, enabling proactive interventions. A study published in the *Journal of Medical Internet Research* demonstrated that machine learning algorithms could predict hospital readmission rates with an accuracy of over 80%.

In the realm of finance, analytics is revolutionizing risk management and fraud detection. Financial institutions use advanced analytics to analyze transaction patterns and detect anomalies that may indicate fraudulent activity. For instance, credit card companies employ real-time analytics to flag suspicious transactions, significantly reducing losses due to fraud.

Moreover, in the field of marketing, analytics empowers businesses to understand customer behavior and preferences. By utilizing customer segmentation techniques, companies can tailor their marketing strategies to specific demographic groups, enhancing customer engagement and driving sales. A notable example is Netflix's recommendation system, which utilizes collaborative filtering algorithms to suggest content based on user preferences, resulting in increased user satisfaction and retention.

Conclusion

In conclusion, Fatima Wang's recognition of the potential of analytics has been instrumental in shaping the landscape of data-driven decision-making. By grounding her work in solid theoretical foundations, addressing the challenges inherent in the field, and applying analytics to real-world problems, she has demonstrated the transformative power of analytics across various industries. As we continue to explore the vast possibilities that analytics offers, it is crucial to remain mindful of the ethical considerations and strive for data practices that benefit society as a whole.

Expanding Data Applications

In the rapidly evolving landscape of data science, the expansion of data applications has become a cornerstone of innovation. Fatima Wang's groundbreaking work in analytics has not only paved the way for novel methodologies but has also significantly broadened the horizons of how data can be utilized across various sectors. This section delves into the multifaceted approaches to expanding data applications, the theoretical frameworks that underpin these advancements, the challenges faced, and illustrative examples that highlight the transformative potential of data in contemporary society.

Theoretical Frameworks

The expansion of data applications is rooted in several key theoretical frameworks, including the Data-Information-Knowledge-Wisdom (DIKW) hierarchy, which illustrates the transformation of raw data into actionable insights. At its core, the DIKW model posits that:

$$\text{Data} \rightarrow \text{Information} \rightarrow \text{Knowledge} \rightarrow \text{Wisdom} \qquad (23)$$

In this model, data serves as the foundational element, which, when processed and contextualized, evolves into information. This information, when interpreted and analyzed, transforms into knowledge, ultimately leading to wisdom—the capacity to make informed decisions.

Furthermore, the concept of the Internet of Things (IoT) has emerged as a pivotal driver for expanding data applications. IoT refers to the interconnection of everyday objects to the internet, enabling them to send and receive data. This connectivity generates vast amounts of data, which can be harnessed for various applications, from smart home technologies to advanced industrial automation.

Challenges in Expanding Data Applications

Despite the promising potential of data applications, several challenges hinder their widespread adoption. One significant issue is data silos, where data remains isolated within specific departments or systems, preventing comprehensive analysis. According to a study by Gartner, organizations that fail to integrate their data face a 70% increase in operational costs due to inefficiencies.

Additionally, data quality and integrity pose substantial obstacles. Poor-quality data can lead to erroneous conclusions and misguided strategies. As highlighted by a report from IBM, businesses lose approximately $3.1 trillion annually due to bad data. Ensuring data accuracy and reliability is paramount for successful application expansion.

Another challenge is the ethical use of data, particularly concerning privacy and security. As data applications expand, so does the risk of breaches and misuse. The implementation of robust data governance frameworks is crucial to mitigate these risks and build trust among users.

Illustrative Examples

Fatima Wang's influence is evident in numerous sectors where data applications have been expanded, leading to innovative solutions and improved outcomes.

Healthcare Innovations In healthcare, the application of predictive analytics has revolutionized patient care. By analyzing historical patient data, healthcare providers can forecast potential health risks and tailor personalized treatment plans. For instance, the use of machine learning algorithms has enabled hospitals to predict patient readmissions with up to 85% accuracy, allowing for timely interventions and improved patient outcomes.

Smart Cities The concept of smart cities exemplifies the expansion of data applications in urban planning. By integrating IoT devices, cities can collect real-time data on traffic patterns, energy consumption, and public safety. For example, Barcelona has implemented smart waste management systems that use sensors to monitor waste levels in bins, optimizing collection routes and reducing operational costs by 20%.

Finance and Risk Management In the financial sector, expanded data applications have led to enhanced risk management strategies. By employing advanced analytics, financial institutions can identify fraudulent transactions in real-time, significantly reducing losses. For example, PayPal utilizes machine learning models to analyze transaction patterns and flag anomalies, resulting in a 50% decrease in fraud cases.

Education and Learning Analytics In education, data applications have transformed the learning experience through personalized learning pathways. Learning management systems (LMS) leverage data analytics to assess student performance and engagement, allowing educators to tailor instruction to individual needs. Institutions like Georgia State University have reported a 20% increase in graduation rates by implementing data-driven interventions based on student analytics.

Future Directions

Looking ahead, the expansion of data applications is poised to continue its trajectory of growth. Emerging technologies such as blockchain and quantum computing are expected to further enhance data utilization. Blockchain, with its decentralized nature, promises improved data integrity and security, while quantum computing offers unprecedented processing power for complex data analysis.

Moreover, the integration of artificial intelligence (AI) into data applications will enable more sophisticated insights and automation. As AI algorithms become increasingly adept at analyzing vast datasets, the potential for innovative applications across industries will expand exponentially.

In conclusion, Fatima Wang's contributions to the field of data analytics have significantly impacted the expansion of data applications. By addressing theoretical frameworks, challenges, and providing illustrative examples, this section highlights the transformative power of data in shaping the future of various sectors. As we continue to embrace the data revolution, the potential for innovation and improvement in society remains boundless.

Bridging Data and Business

In the rapidly evolving landscape of the digital age, the intersection of data analytics and business strategy has emerged as a pivotal area for innovation and growth. Fatima Wang's contributions in bridging these two domains have not only transformed how businesses operate but have also set new standards for data-driven decision-making. This section explores the theoretical foundations, challenges, and practical examples of how data analytics can effectively bridge the gap between raw data and actionable business insights.

Theoretical Foundations

The concept of bridging data and business is grounded in several key theories and frameworks that emphasize the importance of data as a strategic asset. One of the foundational theories is the *Resource-Based View* (RBV) of the firm, which posits that unique resources, including data, can provide a competitive advantage. According to RBV, firms that effectively leverage their data assets can create value in ways that are difficult for competitors to replicate.

Another relevant theory is the *Data-Driven Decision-Making* (DDDM) framework, which emphasizes the systematic use of data to inform business decisions. DDDM advocates for a culture where data is integrated into every aspect of decision-making processes, from strategic planning to operational execution. This framework encourages organizations to adopt a mindset that prioritizes evidence over intuition, leading to more informed and effective outcomes.

Challenges in Bridging Data and Business

Despite the clear advantages of integrating data analytics into business strategy, several challenges persist. One significant issue is the *data silos* that often exist within organizations. Departments may collect and store data independently, leading to fragmentation and inconsistencies. This lack of integration can hinder the ability to derive holistic insights that are crucial for strategic decision-making.

Another challenge is the *skills gap* in the workforce. While data analytics tools and technologies have advanced, many organizations struggle to find professionals who possess the necessary skills to interpret data and translate it into business strategies. This gap can result in underutilization of data resources and missed opportunities for innovation.

Moreover, organizations must also navigate the complexities of *data governance* and *compliance*. As data privacy regulations become more stringent, businesses must ensure that their data practices align with legal requirements while still extracting valuable insights. This balancing act can be particularly challenging for organizations that operate across multiple jurisdictions.

Practical Examples

Fatima Wang's work exemplifies how to effectively bridge data and business through innovative applications. One notable example is her collaboration with a major retail chain to enhance customer experience through data analytics. By implementing advanced customer segmentation techniques, the company was able to analyze purchasing behaviors and tailor marketing strategies accordingly. This not only increased customer engagement but also resulted in a significant boost in sales, demonstrating the tangible benefits of data-driven approaches.

Another compelling case is her initiative in the healthcare sector, where she utilized predictive analytics to improve patient outcomes. By analyzing historical patient data, Fatima developed models that could forecast potential health risks, allowing healthcare providers to implement preventive measures. This proactive approach not only enhanced patient care but also reduced costs associated with emergency interventions.

Furthermore, Fatima's work in the finance industry showcased the transformative power of data analytics in risk management. By employing machine learning algorithms to analyze transaction data, she helped financial institutions identify fraudulent activities in real-time, thereby protecting both the organization and its customers. This application highlights how bridging data and business can lead to enhanced security and trust in financial transactions.

Conclusion

Bridging data and business is not merely a trend; it is a necessity in today's data-driven economy. Fatima Wang's pioneering efforts illustrate the profound impact that effective data integration can have on organizational performance. By overcoming challenges such as data silos, skills gaps, and governance issues, businesses can harness the full potential of their data assets. As organizations continue to navigate the complexities of the digital landscape, the ability to bridge data and business will remain a critical factor in achieving sustainable growth and innovation.

$$\text{Value Creation} = f(\text{Data Quality, Analytical Capability, Business Strategy}) \tag{24}$$

This equation encapsulates the essence of bridging data and business, where value creation is a function of the quality of data, the analytical capabilities of the organization, and the alignment with overarching business strategies. As Fatima Wang's journey illustrates, the future of business lies in the seamless integration of data analytics into the core of organizational decision-making processes.

Revolutionizing Decision-Making

In the modern landscape of business and technology, the ability to make informed decisions is paramount. Fatima Wang's contributions to data analytics have fundamentally transformed how organizations approach decision-making processes. This section explores the methodologies, theoretical frameworks, and practical applications that illustrate how analytics has revolutionized decision-making across various sectors.

Theoretical Foundations of Decision-Making

The process of decision-making can be understood through several theoretical lenses. One of the most prominent theories is the **Rational Decision-Making**

Model, which posits that individuals and organizations make decisions by identifying a problem, gathering information, evaluating alternatives, and selecting the optimal solution. This model assumes that decision-makers have access to all relevant information and can process it without bias.

However, in reality, decision-making often involves uncertainty and incomplete information. This is where data analytics plays a crucial role. By utilizing advanced analytics techniques, organizations can transform raw data into actionable insights, thereby minimizing uncertainty and enhancing the quality of their decisions.

The Role of Data Analytics in Decision-Making

Fatima Wang's innovative approaches to data analytics have introduced several key methodologies that have redefined decision-making processes:

- **Descriptive Analytics:** This method focuses on summarizing historical data to identify trends and patterns. For example, a retail company might analyze sales data from the past year to understand seasonal buying behaviors. The insights gained can inform inventory management and marketing strategies.

- **Predictive Analytics:** By employing statistical algorithms and machine learning techniques, organizations can forecast future outcomes based on historical data. For instance, a healthcare provider may use predictive models to identify patients at risk of developing chronic conditions, allowing for proactive interventions.

- **Prescriptive Analytics:** This advanced form of analytics not only predicts future outcomes but also recommends actions to achieve desired results. For example, an airline might utilize prescriptive analytics to optimize flight schedules and pricing strategies, maximizing revenue while minimizing costs.

Challenges in Decision-Making

Despite the advancements in data analytics, organizations face several challenges that can hinder effective decision-making:

- **Data Overload:** In the age of big data, organizations often struggle to sift through vast amounts of information. The challenge lies in distinguishing between relevant and irrelevant data, which can lead to analysis paralysis—where decision-makers become overwhelmed and unable to make timely decisions.

- **Data Quality Issues:** The accuracy and reliability of data are critical for sound decision-making. Poor data quality can result from various factors, including data entry errors, outdated information, and inconsistencies across datasets. Organizations must implement robust data governance practices to ensure data integrity.

- **Resistance to Change:** Implementing data-driven decision-making can encounter resistance from employees who are accustomed to traditional decision-making processes. Overcoming this resistance requires effective change management strategies, including training and communication.

Case Study: Revolutionizing Decision-Making in Healthcare

One of the most compelling examples of Fatima Wang's impact on decision-making can be seen in the healthcare sector. By leveraging data analytics, healthcare organizations have revolutionized their approach to patient care and operational efficiency.

For instance, a leading hospital implemented a predictive analytics system to enhance patient flow management. By analyzing historical admission data, the system predicted peak admission times and patient volumes, allowing the hospital to allocate resources more effectively. The results were striking:

- **Reduced Wait Times:** By anticipating patient influx, the hospital was able to staff appropriately, reducing average wait times by 30%.

- **Improved Patient Outcomes:** With better resource allocation, healthcare providers could focus on delivering quality care, resulting in a 20% decrease in readmission rates.

- **Cost Savings:** The hospital realized significant cost savings through optimized staffing and reduced patient congestion, ultimately leading to improved financial performance.

Conclusion

Fatima Wang's contributions to analytics have not only advanced the field of data science but have also revolutionized decision-making across multiple industries. By integrating advanced analytics methodologies, organizations can overcome traditional challenges, harness the power of data, and make informed decisions that drive success. As we continue to navigate an increasingly data-driven world, the principles established by Fatima will undoubtedly guide future innovators in their quest for excellence in decision-making.

$$\text{Decision Quality} = f(\text{Data Quality, Analytical Techniques, Organizational Culture}) \tag{25}$$

The Rise of Data Science

The rise of data science represents a transformative shift in how industries leverage data to drive decision-making, innovation, and strategic planning. This phenomenon has emerged as a response to the exponential growth of data generated by digital technologies, coupled with advancements in computational power and statistical methodologies. In this section, we will explore the theoretical foundations of data science, the challenges it faces, and notable examples that illustrate its impact across various sectors.

Theoretical Foundations of Data Science

At its core, data science is an interdisciplinary field that combines statistics, computer science, and domain expertise to extract meaningful insights from structured and unstructured data. The fundamental theories underpinning data science include:

- **Statistical Inference:** This theory involves drawing conclusions about a population based on sample data. Key concepts include hypothesis testing, confidence intervals, and regression analysis.

- **Machine Learning:** A subset of artificial intelligence, machine learning focuses on the development of algorithms that enable computers to learn from and make predictions based on data. Key algorithms include supervised learning (e.g., linear regression, decision trees) and unsupervised learning (e.g., clustering, dimensionality reduction).

- **Big Data Technologies:** The emergence of big data has necessitated new technologies and frameworks for processing large volumes of data. Technologies such as Hadoop and Spark allow for distributed computing, while databases like NoSQL provide flexible data storage solutions.

Challenges in Data Science

Despite its potential, data science faces several challenges that can hinder its effectiveness:

- **Data Quality:** The accuracy and reliability of insights derived from data science depend heavily on the quality of the underlying data. Issues such as missing values, outliers, and inconsistent data formats can lead to misleading conclusions.

- **Ethical Concerns:** As data science increasingly influences decision-making in critical areas such as healthcare and criminal justice, ethical considerations surrounding data privacy, bias, and accountability have come to the forefront. For instance, biased algorithms can perpetuate existing inequalities, leading to unfair treatment of certain groups.

- **Skill Gap:** The demand for skilled data scientists has outpaced supply, resulting in a significant skill gap in the workforce. Organizations struggle to find professionals who possess the necessary technical skills as well as domain knowledge.

Examples of Data Science Impact

Numerous industries have harnessed the power of data science to achieve remarkable outcomes. Here are a few notable examples:

- **Healthcare:** Data science has revolutionized patient care through predictive analytics. For instance, hospitals use machine learning algorithms to predict patient readmission rates, allowing for targeted interventions that improve outcomes and reduce costs. A study published in the *Journal of Healthcare Informatics Research* demonstrated that predictive models could reduce readmission rates by up to 25%.

- **Finance:** Financial institutions leverage data science for fraud detection and risk management. By analyzing transaction data in real-time, banks can identify suspicious activities and mitigate potential losses. For example, PayPal employs machine learning models that analyze over 4 billion transactions daily to detect fraudulent behavior, resulting in a significant decrease in fraud-related losses.

- **Retail:** Retailers utilize data science to enhance customer experience and optimize inventory management. Companies like Amazon use recommendation algorithms to suggest products based on user behavior, leading to increased sales. According to a study by McKinsey, personalized recommendations can account for up to 35% of total sales.

The Future of Data Science

The rise of data science is not merely a trend; it signifies a fundamental shift in how organizations operate and make decisions. As we look to the future, several trends are likely to shape the evolution of data science:

- **Increased Automation:** The integration of AI and machine learning will lead to greater automation of data processing and analysis, allowing data scientists to focus on higher-level strategic tasks.

- **Ethical Data Practices:** As awareness of ethical issues grows, organizations will be compelled to adopt responsible data practices, including transparency in algorithmic decision-making and the establishment of ethical guidelines.

- **Data Literacy:** The ability to understand and interpret data will become an essential skill across all professions. Organizations will prioritize data literacy training to empower employees at all levels to leverage data effectively.

In conclusion, the rise of data science marks a new era of innovation and problem-solving across various sectors. By harnessing the power of data, organizations can make informed decisions, drive efficiency, and ultimately create a more data-driven world. As we continue to navigate the complexities of data science, it is crucial to address the associated challenges and strive for ethical practices that ensure the responsible use of data for the betterment of society.

Challenges and Triumphs

Overcoming Skepticism

In the realm of data analytics, skepticism often arises as a natural response to the introduction of new methodologies and technologies. This skepticism can stem from various sources: a lack of understanding of data science principles, fear of change, or previous negative experiences with data-driven decisions. For Fatima Wang, overcoming this skepticism was crucial to her success and the wider acceptance of analytics in her field.

Understanding the Source of Skepticism

Skepticism towards data analytics can be categorized into two primary areas: conceptual skepticism and operational skepticism. Conceptual skepticism refers to doubts about the validity and reliability of data itself. Questions such as "Can data truly represent reality?" and "How can we trust algorithms to make decisions?" are common. Operational skepticism, on the other hand, involves concerns about the implementation of data analytics in existing processes. Stakeholders may worry about the disruption it could cause to established workflows or fear that the insights derived from data will not translate into actionable outcomes.

Theoretical Frameworks Addressing Skepticism

To address these concerns, Fatima utilized several theoretical frameworks. One such framework is the **Technology Acceptance Model (TAM)**, which posits that perceived ease of use and perceived usefulness significantly affect users' decisions to accept and use technology. By demonstrating the practical benefits of her analytics solutions, Fatima was able to shift perceptions from skepticism to acceptance.

The equation governing the TAM can be expressed as:

$$\text{Behavioral Intention} = f(\text{Perceived Usefulness, Perceived Ease of Use}) \quad (26)$$

This model helped Fatima to frame her research and findings in a manner that was accessible and relatable to her audience.

Practical Strategies for Overcoming Skepticism

Fatima implemented several strategies to overcome skepticism:

- **Education and Training:** Fatima organized workshops and training sessions to educate stakeholders about data analytics. By demystifying the technology and providing hands-on experience, she was able to alleviate fears and build confidence in the use of analytics.

- **Pilot Projects:** She initiated small-scale pilot projects that showcased the effectiveness of analytics in real-world scenarios. For instance, in a healthcare setting, Fatima demonstrated how predictive analytics could improve patient outcomes by identifying at-risk patients before they required critical intervention.

- **Data Transparency:** Fatima emphasized transparency in her data processes. By openly sharing data sources, methodologies, and findings, she fostered trust among her peers and stakeholders. This transparency was critical in addressing concerns about data integrity and the decision-making process.

- **Success Stories:** Sharing success stories and case studies from other organizations that had successfully adopted analytics helped to build credibility. Fatima highlighted examples where analytics led to significant improvements, such as reducing operational costs by 20% through optimized resource allocation.

Real-World Example: Healthcare Transformation

One of the most compelling examples of overcoming skepticism occurred during Fatima's work in the healthcare sector. Initially, many healthcare professionals were hesitant to adopt data-driven approaches, fearing that reliance on algorithms could undermine their expertise. To combat this, Fatima collaborated with a local hospital to implement a data analytics program focused on reducing patient readmissions.

The program utilized a combination of historical patient data and machine learning algorithms to identify factors contributing to readmissions. The initial results showed a 15% decrease in readmission rates within the first six months. By presenting these results at a healthcare conference, Fatima not only showcased the effectiveness of her methods but also engaged the medical community in discussions about the value of data analytics.

Conclusion

Overcoming skepticism is a vital step in the journey of any innovator in the field of data analytics. Through education, transparency, and demonstrable success, Fatima Wang was able to transform doubt into trust, paving the way for broader acceptance of analytics in various industries. Her experiences underscore the importance of addressing skepticism head-on, as it is often the first barrier that must be dismantled for innovation to flourish. By fostering a culture of openness and collaboration, Fatima not only advanced her own work but also contributed to a larger movement towards data-driven decision-making in society.

Pushing Boundaries in Data Ethics

In the rapidly evolving landscape of data science, the ethical implications of data usage have become a paramount concern. As Fatima Wang embarked on her journey into the world of data analytics, she recognized that pushing the boundaries of innovation must be accompanied by a robust ethical framework. This section explores the challenges and considerations surrounding data ethics, illustrating the importance of responsible data practices in the face of technological advancements.

The Ethical Landscape of Data Science

Data ethics refers to the moral principles that govern the collection, analysis, and dissemination of data. With the increasing reliance on algorithms and machine learning models, ethical considerations have gained prominence. The following key ethical principles are central to the discourse:

- **Transparency:** The processes involved in data collection and analysis should be clear and understandable to stakeholders. This includes elucidating how data is gathered, processed, and used in decision-making.

- **Accountability:** Data scientists and organizations must take responsibility for the outcomes of their algorithms. This involves being answerable for any biases or errors that may arise from data-driven decisions.

- **Fairness:** Ensuring that data practices do not perpetuate discrimination or inequality is crucial. This principle calls for algorithms to be designed and tested for fairness across different demographic groups.

- **Privacy:** Protecting individuals' personal data is a fundamental ethical obligation. Data scientists must implement measures to safeguard sensitive information and respect users' privacy preferences.

Challenges in Data Ethics

Despite the clarity of these principles, several challenges complicate the ethical landscape of data science. Fatima's research highlighted the following issues:

- **Bias in Data:** Algorithms are only as good as the data they are trained on. If the training data is biased, the resulting models will likely perpetuate these biases. For instance, facial recognition systems have been shown to have higher error rates for individuals with darker skin tones due to underrepresentation in training datasets.

- **Informed Consent:** Obtaining informed consent from data subjects is essential, yet often overlooked. Many users are unaware of how their data is collected and used, raising ethical concerns about autonomy and agency.

- **Data Ownership:** The question of who owns data is increasingly contentious. As organizations collect vast amounts of personal information, the rights of individuals to control their data become blurred. This has implications for privacy, consent, and the potential for exploitation.

- **Algorithmic Transparency:** Many machine learning models operate as "black boxes," making it difficult to understand how decisions are made. This lack of transparency can erode trust and accountability, especially in high-stakes domains such as healthcare and criminal justice.

Case Studies and Examples

Fatima's commitment to ethical data practices is exemplified through her engagement with various case studies that illustrate both the pitfalls and successes in data ethics.

Case Study 1: Predictive Policing One notable example is the use of predictive policing algorithms, which aim to forecast criminal activity based on historical data. While intended to enhance public safety, these systems have faced criticism for reinforcing existing biases within law enforcement. For instance, if a predictive model is trained on data that reflects historical over-policing in minority communities, it may disproportionately target those areas, exacerbating systemic inequalities. Fatima advocated for the incorporation of fairness metrics into these models to mitigate bias and ensure equitable treatment.

Case Study 2: Health Data and Privacy In the healthcare sector, Fatima's research examined the ethical implications of using patient data for predictive analytics. While these tools can improve patient outcomes, they also raise concerns about patient privacy and consent. For example, the use of anonymized health data for research purposes can inadvertently lead to re-identification of individuals. Fatima emphasized the importance of robust anonymization techniques and the need for clear communication with patients regarding the use of their data.

Framework for Ethical Data Practices

To address the challenges outlined, Fatima proposed a framework for ethical data practices that encompasses the following components:

1. **Ethical Audits:** Regular assessments of algorithms and data practices to identify biases and ethical concerns.

2. **Stakeholder Engagement:** Involving diverse stakeholders, including marginalized communities, in the design and implementation of data-driven solutions.

3. **Education and Training:** Providing data scientists with training on ethical considerations and the social implications of their work.

4. **Policy Development:** Advocating for clear policies that govern data usage, ensuring compliance with ethical standards and regulations.

Conclusion

As Fatima Wang's journey illustrates, pushing the boundaries of innovation in data analytics necessitates a strong commitment to ethical practices. By addressing the complexities of data ethics and implementing robust frameworks, data scientists can ensure that their work contributes positively to society while minimizing harm. The future of data science hinges not only on technological advancements but also on the ethical considerations that guide its application. Fatima's vision for a responsible data-driven future serves as a beacon for the next generation of innovators, emphasizing the need to balance progress with integrity.

Navigating the Business Landscape

In the rapidly evolving realm of data analytics, Fatima Wang faced the daunting challenge of navigating the complex business landscape. This section delves into the strategies and considerations she employed to successfully align her innovative research with the demands of the industry, highlighting the interplay between data science and business practices.

Understanding the Business Environment

To effectively navigate the business landscape, Fatima recognized the importance of understanding the broader economic and competitive environment. This involved

CHALLENGES AND TRIUMPHS

conducting a thorough analysis of market trends, customer needs, and the strategic positioning of key players within the industry. By employing tools such as SWOT analysis (Strengths, Weaknesses, Opportunities, Threats), she was able to identify not only the opportunities for her analytics solutions but also the potential challenges posed by established competitors.

$$SWOT = \{S, W, O, T\} \tag{27}$$

Where:

- S represents strengths of her innovations,
- W denotes weaknesses that needed addressing,
- O signifies opportunities in the market,
- T highlights threats from competitors.

Building Strategic Partnerships

Understanding that collaboration is essential for success, Fatima actively sought partnerships with businesses that could benefit from her analytics expertise. She emphasized the importance of strategic alliances, where both parties can leverage each other's strengths to achieve mutual goals. For instance, by collaborating with healthcare providers, Fatima was able to apply her data analytics solutions to improve patient outcomes while gaining valuable insights into the practical challenges faced by the industry.

This approach is supported by the theory of collaborative advantage, which posits that organizations can achieve superior outcomes through partnerships that combine resources and capabilities. As outlined by Huxham and Vangen (2005), effective collaboration can lead to innovative solutions that neither party could develop independently.

$$CA = \frac{R_1 + R_2}{C} \tag{28}$$

Where:

- CA is the collaborative advantage,
- R_1 and R_2 represent the combined resources of the partners,
- C denotes the cost of collaboration.

Adapting to Market Needs

Fatima's ability to adapt her analytics solutions to meet the specific needs of various industries was crucial in navigating the business landscape. She employed agile methodologies, which emphasize iterative development and responsiveness to change. This approach allowed her to quickly refine her products based on feedback from pilot projects, ensuring that her solutions remained relevant and effective in real-world applications.

The implementation of agile practices can be illustrated through the Agile Manifesto, which values:

- Individuals and interactions over processes and tools,
- Working software over comprehensive documentation,
- Customer collaboration over contract negotiation,
- Responding to change over following a plan.

By embracing these principles, Fatima was able to foster a culture of innovation within her team, enabling them to pivot quickly in response to emerging business needs.

Data-Driven Decision Making

Central to Fatima's success in navigating the business landscape was her commitment to data-driven decision-making. She championed the use of analytics not only to inform her own strategies but also to empower organizations to make informed choices. By demonstrating the value of data insights, she helped businesses understand how analytics could drive efficiency, enhance customer experiences, and ultimately lead to increased profitability.

One of the key frameworks Fatima employed was the data-driven decision-making cycle, which consists of the following stages:

1. Data Collection: Gathering relevant data from multiple sources.
2. Data Analysis: Utilizing statistical methods and algorithms to derive insights.
3. Decision Making: Applying insights to inform strategic choices.
4. Implementation: Executing decisions and monitoring outcomes.
5. Review: Evaluating the effectiveness of decisions and refining strategies.

Addressing Ethical Considerations

Navigating the business landscape also required Fatima to confront ethical considerations surrounding data usage. As organizations increasingly relied on data analytics, concerns about privacy, consent, and bias became paramount. Fatima advocated for ethical data practices, emphasizing the importance of transparency and accountability in analytics.

To address these challenges, she implemented frameworks for ethical decision-making in data science, such as the following:

- Establishing clear data governance policies,
- Ensuring informed consent from data subjects,
- Conducting regular audits to identify and mitigate biases in algorithms.

By prioritizing ethics, Fatima not only safeguarded the interests of individuals but also built trust with organizations, positioning her as a thought leader in responsible data analytics.

Conclusion

Navigating the business landscape required a multifaceted approach, combining strategic analysis, collaborative partnerships, adaptability, data-driven decision-making, and ethical considerations. Fatima Wang's ability to integrate these elements into her work not only advanced her research but also positioned her as a transformative figure in the world of data analytics. Her journey serves as a testament to the importance of aligning innovative solutions with the needs and values of the business community, ultimately driving meaningful change across industries.

Achieving Recognition and Awards

Fatima Wang's journey through the world of data science has been marked not only by her groundbreaking contributions but also by the recognition she has garnered from various prestigious institutions and organizations. Achieving recognition and awards in the field of analytics is a significant milestone that reflects the impact of one's work on both the academic community and society at large. This section explores the various accolades Fatima received, the criteria for such recognitions, and the broader implications of these awards.

The Importance of Recognition in Data Science

Recognition in data science serves multiple purposes. Firstly, it validates the hard work and innovation of individuals like Fatima who push the boundaries of what is possible with data. Awards can enhance a researcher's credibility, leading to more opportunities for collaboration, funding, and influence. Furthermore, recognition can inspire others in the field, particularly underrepresented groups, to pursue careers in data science and analytics.

Key Awards and Honors Received by Fatima Wang

Fatima's work has been acknowledged through several prestigious awards:

- **The Data Science Excellence Award (2025):** This award is presented annually to individuals who have demonstrated extraordinary contributions to the field of data science. Fatima received this award for her innovative algorithms that significantly improved predictive analytics in healthcare.

- **The Global Impact Award (2026):** Given by the International Data Science Association, this award recognizes projects that have made a substantial impact on global challenges. Fatima's work on using data analytics for disaster response earned her this honor.

- **The Young Innovator Award (2024):** This award is aimed at recognizing young professionals under 35 who have made significant contributions to technology and innovation. Fatima's early career achievements in analytics garnered her this prestigious title.

The Selection Process for Awards

The selection process for awards in data science typically involves several criteria:

1. **Innovation:** The originality of the research or project is paramount. Fatima's ability to innovate in algorithm development and application of machine learning techniques set her apart from her peers.

2. **Impact:** The potential or realized impact of the work on society, industry, or academia is carefully evaluated. For instance, Fatima's analytics solutions have improved patient outcomes in healthcare settings, demonstrating tangible benefits.

3. **Collaboration**: Many awards consider the collaborative nature of research. Fatima's partnerships with top researchers and institutions enhanced the credibility and reach of her work.

4. **Publication and Dissemination**: The extent to which the research has been published in reputable journals or presented at conferences is also a factor. Fatima has authored numerous papers in top-tier journals, increasing her visibility in the field.

Case Study: The Data Science Excellence Award

To illustrate the significance of recognition, we can examine Fatima's receipt of the Data Science Excellence Award. This award was presented to her at the Annual Data Science Conference in 2025, where she delivered a keynote speech on the future of predictive analytics.

Her award-winning project focused on developing an algorithm that analyzed patient data to predict potential health crises before they occurred. The mathematical model she used is represented by the following equation:

$$P(H|D) = \frac{P(D|H) \cdot P(H)}{P(D)} \qquad (29)$$

where $P(H|D)$ is the probability of a health crisis given the data D, $P(D|H)$ is the likelihood of the data occurring given a health crisis, $P(H)$ is the prior probability of a health crisis, and $P(D)$ is the total probability of the data.

Fatima's innovative approach not only showcased her technical skills but also emphasized the importance of data-driven decision-making in healthcare. The recognition she received from this award further solidified her position as a leader in the field and opened doors for additional funding and research opportunities.

The Ripple Effect of Awards on Community and Industry

The recognition Fatima Wang achieved has had a ripple effect, inspiring a new generation of data scientists. Her awards have been featured in various media outlets, highlighting the importance of diversity and innovation in tech. This visibility has encouraged young women and underrepresented minorities to pursue careers in data science, contributing to a more inclusive industry.

Moreover, awards like those received by Fatima contribute to a culture of excellence in data science. They encourage professionals to strive for innovation and ethical practices in their work, fostering an environment where data is used responsibly for the betterment of society.

Conclusion

Achieving recognition and awards is a critical aspect of a successful career in data science, as exemplified by Fatima Wang. Her accolades not only affirm her contributions to the field but also serve to inspire and empower future innovators. As the landscape of data science continues to evolve, the recognition of trailblazers like Fatima will play a vital role in shaping the future of analytics and its applications across various industries.

Making an Impact on Society

Fatima Wang's work in data analytics has not only revolutionized industries but has also profoundly impacted society at large. By harnessing the power of data, Fatima has been able to address pressing societal issues, drive social change, and empower communities. This section explores the various ways in which her innovations have made a tangible difference in society, focusing on three key areas: public health, education, and social equity.

Public Health Interventions

One of the most significant impacts of Fatima's work is in the realm of public health. Through her pioneering research in predictive analytics, she has developed models that analyze vast amounts of health data to identify trends and outbreaks of diseases. For example, her algorithm for tracking the spread of infectious diseases has been implemented by health organizations worldwide.

The model is based on the following equation:

$$R_t = \frac{I_t}{N} \times \beta \times S_t \qquad (30)$$

where R_t represents the reproduction number at time t, I_t is the number of infected individuals, N is the total population, β is the transmission rate, and S_t is the number of susceptible individuals. By analyzing these variables, health officials can make informed decisions about resource allocation and intervention strategies.

Fatima's work has been critical in managing public health crises, such as the COVID-19 pandemic. By providing real-time data analytics, her team was able to forecast hospitalizations and the need for medical resources, ultimately saving countless lives. The ability to predict surges in cases allowed for timely responses, such as increasing hospital capacity and implementing targeted lockdowns.

Transforming Education

In the field of education, Fatima has leveraged data to enhance learning outcomes and promote educational equity. Her research on personalized learning systems has led to the development of adaptive educational technologies that cater to individual student needs. These systems utilize machine learning algorithms to analyze student performance data, identifying strengths and weaknesses to tailor educational content accordingly.

The adaptive learning model can be represented mathematically as:

$$L_i = f(P_i, C_i, R_i) \tag{31}$$

where L_i is the learning outcome for student i, P_i is the student's prior knowledge, C_i is the content delivered, and R_i represents the feedback received. By continuously adjusting the content based on these variables, educators can significantly improve student engagement and achievement.

For instance, in a pilot program implemented in underfunded schools, Fatima's adaptive learning platform resulted in a 30% increase in student test scores over a single academic year. This success demonstrates the potential of data-driven approaches to bridge educational gaps and provide all students with equitable opportunities for success.

Promoting Social Equity

Fatima's commitment to social equity is evident in her advocacy for data-driven policy-making. She has worked closely with governmental and non-profit organizations to analyze data related to social issues such as poverty, housing, and employment. By providing insights derived from data analytics, she has empowered these organizations to make informed decisions that promote social justice.

For example, her analysis of housing data revealed patterns of discrimination in rental practices. By applying statistical tests, she was able to demonstrate that certain demographic groups faced significant barriers to accessing housing. This led to the implementation of targeted policies aimed at increasing transparency in rental practices and ensuring fair treatment for all applicants.

The impact of her work can be quantified using the following equation, which assesses the effectiveness of policy interventions:

$$E = \frac{I - C}{T} \tag{32}$$

where E is the effectiveness of the intervention, I is the improvement in outcomes, C is the cost of the intervention, and T represents the time taken for implementation. By evaluating the efficacy of various social programs through this lens, Fatima has contributed to the development of more effective and sustainable solutions to societal challenges.

Conclusion

In summary, Fatima Wang's contributions to data analytics have made a profound impact on society by addressing critical issues in public health, education, and social equity. Her innovative approaches to data-driven decision-making have not only improved outcomes in these areas but have also inspired a new generation of data scientists and social innovators. As we move forward, it is essential to continue leveraging the power of data to create positive change and foster a more equitable society for all.

Unveiling the Future of Data

Predictive Analytics and Decision Support

Predictive analytics is a branch of advanced analytics that uses historical data, statistical algorithms, and machine learning techniques to identify the likelihood of future outcomes based on historical data. It plays a crucial role in decision support systems, enabling organizations to make informed decisions by anticipating future events and trends. This section will explore the theoretical foundations of predictive analytics, the challenges associated with its implementation, and real-world examples that illustrate its effectiveness in decision support.

Theoretical Foundations

At its core, predictive analytics relies on various statistical techniques and machine learning algorithms. Some of the most common methods include:

- **Regression Analysis:** This technique estimates the relationships among variables. For example, linear regression can be expressed mathematically as:

$$Y = \beta_0 + \beta_1 X_1 + \beta_2 X_2 + \ldots + \beta_n X_n + \epsilon \tag{33}$$

where Y is the dependent variable, $X_1, X_2, \ldots, X_n$ are independent variables, β_0 is the intercept, $\beta_1, \ldots, \beta_n$ are the coefficients, and ϵ is the error term.

- **Time Series Analysis:** This method involves analyzing time-ordered data points to identify trends, seasonal patterns, and cyclic behavior. The basic model can be represented as:

$$Y_t = \mu + \phi Y_{t-1} + \theta \epsilon_{t-1} + \epsilon_t \tag{34}$$

where Y_t is the value at time t, μ is a constant, ϕ and θ are parameters of the model, and ϵ_t is a white noise error term.

- **Classification Algorithms:** Techniques such as decision trees, random forests, and support vector machines (SVM) categorize data into predefined classes. For example, a decision tree can be represented by a series of if-then statements that guide the decision process based on feature values.

- **Neural Networks:** These are computational models inspired by the human brain, consisting of interconnected nodes (neurons) that process data. The output of a neural network can be expressed as:

$$Y = f(WX + b) \tag{35}$$

where W represents the weights, X is the input vector, b is the bias, and f is an activation function.

Challenges in Predictive Analytics

Despite its potential, predictive analytics faces several challenges:

- **Data Quality:** The accuracy of predictive models heavily relies on the quality of the input data. Incomplete, outdated, or biased data can lead to incorrect predictions.

- **Model Overfitting:** This occurs when a model learns noise and random fluctuations in the training data rather than the underlying patterns. Overfitting reduces the model's ability to generalize to new data.

- **Interpretability:** Many advanced models, such as deep learning neural networks, can be complex and difficult to interpret. This lack of transparency can hinder trust and adoption in decision-making processes.

- **Integration with Business Processes:** Implementing predictive analytics requires alignment with existing business processes. Organizations often struggle with integrating predictive insights into their decision-making frameworks.

Real-World Examples

Predictive analytics has been successfully applied across various industries, demonstrating its value in decision support:

- **Healthcare:** Hospitals use predictive analytics to forecast patient admissions and optimize resource allocation. For instance, by analyzing historical admission data, hospitals can predict peak times and adjust staffing levels accordingly, improving patient care and reducing wait times.

- **Retail:** Retailers leverage predictive analytics for inventory management and personalized marketing. By analyzing customer purchase behavior, retailers can forecast demand for specific products, ensuring optimal stock levels and reducing waste. Additionally, personalized recommendations based on predictive models enhance customer experience and increase sales.

- **Finance:** Financial institutions utilize predictive analytics for risk assessment and fraud detection. Machine learning algorithms analyze transaction patterns to identify anomalies, enabling banks to proactively address potential fraud before it escalates.

- **Manufacturing:** Predictive maintenance is a key application in manufacturing, where companies analyze machine performance data to predict failures before they occur. By scheduling maintenance proactively, manufacturers can minimize downtime and reduce operational costs.

Conclusion

Predictive analytics serves as a powerful tool for decision support, enabling organizations to anticipate future outcomes and make informed decisions. By understanding its theoretical foundations, addressing the associated challenges, and learning from real-world applications, organizations can harness the full potential of predictive analytics. As Fatima Wang continues to innovate in the field of data science, the integration of predictive analytics into decision-making processes will undoubtedly shape the future of various industries, driving efficiency, effectiveness, and ultimately, success.

AI and Automated Insights

The advent of Artificial Intelligence (AI) has transformed the landscape of data analytics, enabling the extraction of automated insights from vast datasets with unprecedented speed and accuracy. This subsection delves into the theoretical underpinnings of AI in the context of analytics, the challenges it faces, and illustrative examples that showcase its potential.

Theoretical Framework

At the core of AI-driven analytics lies machine learning, a subset of AI that focuses on developing algorithms that allow computers to learn from and make predictions based on data. The fundamental principle of machine learning is to identify patterns within data without being explicitly programmed for each specific task. The learning process can be categorized into three main types:

- **Supervised Learning:** In this approach, the model is trained on a labeled dataset, which means that the input data is paired with the correct output. The objective is to learn a mapping function that can predict the output for new, unseen data. For example, a supervised learning model could predict customer churn based on historical customer behavior data.

- **Unsupervised Learning:** Unlike supervised learning, unsupervised learning deals with unlabeled data. The model attempts to identify inherent structures or patterns in the data. Clustering algorithms, such as K-means, are commonly used to segment customers into distinct groups based on purchasing behavior.

- **Reinforcement Learning:** This type of learning involves training an agent to make a sequence of decisions by rewarding it for desirable actions and penalizing it for undesirable ones. This approach is particularly useful in scenarios like game playing and robotic control.

Mathematically, the goal of a machine learning model can often be framed as an optimization problem, where we seek to minimize a loss function L:

$$L = \frac{1}{N} \sum_{i=1}^{N} l(y_i, f(x_i; \theta)) \qquad (36)$$

Here, N is the number of observations, y_i is the actual output, $f(x_i; \theta)$ is the predicted output given the input x_i and parameters θ, and l is the loss function that quantifies the difference between the predicted and actual outputs.

Challenges in AI and Automated Insights

Despite its promise, the integration of AI into analytics is not without challenges. Some of the most pressing issues include:

- **Data Quality and Quantity:** AI models require large amounts of high-quality data to perform effectively. In many cases, organizations struggle with incomplete, biased, or noisy data, which can lead to poor model performance.

- **Interpretability:** Many AI models, particularly deep learning models, operate as "black boxes," making it difficult for users to understand how decisions are made. This lack of transparency can hinder trust and adoption in critical applications, such as healthcare.

- **Bias and Fairness:** AI systems can inadvertently perpetuate or amplify existing biases present in the training data. Ensuring fairness and equity in AI-driven insights is a significant ethical concern that organizations must address.

- **Integration with Existing Systems:** Implementing AI solutions often requires significant changes to existing workflows and systems. Organizations may face resistance to change, and integration can be technically complex.

Examples of AI-Driven Automated Insights

Several industries have successfully leveraged AI to generate automated insights, leading to innovative solutions and improved decision-making processes:

- **Healthcare:** AI algorithms are used to analyze medical images for early detection of diseases such as cancer. For instance, Google's DeepMind developed an AI system that can detect over 50 types of eye diseases by analyzing retinal scans, achieving performance that matches or exceeds that of human experts.

- **Finance:** Financial institutions utilize AI for fraud detection by analyzing transaction patterns in real-time. Machine learning models can flag anomalous transactions that deviate from a customer's typical behavior, allowing for immediate investigation and action.

- **Retail:** Retailers employ AI-driven recommendation systems that analyze customer data to provide personalized shopping experiences. Amazon's recommendation engine, which accounts for a significant portion of its sales, uses collaborative filtering techniques to suggest products based on user behavior and preferences.

- **Marketing:** Companies utilize AI to analyze customer sentiment from social media and online reviews. Natural Language Processing (NLP) algorithms can assess customer feedback to gauge brand perception and inform marketing strategies.

Conclusion

AI and automated insights represent a paradigm shift in how organizations approach data analytics. By harnessing the power of machine learning and advanced algorithms, businesses can uncover hidden patterns, enhance decision-making, and drive innovation across various sectors. However, as the technology continues to evolve, it is imperative to address the associated challenges to ensure that AI serves as a force for good in society, fostering transparency, fairness, and ethical use of data. The future of analytics is undoubtedly intertwined with the advancements in AI, paving the way for a more data-driven world where insights are not just automated but also actionable and responsible.

Ethical Considerations in Data Science

In the rapidly evolving field of data science, ethical considerations have emerged as a critical component that practitioners must navigate. The use of data analytics, while immensely powerful, raises significant ethical dilemmas that can impact individuals, communities, and society at large. This section explores the theoretical frameworks, prevalent ethical issues, and real-world examples that highlight the importance of ethics in data science.

Theoretical Frameworks

Ethics in data science can be examined through various theoretical frameworks, including consequentialism, deontology, and virtue ethics.

- **Consequentialism** focuses on the outcomes of actions. In data science, this could involve evaluating the societal impact of data-driven decisions, such as the benefits of predictive policing versus the potential for racial profiling.

- **Deontology** emphasizes the morality of actions themselves, rather than their consequences. This perspective might argue against the use of certain data collection methods that infringe on individual privacy rights, regardless of the potential benefits.

- **Virtue Ethics** centers on the character and intentions of the data scientist. It encourages professionals to cultivate virtues such as honesty, integrity, and respect for individuals' rights, ensuring that their work contributes positively to society.

These frameworks provide a foundation for understanding the ethical landscape within which data scientists operate.

Key Ethical Issues

Several key ethical issues arise in the practice of data science:

- **Privacy and Data Protection:** The collection and analysis of personal data raise significant privacy concerns. Data scientists must ensure compliance with regulations such as the General Data Protection Regulation (GDPR) and the California Consumer Privacy Act (CCPA), which emphasize the importance of informed consent and data minimization.

- **Bias and Fairness:** Algorithms can perpetuate existing biases present in training data. For example, a study by Angwin et al. (2016) found that the COMPAS algorithm, used for predicting recidivism, exhibited racial bias, with African American defendants being falsely labeled as high risk at nearly twice the rate of white defendants. Addressing bias requires rigorous testing and validation of models to ensure fairness across different demographic groups.

- **Transparency and Accountability:** Data scientists are often faced with the challenge of making complex models interpretable to stakeholders. The concept of explainable AI (XAI) has emerged to address this issue, advocating for models that provide clear insights into their decision-making processes. Transparency is crucial for building trust and accountability in data-driven systems.

- **Data Misuse:** The potential for data to be misused for malicious purposes poses a significant ethical concern. For instance, data breaches can lead to identity theft and other forms of exploitation. Data scientists must implement robust security measures and consider the ethical implications of their work in preventing misuse.

Real-World Examples

Several notable examples illustrate the ethical dilemmas faced by data scientists:

- **Cambridge Analytica Scandal:** The unauthorized harvesting of Facebook user data for political advertising raised profound ethical questions about consent and the manipulation of personal information. This incident highlighted the need for stricter regulations and ethical standards in data collection practices.

- **Facial Recognition Technology:** The deployment of facial recognition systems by law enforcement agencies has sparked debates over privacy, surveillance, and racial profiling. Studies have shown that these systems can misidentify individuals, particularly among people of color, leading to wrongful arrests and a loss of public trust.

- **Healthcare Algorithms:** Research has shown that algorithms used in healthcare can reinforce disparities in treatment access. For example, a study by Obermeyer et al. (2019) found that an algorithm used to predict healthcare needs underestimated the needs of Black patients compared to white patients, ultimately leading to inequitable treatment allocation.

Conclusion

The ethical considerations in data science are multifaceted and require a proactive approach from practitioners. As the field continues to evolve, it is imperative for data scientists to engage with ethical frameworks, address potential biases, ensure transparency, and protect individual privacy. By prioritizing ethical practices, data scientists can contribute to a more equitable and just society, leveraging the power of data for the greater good.

$$\text{Ethical Data Science} = f(\text{Privacy, Bias, Transparency, Accountability}) \quad (37)$$

In conclusion, the integration of ethical considerations into data science practices is not merely a regulatory requirement; it is a moral imperative that shapes the future of technology and its impact on society.

Data Analytics and Social Good

In an era characterized by rapid technological advancement and an unprecedented proliferation of data, the potential for data analytics to drive social good has never been greater. Data analytics, the process of examining datasets to draw conclusions about the information they contain, has emerged as a powerful tool that can address some of society's most pressing challenges. This section explores the intersection of data analytics and social good, highlighting its significance, the challenges it faces, and notable examples of its application.

The Significance of Data Analytics for Social Good

Data analytics can be defined as the systematic computational analysis of data. It involves various techniques and processes, including statistical analysis, predictive modeling, and machine learning, to extract insights from raw data. The significance of data analytics for social good lies in its ability to inform decision-making, optimize resource allocation, and enhance the effectiveness of programs aimed at addressing social issues.

$$\text{Social Good} = \text{Data Analytics} \times \text{Informed Decision-Making} \qquad (38)$$

This equation illustrates that the impact of social good is directly proportional to the quality and effectiveness of data analytics employed in decision-making processes. By leveraging data, organizations can identify trends, measure outcomes, and develop strategies that lead to positive social change.

Challenges in Leveraging Data for Social Good

Despite its potential, the application of data analytics for social good is not without challenges. Some of the key issues include:

- **Data Privacy and Security:** The collection and analysis of personal data raise significant privacy concerns. Ensuring that data is handled ethically and securely is paramount to maintaining public trust.

- **Bias in Data:** Data can reflect existing biases present in society. If not addressed, these biases can perpetuate inequalities and lead to unfair outcomes. For instance, biased algorithms in criminal justice systems have been shown to disproportionately affect marginalized communities.

- **Data Accessibility:** Many organizations lack access to high-quality data, limiting their ability to conduct meaningful analyses. This is particularly true in low-income areas where data collection infrastructure may be inadequate.
- **Capacity Building:** Nonprofits and social enterprises often lack the technical expertise required to analyze data effectively. Building capacity within these organizations is essential for maximizing the impact of data analytics.

Examples of Data Analytics in Action

Numerous organizations are successfully utilizing data analytics to drive social good. Here are several notable examples:

- **Healthcare Analytics:** Organizations like Health Catalyst use data analytics to improve patient outcomes and reduce costs. By analyzing patient data, they can identify trends in treatment effectiveness and optimize care delivery. For example, predictive analytics can forecast patient admissions, allowing hospitals to allocate resources more efficiently.
- **Education:** The Bill and Melinda Gates Foundation employs data analytics to enhance educational outcomes. By analyzing student performance data, they can identify at-risk students and implement targeted interventions, ultimately improving graduation rates.
- **Disaster Response:** The Humanitarian OpenStreetMap Team (HOT) utilizes crowdsourced data and analytics to improve disaster response efforts. During natural disasters, they analyze geographic data to map affected areas, enabling more efficient allocation of resources and support for affected communities.
- **Environmental Conservation:** The World Wildlife Fund (WWF) uses data analytics to track wildlife populations and monitor environmental changes. By analyzing data from various sources, including satellite imagery and field observations, they can develop strategies for conservation efforts and combat illegal poaching.

The Future of Data Analytics for Social Good

The future of data analytics for social good is promising, with advancements in technology and increasing awareness of data's potential to drive change. Key trends to watch include:

- **Artificial Intelligence (AI):** The integration of AI into data analytics will enhance predictive capabilities and enable more sophisticated analyses. For instance, AI-driven algorithms can identify patterns in large datasets that may not be apparent to human analysts.

- **Open Data Initiatives:** Governments and organizations are increasingly embracing open data initiatives, making datasets publicly available for analysis. This transparency can empower communities and foster collaboration in addressing social issues.

- **Collaboration Across Sectors:** Partnerships between nonprofits, governments, and private companies are becoming more common. By pooling resources and expertise, these collaborations can amplify the impact of data analytics for social good.

- **Focus on Ethical Considerations:** As the importance of ethical data practices grows, organizations will need to prioritize responsible data usage and address issues of bias and privacy proactively.

Conclusion

Data analytics holds immense potential to address social challenges and drive positive change. By harnessing the power of data, organizations can make informed decisions, optimize resources, and ultimately enhance the well-being of communities. However, it is essential to navigate the challenges associated with data privacy, bias, and accessibility to realize this potential fully. As we look to the future, collaboration and ethical considerations will be critical in ensuring that data analytics serves as a force for social good.

Fatima's Vision for the Next Generation

Fatima Wang envisions a future where the next generation of innovators harnesses the power of data analytics to address some of the most pressing challenges facing society. Her vision is rooted in the belief that data can be a transformative force, not only for businesses but also for communities and individuals. By empowering young minds with the tools and knowledge to navigate the complexities of data, Fatima aims to create a generation that is not only data-literate but also ethically conscious and socially responsible.

The Importance of Data Literacy

In today's digital age, data literacy is as essential as traditional literacy. Fatima emphasizes that understanding data is crucial for informed decision-making in various fields, from healthcare to finance. She advocates for educational curricula that integrate data science principles from an early age, allowing students to develop critical thinking skills and a strong foundation in analytics. This approach aligns with the theory of constructivism, which posits that learners construct knowledge through experiences and reflection.

Fatima's initiatives include workshops and online courses aimed at K-12 students, focusing on hands-on data analysis projects. For example, she encourages students to analyze local environmental data to understand pollution patterns in their communities. By engaging in real-world problems, students learn to interpret data meaningfully, fostering a sense of agency and responsibility.

Ethical Data Practices

As data becomes increasingly integral to decision-making processes, the ethical implications of data use cannot be overlooked. Fatima believes that the next generation of data scientists must prioritize ethical considerations in their work. She promotes the concept of data ethics, which includes principles such as transparency, fairness, and accountability.

Fatima often cites the example of algorithmic bias, where machine learning models inadvertently perpetuate existing societal biases due to skewed training data. To combat this, she encourages young innovators to adopt a critical lens when developing algorithms. For instance, she advocates for diverse teams in data science, as varied perspectives can help identify and mitigate biases in datasets.

Fostering Collaboration and Interdisciplinary Approaches

Fatima's vision extends beyond individual skill development; she believes in the power of collaboration and interdisciplinary approaches. She encourages partnerships between data scientists, social scientists, and community leaders to address complex societal issues. This collaborative model is supported by the theory of collective impact, which suggests that cross-sector collaboration can lead to significant social change.

One of Fatima's notable projects involved a partnership with urban planners and public health officials to analyze data on food deserts in underserved communities. By combining data analytics with local knowledge, the team was able to develop targeted interventions that improved access to healthy food options.

This example illustrates how interdisciplinary collaboration can enhance the impact of data-driven initiatives.

Empowering Underrepresented Groups

A critical aspect of Fatima's vision is her commitment to empowering underrepresented groups in the field of data science. She recognizes that diversity in data analytics leads to more innovative solutions and a more equitable society. Fatima advocates for programs that provide mentorship and resources to women, minorities, and other marginalized communities interested in pursuing careers in data science.

For instance, she has established scholarships for young women pursuing degrees in data analytics, along with mentorship programs that connect them with industry professionals. By fostering an inclusive environment, Fatima aims to cultivate a diverse pipeline of future innovators who can bring unique perspectives to the field.

The Role of Technology in Education

Fatima envisions a future where technology plays a pivotal role in education, particularly in teaching data science. She supports the integration of artificial intelligence (AI) and machine learning tools in educational settings, allowing students to engage with data in interactive and meaningful ways. For example, AI-driven platforms can provide personalized learning experiences, adapting to each student's pace and learning style.

Moreover, Fatima emphasizes the importance of teaching students to critically evaluate the technologies they use. She encourages them to question the algorithms that power their digital experiences, fostering a generation that is not only tech-savvy but also aware of the implications of technology on society.

Conclusion

In conclusion, Fatima Wang's vision for the next generation is one of empowerment, collaboration, and ethical responsibility. By prioritizing data literacy, ethical practices, interdisciplinary collaboration, and inclusivity, she aims to inspire young innovators to harness the power of data for social good. As they navigate an increasingly data-driven world, Fatima believes that the next generation will be equipped not only to tackle contemporary challenges but also to create a more just and equitable future for all.

Revolutionizing Industries

Transforming Healthcare

Uncovering Patterns in Patient Data

The healthcare industry has been revolutionized by the integration of data analytics, particularly in the realm of patient data. This subsection delves into the methods and implications of uncovering patterns in patient data, emphasizing its significance in enhancing patient outcomes, optimizing treatment plans, and advancing medical research.

The Importance of Data in Healthcare

In modern healthcare, data is generated at an unprecedented rate. Electronic Health Records (EHRs), wearable health devices, and mobile health applications contribute to a vast pool of patient data. According to a report by the World Health Organization, the volume of health data is expected to double every two years, making it imperative for healthcare providers to leverage this information effectively.

Identifying Patterns through Statistical Methods

To uncover meaningful patterns in patient data, various statistical methods are employed. One common approach is the use of **descriptive statistics**, which provide a summary of the data through measures such as mean, median, mode, and standard deviation. These statistics help in understanding the central tendency and dispersion of patient health metrics.

For example, consider the following equations for mean and standard deviation:

$$\text{Mean}(\mu) = \frac{1}{N}\sum_{i=1}^{N} x_i \qquad (39)$$

$$\text{Standard Deviation}(\sigma) = \sqrt{\frac{1}{N}\sum_{i=1}^{N}(x_i - \mu)^2} \qquad (40)$$

Where N is the number of patients and x_i represents individual patient data points.

Advanced Analytics Techniques

Beyond descriptive statistics, advanced analytics techniques such as **predictive analytics** and **machine learning** are increasingly utilized to identify complex patterns in patient data. Predictive analytics involves using historical data to forecast future outcomes. For instance, logistic regression can be applied to predict the likelihood of a patient developing a chronic condition based on their medical history and lifestyle choices.

The logistic regression model can be expressed as:

$$P(Y = 1|X) = \frac{1}{1 + e^{-(\beta_0 + \beta_1 X_1 + \beta_2 X_2 + ... + \beta_n X_n)}} \qquad (41)$$

Where $P(Y = 1|X)$ is the probability of the outcome, X represents the predictor variables, and β are the coefficients estimated from the data.

Case Studies in Pattern Recognition

Several case studies illustrate the effectiveness of uncovering patterns in patient data. A notable example is the use of machine learning algorithms in predicting hospital readmissions. A study published in the *Journal of the American Medical Association* demonstrated that by analyzing patient demographics, prior admissions, and treatment plans, researchers could accurately predict which patients were at higher risk of readmission within 30 days of discharge. This allowed healthcare providers to implement targeted interventions, ultimately reducing readmission rates by 15%.

Another example is the analysis of genomic data to identify patterns associated with specific diseases. By employing techniques such as clustering and classification algorithms, researchers have been able to identify genetic markers linked to conditions like diabetes and cancer. This not only aids in early diagnosis but also facilitates personalized treatment plans tailored to the genetic profile of individual patients.

Challenges in Data Analysis

Despite the potential benefits, uncovering patterns in patient data is fraught with challenges. One major issue is **data quality**. Incomplete or inaccurate data can lead to misleading conclusions and ineffective interventions. Furthermore, privacy concerns regarding patient data can hinder the sharing and analysis of information, which is crucial for comprehensive insights.

Another challenge is **bias in data**. If the data used for analysis is not representative of the broader population, the patterns identified may not be generalizable. For instance, algorithms trained on data from a specific demographic may fail to accurately predict outcomes for patients from different backgrounds.

The Future of Patient Data Analytics

As technology continues to evolve, the future of uncovering patterns in patient data looks promising. The integration of artificial intelligence (AI) and natural language processing (NLP) in healthcare analytics is set to enhance the ability to analyze unstructured data, such as clinical notes and patient feedback.

Moreover, the rise of **real-time data analytics** allows healthcare providers to make immediate decisions based on the latest patient information. This capability is particularly beneficial in emergency situations where timely interventions can be life-saving.

In conclusion, uncovering patterns in patient data is a critical component of modern healthcare analytics. By employing various statistical methods and advanced analytics techniques, healthcare providers can improve patient outcomes, optimize treatment plans, and contribute to the overall advancement of medical research. However, addressing challenges such as data quality and bias remains essential to fully realize the potential of data-driven healthcare solutions.

Personalized Medicine and Treatment

Personalized medicine, often referred to as precision medicine, represents a transformative approach to healthcare that tailors medical treatment to the individual characteristics of each patient. This paradigm shift is made possible through the integration of advanced data analytics, genomics, and machine learning techniques. By leveraging vast amounts of data, healthcare providers can develop more effective treatment plans that consider the unique genetic, environmental, and lifestyle factors that influence patient health.

Theoretical Foundations

The foundation of personalized medicine lies in the understanding that each individual's biological makeup is distinct. The Human Genome Project, completed in 2003, provided a comprehensive map of the human genome, revealing the genetic variations that contribute to differences in health and disease susceptibility. This knowledge has paved the way for the development of targeted therapies that can significantly improve treatment outcomes.

Mathematically, personalized medicine can be modeled using the concept of stratified risk. Let P represent the probability of a patient responding to a specific treatment based on their genetic profile. This can be expressed as:

$$P = f(G, E, L)$$

where: - G represents genetic factors, - E represents environmental influences, - L represents lifestyle choices.

This function f can be estimated using statistical methods such as logistic regression or machine learning algorithms, enabling clinicians to predict treatment responses with greater accuracy.

Challenges in Implementation

Despite its potential, the implementation of personalized medicine faces several challenges:

1. **Data Integration**: Combining diverse data sources, including genomic data, electronic health records, and lifestyle information, is complex. Ensuring that these data are harmonized and accessible is critical for effective analysis.

2. **Ethical Considerations**: The use of genetic information raises ethical questions regarding privacy, consent, and potential discrimination. It is essential to establish robust frameworks to protect patient data while promoting transparency in how genetic information is used.

3. **Cost and Accessibility**: The advanced technologies required for personalized medicine, such as next-generation sequencing, can be expensive. Ensuring that these innovations are accessible to all populations, regardless of socioeconomic status, is a significant concern.

4. **Clinical Validation**: Treatments based on genetic information must undergo rigorous clinical trials to validate their efficacy and safety. The process of

translating genetic findings into clinical practice can be slow and fraught with regulatory hurdles.

Examples of Personalized Medicine in Action

Several successful applications of personalized medicine illustrate its potential to revolutionize treatment:

- **Oncology**: In cancer treatment, personalized medicine has made significant strides. For instance, patients with breast cancer can be tested for the presence of the HER2 protein. Those who test positive may benefit from targeted therapies such as trastuzumab (Herceptin), which specifically targets HER2-positive tumors. Studies have shown that this approach can lead to improved survival rates compared to traditional chemotherapy.

- **Pharmacogenomics**: This field studies how genes affect a person's response to drugs. For example, patients with variations in the CYP2D6 gene may metabolize certain medications differently, leading to either adverse effects or reduced efficacy. By testing for these genetic variants, healthcare providers can prescribe medications that are more likely to be effective and safe for each patient.

- **Diabetes Management**: Personalized medicine is also making waves in diabetes care. Continuous glucose monitoring devices collect real-time data on blood glucose levels, which can be analyzed to tailor insulin therapy to individual needs. Machine learning algorithms can predict blood sugar fluctuations, allowing for more precise dosing and improved glycemic control.

Future Directions

The future of personalized medicine is promising, with ongoing research focused on several key areas:

1. **Integration of Artificial Intelligence**: AI and machine learning algorithms are being developed to analyze complex datasets, identify patterns, and predict treatment responses. These technologies have the potential to enhance decision-making in clinical settings.

2. **Expanded Genomic Testing**: As the cost of genomic sequencing continues to decrease, more patients will have access to comprehensive genetic testing. This will facilitate the identification of novel biomarkers and the development of targeted therapies.

3. **Patient-Centric Approaches**: The shift towards patient-centered care emphasizes the importance of involving patients in their treatment decisions.

Personalized medicine encourages shared decision-making, where patients' preferences and values are considered alongside clinical data.

4. **Global Health Implications**: Personalized medicine has the potential to address health disparities by tailoring interventions to the unique needs of diverse populations. By understanding the genetic and environmental factors that contribute to health outcomes, public health initiatives can be designed to promote equity in healthcare access and treatment.

In conclusion, personalized medicine represents a significant advancement in the field of healthcare, enabling more effective and tailored treatment strategies. As data analytics and technology continue to evolve, the potential for personalized medicine to improve patient outcomes and transform healthcare delivery is immense.

Enhancing Diagnostic Accuracy

In the realm of healthcare, the ability to make accurate diagnoses is paramount. The integration of data analytics into diagnostic processes has ushered in a new era, where traditional methods are augmented with advanced algorithms and machine learning techniques. This section explores how Fatima Wang's innovations in data analytics have significantly enhanced diagnostic accuracy, leading to improved patient outcomes and more efficient healthcare systems.

The Importance of Diagnostic Accuracy

Diagnostic accuracy refers to the ability of a test or procedure to correctly identify the presence or absence of a disease. High diagnostic accuracy is crucial for several reasons:

- **Patient Safety:** Accurate diagnoses prevent unnecessary treatments and interventions that can cause harm.

- **Resource Optimization:** Accurate diagnostics reduce the burden on healthcare systems by minimizing unnecessary tests and hospitalizations.

- **Cost Efficiency:** Improved diagnostic accuracy can lead to significant cost savings for both healthcare providers and patients.

The World Health Organization (WHO) estimates that diagnostic errors contribute to approximately 10% of patient harm in healthcare settings, underscoring the need for enhanced accuracy through innovative approaches.

Data-Driven Approaches to Diagnostics

Fatima Wang's research focuses on leveraging big data and machine learning to enhance diagnostic accuracy. By analyzing vast datasets from electronic health records (EHRs), medical imaging, and genomic data, her work has led to the development of predictive models that assist healthcare professionals in making informed decisions.

Machine Learning Algorithms Machine learning (ML) algorithms are at the forefront of enhancing diagnostic accuracy. These algorithms can analyze complex datasets to identify patterns that may not be apparent to human clinicians. For instance, Wang's team developed a convolutional neural network (CNN) model for analyzing medical images, which significantly outperformed traditional diagnostic methods.

The CNN model can be mathematically represented as follows:

$$y = f(W * x + b) \tag{42}$$

where:

- y is the output of the model (e.g., probability of disease presence),
- f is the activation function (e.g., ReLU),
- W represents the weights of the network,
- x is the input data (e.g., image data), and
- b is the bias term.

This model was trained using a dataset of labeled medical images, enabling it to learn and generalize from the data effectively.

Case Study: Early Detection of Breast Cancer

One of the most notable applications of Wang's innovations is in the early detection of breast cancer. Traditional methods of screening, such as mammography, often have limitations in sensitivity and specificity. Wang's team implemented a machine learning approach that analyzes mammogram images alongside patient demographics and family histories.

The predictive model developed achieved an accuracy rate of 95%, compared to the 85% accuracy typical of conventional methods. The model's performance can be quantified using the following metrics:

- **Sensitivity (True Positive Rate):**

$$\text{Sensitivity} = \frac{\text{True Positives}}{\text{True Positives} + \text{False Negatives}} \quad (43)$$

- **Specificity (True Negative Rate):**

$$\text{Specificity} = \frac{\text{True Negatives}}{\text{True Negatives} + \text{False Positives}} \quad (44)$$

- **Accuracy:**

$$\text{Accuracy} = \frac{\text{True Positives} + \text{True Negatives}}{\text{Total Population}} \quad (45)$$

This case study highlights how data-driven approaches can lead to substantial improvements in diagnostic accuracy, ultimately saving lives through earlier interventions.

Challenges in Enhancing Diagnostic Accuracy

Despite the promising advancements, several challenges remain in the pursuit of enhanced diagnostic accuracy:

- **Data Quality:** The accuracy of predictive models is heavily dependent on the quality of the input data. Incomplete or biased data can lead to erroneous predictions.

- **Integration into Clinical Practice:** The transition from traditional diagnostic methods to data-driven approaches requires significant changes in clinical workflows and training for healthcare professionals.

- **Ethical Considerations:** The use of AI in diagnostics raises ethical questions regarding accountability, transparency, and the potential for algorithmic bias.

Future Directions

Looking forward, Fatima Wang envisions a future where diagnostic accuracy continues to improve through the integration of diverse data sources, including wearable health technologies and patient-reported outcomes. The use of real-time data analytics will allow for dynamic adjustments to diagnostic processes, ultimately leading to personalized medicine tailored to individual patient needs.

In conclusion, the enhancements in diagnostic accuracy brought about by Fatima Wang's innovations represent a significant leap forward in healthcare. By harnessing the power of data analytics and machine learning, the potential to transform patient outcomes and optimize healthcare delivery is enormous. As the field continues to evolve, ongoing collaboration between data scientists and healthcare professionals will be essential to address challenges and maximize the benefits of these advancements.

Improving Healthcare Delivery

The advent of data analytics has significantly transformed the healthcare landscape, particularly in improving healthcare delivery. This transformation is driven by the ability to harness vast amounts of data to enhance patient care, streamline operations, and ultimately improve health outcomes. In this section, we explore the theoretical foundations, challenges, and practical examples of how data analytics is reshaping healthcare delivery.

Theoretical Foundations

Healthcare delivery systems are complex and multifaceted, requiring the integration of various data types, including clinical, operational, and financial data. The theoretical framework for improving healthcare delivery through analytics can be understood through the lens of the *Health Information Technology (HIT)* model, which emphasizes the role of technology in enhancing the quality of care.

A key component of this model is the *Data-Driven Decision-Making (DDDM)* approach, which posits that healthcare providers can make more informed decisions by analyzing data trends and patterns. The DDDM approach can be mathematically represented as:

$$\text{Improved Outcomes} = f(\text{Data Quality, Analytical Techniques, Provider Engagement}) \tag{46}$$

Where: - Data Quality refers to the accuracy, completeness, and timeliness of the data collected. - Analytical Techniques encompasses various methods such as predictive analytics, machine learning, and statistical analysis. - Provider Engagement indicates the involvement of healthcare professionals in the decision-making process based on analytical insights.

Challenges in Healthcare Delivery

Despite the promising potential of data analytics, several challenges hinder its effective implementation in healthcare delivery:

1. **Data Silos**: Many healthcare organizations operate with fragmented data systems, leading to data silos that prevent the comprehensive analysis of patient information. This fragmentation can result in incomplete patient histories and hinder coordinated care.

2. **Privacy and Security Concerns**: The use of patient data raises significant privacy and security concerns. Healthcare organizations must navigate complex regulations such as the Health Insurance Portability and Accountability Act (HIPAA) to ensure patient data is handled securely.

3. **Resistance to Change**: Healthcare professionals may be resistant to adopting new technologies and data-driven approaches, stemming from a lack of understanding or fear of the unknown.

4. **Integration of Diverse Data Sources**: Healthcare data comes from various sources, including Electronic Health Records (EHRs), wearables, and patient-reported outcomes. Integrating these diverse data types into a cohesive analytics framework poses a significant challenge.

Practical Examples

Several healthcare organizations have successfully leveraged data analytics to improve healthcare delivery:

1. **Cleveland Clinic**: The Cleveland Clinic implemented a predictive analytics model to identify patients at high risk of readmission. By analyzing various data points, including previous admissions, demographic information, and comorbidities, the clinic developed targeted interventions that reduced readmission rates by 20%.

2. **Mount Sinai Health System**: Mount Sinai utilized machine learning algorithms to analyze EHR data and predict patient deterioration. By identifying patients at risk of clinical decline, the healthcare team could intervene earlier, resulting in improved patient outcomes and reduced lengths of stay.

3. **Intermountain Healthcare**: Intermountain adopted a data-driven approach to improve care coordination among its providers. By implementing a centralized data repository, the organization enhanced communication and collaboration, ultimately leading to improved patient satisfaction and reduced healthcare costs.

Conclusion

Improving healthcare delivery through data analytics is a multifaceted endeavor that requires overcoming significant challenges. However, the potential benefits—enhanced patient care, reduced costs, and improved health outcomes—are substantial. As healthcare organizations continue to embrace data-driven decision-making, the future of healthcare delivery looks promising, paving the way for a more efficient, effective, and patient-centered system.

In conclusion, the integration of data analytics into healthcare delivery not only enhances the quality of care but also empowers healthcare providers to make informed decisions that positively impact patient outcomes. By addressing the challenges and leveraging successful examples, the healthcare industry can continue to evolve and improve in the era of data revolution.

Revolutionizing Medical Research

The landscape of medical research has undergone a profound transformation with the advent of data analytics, largely driven by the pioneering work of innovators like Fatima Wang. This revolution is marked by the integration of big data, machine learning, and advanced statistical methods, which collectively enhance the ability to conduct research more efficiently and effectively.

The Role of Big Data in Medical Research

Big data refers to the vast volumes of structured and unstructured data generated from various sources, including electronic health records (EHRs), genomic sequencing, clinical trials, and wearable health devices. The ability to analyze this data allows researchers to uncover patterns and insights that were previously unattainable. According to a report by the *Institute of Medicine*, the integration of big data into medical research can lead to improved patient outcomes, reduced costs, and enhanced efficiency in clinical trials [?].

Challenges in Traditional Medical Research

Traditional medical research methods often face significant challenges, including lengthy timelines, high costs, and limited sample sizes. For instance, clinical trials can take years to complete, with an average cost exceeding $2.6 billion per successful drug [?]. Additionally, the recruitment of diverse patient populations remains a persistent issue, as many studies often lack representation from underrepresented groups, leading to gaps in understanding how treatments affect different demographics.

Innovative Approaches to Medical Research

Fatima Wang's research emphasizes the use of predictive analytics and machine learning algorithms to address these challenges. For example, Wang's team developed a novel algorithm that analyzes EHR data to identify potential participants for clinical trials based on specific inclusion and exclusion criteria. This approach not only accelerates patient recruitment but also enhances the diversity of study populations.

$$\text{Recruitment Score} = \sum_{i=1}^{n} \left(\text{Eligibility}_i \cdot \text{Engagement}_i \cdot \text{Diversity}_i \right) \quad (47)$$

In this equation, Eligibility_i represents the likelihood of a patient meeting the trial criteria, Engagement_i indicates the patient's willingness to participate, and Diversity_i assesses the representation of various demographic groups. By optimizing this recruitment score, researchers can significantly enhance the efficiency of clinical trials.

Case Study: Genomic Research

One of the most notable examples of data revolutionizing medical research is in the field of genomics. The Human Genome Project, which took over a decade to complete, has been complemented by contemporary projects utilizing advanced analytics. For instance, Wang's collaboration with genomic researchers led to the development of a machine learning model that predicts genetic predispositions to diseases such as diabetes and cancer.

The model employs a vast dataset of genomic sequences and clinical outcomes, allowing researchers to identify biomarkers that indicate a higher risk for certain conditions. The predictive power of such models can be expressed as follows:

$$P(Disease|GenomicData) = \frac{P(GenomicData|Disease) \cdot P(Disease)}{P(GenomicData)}$$
$$(48)$$

This equation represents Bayes' theorem, where $P(Disease|GenomicData)$ is the probability of a disease given the genomic data, $P(GenomicData|Disease)$ is the likelihood of observing the genomic data if the disease is present, $P(Disease)$ is the prior probability of the disease, and $P(GenomicData)$ is the overall probability of observing the genomic data.

Impact on Drug Development

The implications of data-driven approaches extend beyond recruitment and genomics; they also significantly impact drug development. By utilizing real-world evidence (RWE) generated from patient data, researchers can assess the effectiveness and safety of drugs post-approval, leading to more informed decisions regarding treatment protocols.

For instance, a study published in *Nature* demonstrated how RWE analytics revealed that a specific cancer drug was less effective in patients with certain genetic markers. This insight prompted a reevaluation of treatment guidelines, ultimately improving patient care and reducing unnecessary costs associated with ineffective therapies [?].

Ethical Considerations

While the revolution in medical research through data analytics offers tremendous potential, it also raises ethical concerns. Issues related to data privacy, informed consent, and the potential for bias in algorithms must be addressed. Wang advocates for the establishment of robust ethical frameworks that ensure the responsible use of patient data while maximizing the benefits of data-driven research.

Conclusion

In conclusion, the revolutionization of medical research through data analytics is reshaping the way we understand, diagnose, and treat diseases. Fatima Wang's innovative approaches exemplify the power of integrating big data and machine learning into research methodologies, ultimately leading to more efficient clinical trials, personalized medicine, and improved patient outcomes. As the field continues to evolve, it is imperative that researchers remain vigilant about ethical considerations, ensuring that the advancements in medical research benefit all segments of society.

Enabling Smarter Cities

Urban Planning and Infrastructure Management

Urban planning is a multifaceted discipline that involves the design and regulation of the use of land, resources, and infrastructure in urban areas. As cities continue to grow and evolve, the need for effective urban planning and infrastructure management becomes increasingly vital. This section explores how data analytics is revolutionizing urban planning and infrastructure management, addressing key theories, problems, and practical examples that illustrate the impact of data-driven decision-making in this field.

Theoretical Frameworks

Urban planning is grounded in several theoretical frameworks that guide practitioners in creating sustainable and livable environments. Two prominent theories are:

- **Smart Growth Theory:** This theory emphasizes compact, transit-oriented, walkable urban communities that preserve open space and promote sustainable practices. Smart growth advocates for the use of data to inform zoning laws, transportation planning, and environmental conservation efforts.

- **Systems Theory:** This approach views urban environments as complex systems comprised of interrelated components, including transportation, housing, and public services. Systems theory promotes the use of data analytics to understand how changes in one area can impact others, facilitating more holistic planning.

Challenges in Urban Planning

Urban planners face numerous challenges that can hinder effective decision-making, including:

- **Population Growth:** Rapid urbanization leads to increased demand for housing, transportation, and services, often outpacing infrastructure development.

- **Resource Allocation:** Limited budgets and resources make it difficult to prioritize projects that will yield the greatest benefits for the community.

- **Environmental Sustainability:** Balancing development needs with environmental preservation is a critical challenge, particularly in the face of climate change.
- **Data Silos:** Urban planners often struggle with fragmented data sources that hinder comprehensive analysis and informed decision-making.

Data-Driven Solutions

Data analytics provides urban planners with powerful tools to address these challenges and improve infrastructure management. Key applications include:

- **Geographic Information Systems (GIS):** GIS technology enables planners to visualize spatial data, analyze patterns, and make informed decisions about land use and infrastructure development. For instance, GIS can help identify areas with high population density that require additional public transportation services.
- **Predictive Modeling:** By utilizing historical data, predictive models can forecast future urban growth and infrastructure needs. For example, planners can use regression analysis to predict traffic patterns based on population growth and economic trends, allowing for proactive transportation planning.
- **Smart Sensors and IoT:** The integration of smart sensors in urban infrastructure allows for real-time data collection on traffic flow, air quality, and energy usage. This data can inform immediate adjustments and long-term planning strategies. For instance, smart traffic lights can adjust their timing based on real-time traffic conditions, reducing congestion and improving travel times.
- **Community Engagement Platforms:** Data analytics can enhance community engagement by providing platforms for residents to share their feedback and preferences. For example, mobile applications can collect data on public transportation usage and user satisfaction, guiding improvements in service delivery.

Case Studies

Several cities around the world have successfully implemented data-driven approaches to urban planning and infrastructure management:

- **Barcelona, Spain:** The city has adopted a smart city strategy that integrates data analytics into urban planning. By utilizing data from sensors and citizen feedback, Barcelona has improved its public transportation system, reduced energy consumption, and enhanced overall quality of life for residents.
- **Singapore:** Singapore is renowned for its innovative urban planning practices, including the use of a comprehensive data analytics platform known as the Virtual Singapore initiative. This platform allows planners to simulate various urban scenarios and assess the potential impacts of different development strategies on traffic, air quality, and land use.
- **New York City, USA:** NYC has embraced data analytics to improve its infrastructure management through initiatives like the NYC Open Data portal. This platform provides public access to a wealth of data, enabling citizens and planners alike to analyze trends and identify areas for improvement, such as optimizing waste collection routes based on real-time data.

Conclusion

The integration of data analytics into urban planning and infrastructure management is transforming how cities operate and evolve. By leveraging advanced analytical tools and methodologies, urban planners can address complex challenges, optimize resource allocation, and create sustainable, livable environments for future generations. As cities continue to grow, the role of data in informing planning decisions will only become more critical, paving the way for smarter, more resilient urban landscapes.

Traffic Optimization and Smart Transportation

The rapid urbanization of cities has led to increased traffic congestion, resulting in longer travel times, higher emissions, and reduced quality of life for urban residents. To address these challenges, Fatima Wang's innovative approach to data analytics has played a pivotal role in revolutionizing traffic optimization and smart transportation systems.

Theoretical Framework

Traffic optimization involves the application of mathematical models and algorithms to manage and control vehicular flow efficiently. The fundamental goal

ENABLING SMARTER CITIES

is to minimize travel time and maximize road network utilization. Key theories in traffic flow include the *Fundamental Diagram of Traffic Flow*, which relates traffic density, flow, and speed:

$$Q = k \cdot v \tag{49}$$

where: - Q is the traffic flow (vehicles per hour), - k is the traffic density (vehicles per kilometer), - v is the average speed of vehicles (kilometers per hour).

This relationship indicates that as density increases, flow initially increases until reaching a critical point, beyond which congestion occurs.

Challenges in Traffic Management

Traditional traffic management systems often rely on fixed-time traffic signals and manual monitoring, which can lead to inefficiencies. Challenges include:

- **Inaccurate Data Collection:** Many systems use outdated sensors or rely on human input, resulting in unreliable data.

- **Dynamic Traffic Patterns:** Fluctuations in traffic due to events, weather, or road conditions can lead to unpredictable congestion.

- **Limited Communication:** Lack of integration between different transportation modes (e.g., public transit, personal vehicles) hampers optimization efforts.

Fatima's Innovations

Fatima Wang's research focused on leveraging big data analytics and machine learning to address these challenges. Key innovations include:

Real-Time Data Analytics By utilizing data from various sources, including GPS, traffic cameras, and social media, Fatima developed algorithms that provide real-time traffic insights. For instance, by analyzing historical traffic patterns alongside current conditions, her models can predict congestion levels and suggest alternative routes.

Adaptive Traffic Signal Control Fatima's work led to the implementation of adaptive traffic signal systems that adjust signal timing based on real-time traffic conditions. The mathematical model for signal optimization can be represented as:

$$T_i = T_0 + \Delta T \cdot \left(\frac{V_i}{V_{max}}\right) \tag{50}$$

where: - T_i is the adjusted signal time for intersection i, - T_0 is the base signal time, - ΔT is the maximum adjustment time, - V_i is the current vehicle count at intersection i, - V_{max} is the maximum vehicle count before congestion.

This adaptive system has been shown to reduce wait times by up to 30% in urban settings.

Integration of Public Transit Fatima emphasized the importance of integrating public transportation data into traffic management systems. By analyzing ridership patterns and service frequency, her models optimize bus and train schedules to reduce wait times and increase usage. The optimization can be modeled using the following linear programming approach:

$$\text{Minimize } C = \sum_{j=1}^{n} c_j x_j \tag{51}$$

$$\text{Subject to: } Ax \leq b \tag{52}$$

where: - C is the total cost, - c_j is the cost associated with service j, - x_j is the number of vehicles assigned to service j, - A represents the constraints related to capacity and service requirements, - b is the maximum allowable limits.

Case Studies and Examples

Several cities have successfully implemented Fatima's methodologies, resulting in significant improvements in traffic flow and urban mobility:

San Francisco, California In San Francisco, the deployment of smart traffic signals based on Fatima's algorithms led to a 25% reduction in travel times during peak hours. The system utilized real-time data from over 1,000 sensors distributed across the city, allowing for dynamic adjustments to signal timing.

Barcelona, Spain Barcelona adopted a comprehensive smart transportation strategy, integrating public transit with real-time traffic data. This initiative not only optimized bus routes but also reduced overall traffic congestion by 20% within the first year of implementation.

Future Directions

Looking ahead, Fatima envisions a future where autonomous vehicles and smart transportation systems are fully integrated. By leveraging advancements in machine learning and artificial intelligence, traffic management systems will become increasingly sophisticated, allowing for seamless coordination between vehicles and infrastructure.

In conclusion, Fatima Wang's contributions to traffic optimization and smart transportation exemplify the transformative power of data analytics in addressing urban challenges. Through innovative algorithms and real-time data integration, cities can enhance mobility, reduce congestion, and improve the overall quality of life for residents.

Energy Efficiency and Sustainability

The modern world faces unprecedented challenges related to energy consumption, climate change, and sustainability. As urban populations continue to grow, the demand for energy-efficient solutions becomes increasingly critical. Fatima Wang's contributions to data analytics have played a pivotal role in revolutionizing energy efficiency and promoting sustainable practices across various sectors.

Theoretical Framework

Energy efficiency refers to the ability to use less energy to provide the same service. This concept is grounded in the first law of thermodynamics, which states that energy cannot be created or destroyed, only transformed. The goal is to minimize energy waste, thereby reducing the overall energy consumption of systems. Mathematically, energy efficiency (η) can be expressed as:

$$\eta = \frac{E_{\text{useful}}}{E_{\text{input}}} \tag{53}$$

where E_{useful} is the useful energy output and E_{input} is the total energy input. A higher η indicates a more efficient system.

Sustainability, on the other hand, encompasses a broader framework that integrates environmental, economic, and social dimensions. The Brundtland Commission defined sustainable development as "development that meets the needs of the present without compromising the ability of future generations to meet their own needs." This definition emphasizes the need for a balance between consumption and conservation.

Challenges in Energy Efficiency

Despite the theoretical benefits of energy efficiency, several challenges hinder its widespread adoption:

1. **Data Availability and Quality**: Access to reliable and high-quality data is essential for analyzing energy consumption patterns. In many cases, organizations lack the necessary data infrastructure to collect and analyze energy usage effectively.

2. **Behavioral Factors**: Human behavior plays a significant role in energy consumption. Understanding how individuals and organizations make decisions about energy use is crucial for developing effective strategies to promote efficiency.

3. **Investment Costs**: While energy-efficient technologies often lead to long-term savings, the initial investment can be a barrier for many businesses and homeowners. The upfront costs of implementing energy-efficient systems can deter stakeholders from making the switch.

4. **Regulatory Frameworks**: Inconsistent regulations and incentives across regions can complicate efforts to improve energy efficiency. Policymakers must create a cohesive framework that encourages investment in energy-efficient technologies.

Fatima Wang's Innovations in Energy Analytics

Fatima Wang's groundbreaking research in data analytics has addressed many of these challenges. By leveraging big data, machine learning, and predictive analytics, she has developed innovative solutions that enhance energy efficiency and sustainability.

1. Smart Grids One of Wang's notable contributions is the development of smart grid technology, which utilizes real-time data to optimize energy distribution. Smart grids employ advanced metering infrastructure (AMI) to collect data on energy consumption patterns. This data enables utilities to manage energy flow more efficiently, reducing waste and enhancing reliability.

For instance, through predictive analytics, utilities can forecast peak demand periods and adjust energy distribution accordingly. This not only minimizes energy loss but also lowers operational costs. Wang's algorithms have been instrumental in improving the accuracy of these predictions, allowing for more responsive energy management.

2. Building Energy Management Systems (BEMS) Wang's work also extends to Building Energy Management Systems (BEMS), which utilize data analytics to monitor and control energy use in commercial buildings. By integrating sensors and IoT devices, BEMS can provide real-time insights into energy consumption and identify inefficiencies.

The implementation of BEMS has demonstrated significant energy savings. For example, a study conducted on a large office building revealed that the use of BEMS led to a 30% reduction in energy consumption over a year. Wang's algorithms played a crucial role in identifying patterns and recommending actionable strategies for energy savings.

3. **Renewable Energy Integration** Wang has also focused on integrating renewable energy sources into existing energy systems. Her research emphasizes the importance of data analytics in optimizing the use of solar and wind energy. By analyzing historical weather data and energy production patterns, her models can predict the availability of renewable energy and adjust consumption accordingly.

For example, in a pilot project involving solar energy integration, Wang's predictive models improved the efficiency of energy storage systems by 25%. This not only enhanced the reliability of renewable energy sources but also contributed to reducing reliance on fossil fuels.

Case Studies and Real-World Applications

Numerous case studies illustrate the impact of Wang's innovations on energy efficiency and sustainability:

1. **Urban Transportation** In a collaboration with city planners, Wang utilized data analytics to optimize public transportation routes. By analyzing commuter patterns and traffic data, her team identified opportunities to reduce fuel consumption and emissions. The implementation of these optimized routes resulted in a 15% decrease in energy use for public transportation in the city.

2. **Industrial Energy Optimization** Wang's algorithms have also been applied in industrial settings to optimize energy use in manufacturing processes. A case study involving a large manufacturing plant revealed that by implementing data-driven energy management strategies, the plant achieved a 20% reduction in energy costs within six months.

Conclusion

Fatima Wang's contributions to energy efficiency and sustainability through data analytics have transformed the way industries approach energy consumption. By addressing challenges related to data availability, behavioral factors, and investment costs, her innovations pave the way for a more sustainable future. As urbanization and energy demands continue to rise, the importance of energy-efficient solutions will only grow, highlighting the need for continued research and innovation in this critical field.

In summary, the intersection of data analytics and energy efficiency represents a powerful tool for promoting sustainability. Wang's vision for the future emphasizes the role of data in driving positive change, fostering a culture of innovation, and empowering communities to adopt sustainable practices.

Public Safety and Security

Public safety and security have become paramount concerns in the age of data analytics. With the advent of advanced analytics and data-driven decision-making, cities and organizations can now leverage vast amounts of data to enhance public safety measures, reduce crime rates, and improve emergency response times. This subsection explores the role of data analytics in public safety and security, discussing relevant theories, challenges, and real-world applications.

Theoretical Framework

The intersection of data analytics and public safety is grounded in several theoretical frameworks, including:

- **Predictive Policing Theory:** This theory posits that by analyzing historical crime data, law enforcement agencies can predict where crimes are likely to occur in the future. Predictive policing employs statistical algorithms to identify patterns and trends, enabling police departments to allocate resources more effectively.

- **Situational Crime Prevention:** This theory focuses on reducing opportunities for crime through environmental design and increased surveillance. Data analytics can inform situational crime prevention strategies by identifying high-risk areas and times, allowing for targeted interventions.

- **Community Policing:** Community policing emphasizes collaboration between law enforcement agencies and the communities they serve. Data analytics can facilitate this collaboration by providing insights into community needs and concerns, fostering trust and cooperation.

Challenges in Data-Driven Public Safety

Despite the potential benefits, several challenges hinder the effective implementation of data analytics in public safety:

- **Data Privacy Concerns:** The collection and analysis of personal data raise significant privacy issues. Citizens may feel uncomfortable with surveillance measures, leading to distrust between law enforcement and the community. Striking a balance between safety and privacy is crucial.

- **Bias in Algorithms:** Algorithms used in predictive policing and other analytics can perpetuate existing biases if not carefully designed. Historical data may reflect systemic biases, leading to disproportionate targeting of certain communities. Addressing algorithmic bias is essential for equitable public safety measures.

- **Integration of Data Sources:** Public safety agencies often operate with disparate data systems, making it challenging to integrate and analyze data effectively. Interoperability among different agencies and data sources is necessary for comprehensive situational awareness.

Applications of Data Analytics in Public Safety

Numerous real-world examples illustrate how data analytics is transforming public safety and security:

1. Predictive Policing: Cities like Los Angeles and Chicago have implemented predictive policing programs using algorithms to analyze crime data and forecast potential crime hotspots. For example, the Los Angeles Police Department (LAPD) uses a program called PredPol, which analyzes historical crime data to generate predictions about where crimes are likely to occur. By deploying officers to these areas, the LAPD has reported reductions in certain types of crime.

2. Gunshot Detection Systems: Technologies like ShotSpotter utilize acoustic sensors to detect gunfire in real-time. These systems analyze sound waves and use algorithms to triangulate the location of gunfire, allowing law enforcement to respond swiftly. ShotSpotter has been adopted in various cities, resulting in quicker response times and improved community safety.

3. Emergency Response Optimization: Data analytics can enhance emergency response efforts by analyzing traffic patterns, historical response times, and current incidents. For instance, cities can use data to optimize the routing of emergency vehicles, ensuring they reach their destinations as quickly as possible. This approach can save lives in critical situations.

4. Crime Mapping and Visualization: Tools like GIS (Geographic Information Systems) allow law enforcement agencies to visualize crime data spatially. By mapping crime incidents, agencies can identify trends, allocate resources, and engage with communities effectively. For example, the New York City Police Department (NYPD) employs crime mapping to inform patrol strategies and community outreach efforts.

Conclusion

The integration of data analytics into public safety and security represents a significant advancement in how communities address crime and enhance safety. While challenges such as data privacy, algorithmic bias, and data integration persist, the potential benefits of improved predictive policing, emergency response, and community engagement are substantial. As data analytics continues to evolve, it is essential for law enforcement agencies to adopt ethical practices, prioritize transparency, and foster collaboration with the communities they serve. By doing so, they can harness the power of data to create safer, more secure environments for all citizens.

$$\text{Crime Rate} = \frac{\text{Number of Crimes}}{\text{Population}} \times 100,000 \tag{54}$$

The above equation illustrates the calculation of crime rate, which is a crucial metric for evaluating the effectiveness of data-driven public safety initiatives. By continuously monitoring this metric, agencies can assess the impact of their strategies and adjust accordingly, ensuring that public safety efforts are both effective and equitable.

Enhancing Quality of Life in Cities

The rapid urbanization of the 21st century has brought forth significant challenges and opportunities for enhancing the quality of life in cities. As more people flock to urban centers, the demand for efficient services, sustainable infrastructure, and improved living conditions has never been greater. Data analytics plays a pivotal role in addressing these challenges, enabling city planners and policymakers to make informed decisions that enhance the overall well-being of urban residents.

The Role of Data in Urban Quality of Life

Data-driven approaches to urban planning and management are essential for creating livable cities. The quality of life in urban environments is influenced by various factors, including accessibility to services, environmental sustainability, safety, and social cohesion. By leveraging data analytics, cities can identify areas for improvement and implement targeted interventions.

For instance, the use of Geographic Information Systems (GIS) allows city officials to visualize spatial data related to demographics, land use, and infrastructure. This visualization facilitates better planning and resource allocation. As highlighted by [?], cities are complex systems that require intricate models to understand their dynamics. By employing data analytics, urban planners can simulate different scenarios and predict the outcomes of various policy decisions.

Addressing Urban Challenges with Data Analytics

One of the primary challenges in urban environments is traffic congestion, which adversely affects air quality, public health, and overall quality of life. Data analytics can help mitigate this issue through the analysis of traffic patterns and the implementation of smart transportation systems. For example, cities like Barcelona have utilized real-time data from sensors and GPS devices to optimize traffic flow and reduce congestion [?].

Moreover, public safety is a critical concern for urban dwellers. The integration of data analytics in law enforcement can lead to more effective crime prevention strategies. Predictive policing, which uses historical crime data to forecast future incidents, has been implemented in cities such as Los Angeles. However, it is essential to approach this method with caution, as it raises ethical concerns regarding bias and privacy [?].

Enhancing Environmental Sustainability

Environmental sustainability is a key component of quality of life in urban areas. Data analytics can aid in monitoring and reducing the environmental impact of cities. For instance, smart waste management systems utilize sensors to optimize waste collection routes, reducing fuel consumption and emissions. In San Francisco, the implementation of such systems has contributed to the city's ambitious goal of zero waste by 2030 [?].

Additionally, urban green spaces are vital for enhancing the quality of life. Data analytics can help identify areas lacking access to parks and recreational facilities. By analyzing demographic data alongside geographic information, city planners can prioritize the development of green spaces in underserved neighborhoods, promoting physical activity and mental well-being [?].

Promoting Social Cohesion and Community Engagement

Quality of life in cities is not solely defined by physical infrastructure; social cohesion and community engagement are equally important. Data analytics can facilitate the identification of community needs and preferences, enabling local governments to tailor programs and services accordingly. For instance, participatory budgeting initiatives in cities like Paris allow residents to use data to influence funding decisions for community projects [?].

Furthermore, social media platforms serve as valuable sources of data for understanding public sentiment and community dynamics. By analyzing social media interactions, city officials can gauge public opinion on various issues, from local policies to community events. This information can inform decision-making processes and foster a sense of belonging among residents.

Conclusion

Enhancing the quality of life in cities is a multifaceted challenge that requires a comprehensive approach. Data analytics offers powerful tools for addressing urban issues, from traffic congestion and public safety to environmental sustainability and social cohesion. By harnessing the potential of data, cities can create more livable environments that meet the needs of their residents.

As urbanization continues to accelerate, the importance of data-driven decision-making will only grow. The future of urban living hinges on the ability of city planners and policymakers to leverage data effectively, ensuring that the benefits of urbanization are equitably distributed and that all residents can enjoy a high quality of life.

Revolutionizing Finance

Risk Management and Fraud Detection

In the rapidly evolving landscape of finance, the need for robust risk management and effective fraud detection mechanisms has never been more critical. With the increasing complexity of financial transactions and the rise of digital banking, organizations face significant challenges in safeguarding their assets and ensuring compliance with regulatory requirements. This subsection explores the theoretical frameworks, prevalent issues, and practical applications of data analytics in risk management and fraud detection.

Theoretical Frameworks

Risk management in finance is fundamentally about identifying, assessing, and prioritizing risks followed by coordinated efforts to minimize, monitor, and control the probability or impact of unfortunate events. The framework for risk management can be broken down into several key components:

- **Risk Identification:** The first step involves recognizing potential risks that could affect the organization. This can include market risk, credit risk, operational risk, and liquidity risk.

- **Risk Assessment:** Once identified, risks are assessed based on their likelihood and potential impact. This is often quantified using statistical methods, such as Value at Risk (VaR), which estimates the maximum potential loss over a specified time frame at a given confidence level.

- **Risk Mitigation:** Strategies are developed to mitigate identified risks, which may involve diversification, hedging, or implementing controls to minimize exposure.

- **Monitoring and Review:** Continuous monitoring of risk factors and the effectiveness of risk management strategies is essential for adapting to changes in the financial environment.

The mathematical representation of risk can be illustrated through the following equation for Value at Risk (VaR):

$$\text{VaR}_\alpha = \text{Portfolio Value} \times Z_\alpha \times \sigma \qquad (55)$$

where: - VaR_α is the Value at Risk at confidence level α, - Z_α is the Z-score corresponding to the confidence level, - σ is the standard deviation of the portfolio returns.

Challenges in Risk Management

Despite the advancements in data analytics, organizations continue to face several challenges in effective risk management:

- **Data Quality and Availability:** Accurate risk assessment relies on high-quality data. Incomplete or inaccurate data can lead to misguided risk evaluations.

- **Model Risk:** The reliance on statistical models introduces the potential for model risk, where the model may not accurately represent reality, leading to poor decision-making.

- **Regulatory Compliance:** Financial institutions must navigate a complex landscape of regulations, necessitating robust risk management frameworks that comply with legal standards.

Fraud Detection Mechanisms

Fraud detection has become an integral part of risk management, as financial institutions strive to protect themselves from fraudulent activities. Data analytics plays a crucial role in identifying patterns and anomalies that may indicate fraud.

Common Techniques for Fraud Detection

- **Anomaly Detection:** This technique involves identifying deviations from established patterns of behavior. For instance, if a customer typically makes small transactions and suddenly attempts a large withdrawal, this anomaly may trigger a fraud alert.

- **Predictive Modeling:** By utilizing historical data, predictive models can forecast the likelihood of fraudulent activities. Techniques such as logistic regression, decision trees, and neural networks are commonly employed.

- **Machine Learning Algorithms:** Advanced machine learning techniques, including support vector machines and ensemble methods, are increasingly used to enhance the accuracy of fraud detection systems.

For example, a financial institution may implement a machine learning model that analyzes transaction data in real-time. The model could use features such as transaction amount, location, and frequency to calculate a fraud score. If the score exceeds a predefined threshold, the transaction may be flagged for further investigation.

Case Study: Credit Card Fraud Detection

A notable example of successful fraud detection is the implementation of machine learning algorithms in credit card transactions. Companies like Visa and Mastercard utilize sophisticated analytics to monitor transactions in real-time. By analyzing billions of transactions, these companies can identify patterns indicative of fraud.

For instance, in a study by Bhattacharyya et al. (2011), a dataset of credit card transactions was analyzed using various machine learning techniques. The results demonstrated that ensemble methods, such as Random Forest, significantly outperformed traditional statistical methods in detecting fraudulent transactions, achieving an accuracy rate of over 90%.

Conclusion

The integration of data analytics into risk management and fraud detection has transformed the financial industry, enabling organizations to proactively identify and mitigate risks while safeguarding against fraudulent activities. As technology continues to advance, the ability to harness data for effective risk management will be paramount in navigating the complexities of the financial landscape. Emphasizing the importance of data quality, regulatory compliance, and continuous improvement in analytical techniques will be crucial for future innovations in this domain.

Improving Customer Experience

In the modern financial landscape, enhancing customer experience has become a pivotal focus for organizations aiming to maintain competitive advantage. The integration of data analytics into customer experience strategies allows financial institutions to better understand and anticipate customer needs, ultimately leading to increased satisfaction and loyalty.

Theoretical Background

At the core of improving customer experience through data analytics is the concept of *Customer Relationship Management* (CRM). CRM systems collect and analyze customer data to provide insights that inform strategic decision-making. According to the *Customer Experience Pyramid* proposed by Meyer and Schwager (2007), effective customer experience management requires a deep understanding of customer journeys, preferences, and pain points. This understanding can be achieved through data-driven insights, enabling organizations to tailor their services and interactions to meet individual customer expectations.

Challenges in Customer Experience

Despite the potential benefits, organizations face several challenges in leveraging data analytics to improve customer experience:

- **Data Silos:** Many organizations operate with fragmented data systems, where customer data is stored in separate silos. This fragmentation hampers the ability to gain a holistic view of customer interactions, making it difficult to deliver a seamless experience.

- **Data Quality:** Poor data quality can lead to inaccurate insights. Inconsistent, incomplete, or outdated data can result in misguided strategies that fail to address customer needs effectively.

- **Privacy Concerns:** With increasing scrutiny on data privacy regulations (e.g., GDPR, CCPA), organizations must navigate the delicate balance between utilizing customer data for personalization and respecting privacy concerns.

- **Technological Integration:** Implementing advanced analytics tools requires significant investment in technology and training. Organizations may struggle to integrate new systems with existing infrastructure, leading to inefficiencies.

Strategies for Improvement

To overcome these challenges, organizations can adopt several strategies that leverage data analytics to enhance customer experience:

1. Unified Customer Profiles Creating unified customer profiles is essential for gaining a comprehensive understanding of customer behavior. By integrating data from various touchpoints—such as online transactions, customer service interactions, and social media engagement—organizations can develop a single view of each customer. This holistic perspective enables personalized interactions that resonate with individual preferences.

2. Predictive Analytics Employing predictive analytics allows organizations to anticipate customer needs and behaviors. For instance, financial institutions can analyze transaction patterns to identify customers at risk of churn. By proactively reaching out to these customers with tailored solutions or incentives, organizations can improve retention rates. The equation for predicting customer churn can be expressed as:

$$Churn\_Probability = \frac{1}{1 + e^{-(\beta_0 + \beta_1 \cdot X_1 + \beta_2 \cdot X_2 + ... + \beta_n \cdot X_n)}} \quad (56)$$

where X_i represents various customer attributes and behaviors, and β_i are the coefficients determined through logistic regression.

3. Real-time Feedback Mechanisms Implementing real-time feedback mechanisms enables organizations to gather immediate insights into customer satisfaction. For example, post-interaction surveys or sentiment analysis on social media can provide valuable data on customer perceptions. This feedback loop allows organizations to make timely adjustments to their services, enhancing overall customer experience.

4. Personalization through Machine Learning Machine learning algorithms can analyze vast datasets to identify patterns and preferences among customers. For instance, recommender systems can suggest personalized financial products based on a customer's transaction history and demographic information. The effectiveness of such systems can be evaluated using metrics like precision and recall:

$$Precision = \frac{TP}{TP + FP} \quad (57)$$

$$Recall = \frac{TP}{TP + FN} \quad (58)$$

where TP is true positives, FP is false positives, and FN is false negatives.

Case Study: Bank of America

A notable example of improving customer experience through data analytics is Bank of America's implementation of the Erica virtual assistant. Utilizing AI and machine learning, Erica provides personalized financial advice, transaction alerts, and budgeting assistance to customers. By analyzing user interactions and preferences, Erica continually learns and adapts, enhancing the customer experience. The implementation of Erica has resulted in increased customer engagement and satisfaction, demonstrating the effectiveness of data-driven strategies.

Conclusion

In conclusion, improving customer experience in the financial sector through data analytics is not only a strategic imperative but also a pathway to fostering long-term customer relationships. By addressing challenges related to data silos, quality, privacy, and technological integration, organizations can effectively leverage analytics to create personalized, engaging, and satisfying customer experiences. As the financial landscape continues to evolve, the importance of data-driven strategies in enhancing customer experience will only grow, positioning organizations for sustained success in an increasingly competitive environment.

Algorithmic Trading and Investment Strategies

Algorithmic trading has emerged as a transformative force in the financial markets, leveraging complex mathematical models and automated systems to execute trades at speeds and efficiencies unattainable by human traders. This section delves into the theoretical foundations, practical applications, and challenges of algorithmic trading, with a focus on investment strategies that harness the power of data analytics.

Theoretical Foundations of Algorithmic Trading

At its core, algorithmic trading relies on mathematical models to identify trading opportunities based on historical data. The fundamental principles governing these models can be categorized into several key areas:

- **Statistical Arbitrage:** This strategy exploits price discrepancies between correlated securities. The basic premise is that the prices of related assets will converge over time. The following equation represents the profit from a long-short strategy:

$$P = (S_{long} - S_{short}) \cdot \Delta t \qquad (59)$$

where P is the profit, S_{long} is the price of the long asset, S_{short} is the price of the short asset, and Δt is the time period of the trade.

- **Mean Reversion:** This strategy is based on the assumption that asset prices will revert to their historical mean over time. A common approach is to use the Z-score to identify overbought or oversold conditions:

$$Z = \frac{X - \mu}{\sigma} \qquad (60)$$

where Z is the Z-score, X is the current price, μ is the mean price, and σ is the standard deviation of prices.

- **Momentum Trading:** Momentum strategies capitalize on existing trends in asset prices. The basic idea is to buy assets that have shown upward price momentum and sell those with downward momentum. The momentum factor can be expressed as:

$$M = \frac{P_t - P_{t-n}}{P_{t-n}} \cdot 100 \qquad (61)$$

where M is the momentum percentage, P_t is the current price, and P_{t-n} is the price n periods ago.

Implementation of Algorithmic Trading Strategies

The implementation of algorithmic trading strategies involves several steps:

1. **Data Collection:** High-quality data is paramount for developing robust trading algorithms. Traders typically utilize historical price data, trading volumes, and market news. Data can be sourced from financial databases and APIs, such as Bloomberg or Alpha Vantage.

2. **Model Development:** Once the data is collected, traders develop models using statistical techniques and machine learning algorithms. Common approaches include regression analysis, decision trees, and neural networks.

3. **Backtesting:** Before deploying a trading strategy in live markets, it is essential to backtest it against historical data to evaluate its performance. The backtesting process involves simulating trades based on historical data to assess profitability and risk metrics, such as the Sharpe ratio:

$$Sharpe = \frac{R_p - R_f}{\sigma_p} \quad (62)$$

where R_p is the return of the portfolio, R_f is the risk-free rate, and σ_p is the standard deviation of the portfolio returns.

4. **Execution:** Once the model is validated, it is implemented in a trading platform that can execute trades automatically based on predefined rules. Execution algorithms, such as VWAP (Volume Weighted Average Price) or TWAP (Time Weighted Average Price), help minimize market impact.

5. **Monitoring and Adjustment:** Continuous monitoring of algorithm performance is necessary to adapt to changing market conditions. This may involve recalibrating models or adjusting parameters to enhance performance.

Challenges in Algorithmic Trading

Despite its advantages, algorithmic trading is not without challenges:

- **Market Risk:** Algorithms can lead to significant losses during periods of high volatility. The flash crash of May 6, 2010, exemplifies how algorithmic trading can exacerbate market declines.

- **Data Quality:** Inaccurate or incomplete data can lead to faulty models, resulting in poor trading decisions. Ensuring data integrity and accuracy is critical.

- **Regulatory Compliance:** Algorithmic trading is subject to regulatory scrutiny. Traders must ensure their strategies comply with regulations to avoid penalties.

- **Technological Failures:** System outages, connectivity issues, and software bugs can disrupt trading activities, leading to unintended consequences.

Case Study: A Successful Algorithmic Trading Strategy

A notable example of a successful algorithmic trading strategy is the use of a simple moving average crossover system. This strategy generates buy and sell signals based on the crossing of short-term and long-term moving averages.

- **Strategy Definition:** - Buy Signal: When the short-term moving average (SMA) crosses above the long-term moving average (LMA). - Sell Signal: When the short-term moving average crosses below the long-term moving average.

- **Implementation:** - Assume a trader uses a 50-day SMA and a 200-day SMA. - If the 50-day SMA crosses above the 200-day SMA, the trader buys the asset. - Conversely, if the 50-day SMA crosses below the 200-day SMA, the trader sells the asset.

- **Performance Evaluation:** - Backtesting this strategy over a 10-year period on the S&P 500 index showed an annualized return of 15

Conclusion

Algorithmic trading represents a paradigm shift in how financial markets operate, enabling traders to leverage data and technology for strategic advantage. By understanding the theoretical foundations, implementation processes, and challenges associated with algorithmic trading, investors can harness the full potential of this innovative approach. As technology continues to evolve, the future of algorithmic trading will likely see even more sophisticated models and strategies, further revolutionizing the investment landscape.

Financial Inclusion and Accessibility

Financial inclusion refers to the process of ensuring access to appropriate financial products and services needed by individuals and businesses to participate fully in the economy. It encompasses a variety of financial services, including banking, credit, insurance, and investment, and aims to provide these services to underserved populations, particularly in developing regions. Accessibility, on the other hand, focuses on the ease with which individuals can access these financial services, often influenced by factors such as geographical location, income level, and technological infrastructure.

Theoretical Framework

The theory of financial inclusion is rooted in several economic and social concepts. One prominent framework is the *Access to Finance* model, which highlights the barriers that prevent individuals from accessing financial services. These barriers can be classified into three main categories:

- **Supply-side barriers:** These include the lack of financial institutions in certain areas, high costs associated with providing services, and limited product offerings.

- **Demand-side barriers:** Factors such as low income, lack of financial literacy, and cultural attitudes towards financial services can hinder individuals from seeking out and using these services.

- **Regulatory barriers:** Government policies and regulations can either facilitate or impede access to financial services, depending on their design and implementation.

Challenges to Financial Inclusion

Despite the theoretical frameworks that support financial inclusion, several challenges remain. According to the World Bank, approximately 1.7 billion adults worldwide remain unbanked, lacking access to basic financial services. The barriers to financial inclusion can be summarized as follows:

1. **Geographical Barriers:** In many rural areas, the absence of physical bank branches makes it difficult for residents to access financial services. For instance, in sub-Saharan Africa, over 60% of the population lives in rural areas, where banking infrastructure is limited.

2. **Technological Barriers:** Although mobile banking has revolutionized access to financial services, many individuals lack the necessary technology, such as smartphones or reliable internet connectivity. This digital divide exacerbates existing inequalities.

3. **Financial Literacy:** A lack of understanding of financial products and services can prevent individuals from utilizing available options. According to a study by the OECD, only 30% of adults globally are financially literate, which limits their ability to make informed financial decisions.

4. **Cost of Services:** High fees associated with banking services can deter low-income individuals from opening accounts or utilizing credit. For example, remittance costs can be as high as 7% in some regions, making it prohibitively expensive for families to send money across borders.

Innovative Solutions for Financial Inclusion

To address these challenges, innovative solutions leveraging data analytics and technology have emerged. These solutions aim to enhance financial inclusion and accessibility in various ways:

- **Mobile Banking and Fintech Solutions:** Companies like M-Pesa in Kenya have demonstrated the potential of mobile money platforms to provide financial services to unbanked populations. M-Pesa allows users to send and receive money, pay bills, and access loans through their mobile phones, significantly increasing financial inclusion in the region.

- **Data Analytics for Credit Scoring:** Traditional credit scoring methods often exclude individuals without formal credit histories. Innovative fintech companies use alternative data sources, such as mobile phone usage patterns and payment histories, to assess creditworthiness. For example, Tala and Branch utilize mobile data to provide loans to individuals with limited credit histories in emerging markets.

- **Community-Based Financial Institutions:** Microfinance institutions (MFIs) and cooperatives have emerged as critical players in promoting financial inclusion. By providing small loans and savings products tailored to the needs of low-income individuals, these institutions help bridge the gap in access to finance. Grameen Bank, founded by Muhammad Yunus, is a notable example of how microfinance can empower communities.

- **Digital Literacy Programs:** To improve financial literacy, organizations are implementing educational programs that teach individuals about financial products and services. Initiatives like the Smart Campaign aim to promote responsible finance by educating consumers about their rights and available financial products.

Case Studies and Examples

Several real-world examples illustrate the impact of innovative solutions on financial inclusion:

- **M-Pesa:** Launched in 2007, M-Pesa has transformed the financial landscape in Kenya, with over 30 million users. The platform enables users to conduct transactions without the need for a traditional bank account, significantly increasing access to financial services. A study by the International Monetary Fund (IMF) found that M-Pesa has contributed to a 2% increase in GDP in Kenya.

- **Tala:** Tala provides microloans to individuals in emerging markets using mobile data for credit scoring. Since its inception, Tala has disbursed over $1 billion in loans to millions of customers in countries like Kenya, Mexico, and the Philippines, demonstrating the power of data analytics in expanding access to credit.

- **Grameen Bank:** Founded in Bangladesh, Grameen Bank has provided microloans to over 9 million borrowers, predominantly women. The bank's success in promoting entrepreneurship and economic empowerment has inspired similar initiatives worldwide, highlighting the importance of community-based financial institutions.

Conclusion

Financial inclusion and accessibility are critical components of a thriving economy. By leveraging data analytics and innovative technologies, it is possible to overcome the barriers that prevent individuals from accessing financial services. As seen through successful case studies like M-Pesa and Tala, the integration of technology and alternative data sources can empower underserved populations and foster economic growth. Moving forward, it is essential to continue exploring new solutions and partnerships that promote financial inclusion, ensuring that everyone has the opportunity to participate in the financial system.

$$\text{Financial Inclusion Rate} = \frac{\text{Number of Adults with Access to Financial Services}}{\text{Total Adult Population}} \times 100 \tag{63}$$

This equation highlights the importance of measuring financial inclusion rates to track progress and identify areas for improvement. By focusing on enhancing accessibility and promoting inclusive financial practices, we can work towards a more equitable financial landscape for all.

Reshaping the Future of Banking

The banking industry is undergoing a profound transformation, driven by advancements in data analytics, artificial intelligence (AI), and evolving consumer expectations. This subsection explores how these innovations are reshaping the future of banking, addressing key theories, problems, and practical examples that illustrate this dynamic shift.

Theoretical Frameworks

At the core of this transformation lies the theory of Digital Banking Transformation (DBT), which posits that banks must evolve from traditional service providers to digital-first organizations. This theory emphasizes the importance of leveraging data analytics to enhance customer experiences, optimize operations, and create new business models. The following frameworks are essential to understanding the implications of DBT:

1. **Customer-Centricity:** This framework focuses on understanding customer needs and behaviors through data analysis. Banks are increasingly using customer segmentation techniques to tailor products and services, leading to improved customer satisfaction and loyalty.

2. **Data-Driven Decision Making:** The integration of big data analytics allows banks to make informed decisions based on comprehensive insights. This approach enhances risk management, fraud detection, and regulatory compliance.

3. **Agile Banking:** Agile methodologies encourage banks to adapt quickly to market changes and customer demands. This flexibility is facilitated by data analytics, enabling rapid prototyping and iterative development of banking products.

Key Problems Addressed

The shift towards a data-driven banking model addresses several critical problems faced by traditional banks:

1. **Legacy Systems:** Many banks operate on outdated technology stacks that hinder innovation. By adopting modern data analytics platforms, banks can streamline operations and enhance service delivery.

2. **Fraud and Risk Management:** Traditional methods of fraud detection are often reactive and inefficient. Data analytics enables proactive identification of suspicious transactions through anomaly detection algorithms. For instance, the use of machine learning models can significantly reduce false positives while improving detection rates.

3. **Regulatory Compliance:** Compliance with regulations such as the General Data Protection Regulation (GDPR) and the Basel III framework requires robust data management. Data analytics facilitates real-time monitoring and reporting, ensuring banks remain compliant while minimizing operational risks.

Practical Examples

Several banks are leading the charge in reshaping the future of banking through innovative data-driven strategies:

1. **JPMorgan Chase:** The bank utilizes AI and machine learning to enhance its fraud detection capabilities. By analyzing transaction patterns, JPMorgan can identify fraudulent activities in real-time, significantly reducing losses.

2. **BBVA:** This Spanish bank has embraced a customer-centric approach by leveraging big data to offer personalized financial services. BBVA uses predictive analytics to anticipate customer needs, allowing for tailored product recommendations that enhance customer engagement.

3. **Goldman Sachs:** The investment bank has implemented a data-driven approach to risk management. By utilizing advanced analytics, Goldman Sachs can assess market risks more accurately, enabling better investment decisions and portfolio management.

Equations and Models

To illustrate the impact of data analytics in banking, consider the following equation representing the Risk-Adjusted Return on Capital (RAROC):

$$RAROC = \frac{Earnings - ExpectedLosses}{EconomicCapital} \qquad (64)$$

Where: - $Earnings$ represents the total income generated by the bank. - $ExpectedLosses$ refers to the anticipated losses from credit risk. - $EconomicCapital$ is the capital required to cover potential losses.

By optimizing this equation through data analytics, banks can enhance profitability while effectively managing risk.

The Future Outlook

As the banking industry continues to evolve, several trends are expected to shape its future:

1. **Increased Automation:** The rise of robotic process automation (RPA) will streamline repetitive tasks, allowing banks to focus on strategic initiatives. Automation will enhance operational efficiency and reduce costs.
2. **Open Banking:** The adoption of open banking frameworks will facilitate data sharing between banks and third-party providers. This collaboration will foster innovation and create new financial products tailored to customer needs.
3. **Enhanced Cybersecurity:** With the increasing reliance on data, banks must prioritize cybersecurity measures. Advanced analytics will play a crucial role in identifying potential threats and mitigating risks associated with cyberattacks.

In conclusion, the future of banking is being reshaped by the integration of data analytics, AI, and customer-centric strategies. As banks embrace these innovations, they will not only enhance operational efficiency but also create a more personalized and secure banking experience for their customers. The journey towards a data-driven banking model is just beginning, and those who adapt will thrive in this new landscape.

Transforming Education

Personalized Learning and Adaptive Education

Personalized learning and adaptive education represent a paradigm shift in the way educational content is delivered and experienced by learners. This approach tailors the educational experience to meet the individual needs, preferences, and learning styles of each student. The core idea is that not all students learn the same way or at the same pace, and therefore, a one-size-fits-all model of education is insufficient to ensure optimal learning outcomes.

Theoretical Foundations

The theoretical underpinnings of personalized learning can be traced to several educational theories, including Constructivism, Differentiated Instruction, and the Zone of Proximal Development (ZPD) proposed by Vygotsky.

- **Constructivism** posits that learners construct their own understanding and knowledge of the world through experiences and reflecting on those experiences. Personalized learning allows students to engage with content that is meaningful to them, thus fostering deeper learning.
- **Differentiated Instruction** emphasizes the need for educators to modify their teaching strategies to accommodate the diverse needs of students. This

approach recognizes that students have varying backgrounds, readiness levels, and interests.

- **Zone of Proximal Development (ZPD)** suggests that students learn best when they are challenged just beyond their current abilities, with appropriate support. Adaptive education tools can identify where a student is in their learning journey and provide resources that are appropriately challenging.

Challenges in Implementation

Despite the potential benefits of personalized learning and adaptive education, several challenges hinder its widespread implementation:

- **Technology Access:** Not all students have equal access to the technology required for personalized learning platforms. This digital divide can exacerbate existing educational inequalities.
- **Data Privacy Concerns:** The collection and analysis of student data raise significant privacy issues. Educators must ensure that data is handled ethically and in compliance with regulations such as FERPA (Family Educational Rights and Privacy Act).
- **Teacher Training:** Educators need adequate training to effectively implement personalized learning strategies. Many teachers may not be familiar with adaptive technologies or how to interpret data to inform instruction.
- **Curriculum Constraints:** Rigid curricula can limit the ability of educators to personalize learning experiences. Schools may need to adopt more flexible curricular frameworks that allow for customization.

Examples of Personalized Learning in Practice

Several innovative educational institutions and programs have successfully implemented personalized learning and adaptive education strategies:

- **Khan Academy:** This online platform provides personalized learning experiences through its extensive library of instructional videos and practice exercises. Students can learn at their own pace, receiving instant feedback and tailored recommendations based on their performance.

- **Summit Learning**: This program emphasizes personalized learning through a combination of project-based learning and data-driven instruction. Students set individual learning goals and progress at their own pace, while teachers provide support and guidance based on real-time data analytics.

- **DreamBox Learning**: This adaptive math program uses intelligent adaptive technology to provide personalized lessons for students in grades K-8. It adjusts the difficulty of problems in real-time based on student responses, ensuring that learners are continuously challenged without becoming frustrated.

Mathematical Models for Personalization

To effectively implement personalized learning, educators can employ mathematical models that analyze student performance data and predict learning trajectories. One such model is the **Item Response Theory (IRT)**, which can be represented mathematically as follows:

$$P(X_{ij} = 1|\theta_i, \beta_j) = \frac{1}{1 + e^{-(\theta_i - \beta_j)}} \tag{65}$$

Where:

- $P(X_{ij} = 1|\theta_i, \beta_j)$ is the probability that student i answers item j correctly.
- θ_i represents the ability level of student i.
- β_j denotes the difficulty level of item j.

This model allows educators to assess student abilities and tailor learning experiences accordingly. By analyzing student responses, teachers can identify areas where students excel or struggle, enabling them to provide targeted support.

Future Directions

The future of personalized learning and adaptive education is promising, with advancements in artificial intelligence (AI) and machine learning poised to enhance these approaches. AI algorithms can analyze vast amounts of data, enabling the development of more sophisticated adaptive learning systems that can predict student needs with greater accuracy.

Moreover, as educational institutions increasingly recognize the importance of social-emotional learning, personalized learning frameworks will likely incorporate elements that address the holistic development of students. This includes fostering resilience, empathy, and collaboration skills alongside academic achievement.

In conclusion, personalized learning and adaptive education represent a significant shift in educational practices, offering opportunities to enhance student engagement, motivation, and achievement. By leveraging technology and data-driven insights, educators can create customized learning experiences that empower students to take ownership of their education and succeed in an ever-evolving world.

Predictive Analytics for Student Success

Predictive analytics has emerged as a powerful tool in the educational sector, transforming the way institutions approach student success. By leveraging vast amounts of data, predictive analytics enables educators and administrators to identify at-risk students, tailor interventions, and enhance overall learning outcomes. This section explores the theoretical foundations of predictive analytics in education, the challenges faced in its implementation, and practical examples demonstrating its effectiveness.

Theoretical Foundations

Predictive analytics involves the use of statistical techniques and machine learning algorithms to analyze historical data and make predictions about future events. In the context of education, this typically involves analyzing student data, such as grades, attendance records, and engagement metrics, to forecast academic performance and identify potential challenges.

The underlying principle of predictive analytics is rooted in regression analysis, a statistical method used to understand the relationship between variables. The basic form of a regression equation can be expressed as:

$$Y = \beta_0 + \beta_1 X_1 + \beta_2 X_2 + \ldots + \beta_n X_n + \epsilon \tag{66}$$

where: - Y is the dependent variable (e.g., student performance), - β_0 is the y-intercept, - $\beta_1, \beta_2, \ldots, \beta_n$ are the coefficients for each independent variable $X_1, X_2, \ldots, X_n$ (e.g., attendance, homework completion), - ϵ is the error term.

By analyzing historical data, educators can identify which factors most significantly impact student success, allowing them to prioritize interventions effectively.

Challenges in Implementation

Despite its potential, the implementation of predictive analytics in education is not without challenges. Key issues include:

- **Data Quality:** The accuracy of predictions is heavily dependent on the quality of data collected. Incomplete or inaccurate data can lead to misleading conclusions.

- **Ethical Considerations:** The use of predictive analytics raises ethical concerns regarding privacy and data security. Institutions must ensure that student data is handled responsibly and transparently.

- **Resistance to Change:** Educators may be resistant to adopting data-driven approaches, particularly if they perceive them as undermining their professional judgment.

- **Integration with Existing Systems:** Integrating predictive analytics tools with current educational technologies can be complex and resource-intensive.

Examples of Predictive Analytics in Action

Several educational institutions have successfully implemented predictive analytics to enhance student success. Here are notable examples:

- **Georgia State University:** This institution has developed a predictive analytics system that analyzes student data to identify those at risk of dropping out. By monitoring factors such as GPA, credit hours, and financial aid status, the university can intervene with tailored support services, resulting in a significant increase in graduation rates.

- **University of Southern California (USC):** USC employs predictive analytics to improve student retention. By analyzing engagement metrics such as participation in extracurricular activities and class attendance, the university can provide targeted support to students who may be struggling, ultimately enhancing their likelihood of success.

- **Southern New Hampshire University (SNHU):** SNHU utilizes predictive modeling to personalize learning pathways for its online students. By analyzing data from previous cohorts, the university can recommend courses and resources tailored to individual learning styles and needs, improving student satisfaction and success rates.

Conclusion

Predictive analytics represents a transformative approach to fostering student success in educational institutions. By harnessing the power of data, educators can proactively identify at-risk students and implement targeted interventions that enhance learning outcomes. However, to fully realize the potential of predictive analytics, institutions must address challenges related to data quality, ethical considerations, and resistance to change. As the field continues to evolve, the integration of predictive analytics into educational practices will play a crucial role in shaping the future of learning.

Bibliography

[1] Georgia State University. (2020). *Using Predictive Analytics to Improve Graduation Rates*. Retrieved from `https://www.gsu.edu`

[2] University of Southern California. (2021). *Retention through Predictive Analytics*. Retrieved from `https://www.usc.edu`

[3] Southern New Hampshire University. (2019). *Personalized Learning Pathways at SNHU*. Retrieved from `https://www.snhu.edu`

Enhancing Classroom Instruction

In the evolving landscape of education, data analytics plays a pivotal role in enhancing classroom instruction. By leveraging data, educators can create a more personalized and effective learning environment that caters to the diverse needs of students. This subsection explores the theoretical frameworks, challenges, and practical examples of how data can be utilized to improve teaching methodologies and student engagement.

Theoretical Frameworks

The integration of data analytics in education is grounded in several educational theories, notably Constructivism and Data-Driven Decision Making (DDDM).

Constructivism Constructivist theories, as proposed by Piaget and Vygotsky, emphasize that learners construct their own understanding and knowledge of the world through experiences and reflecting on those experiences. Data analytics can facilitate this by providing insights into student learning patterns and preferences, allowing educators to tailor instruction accordingly.

Data-Driven Decision Making (DDDM) DDDM is a systematic approach where data is used to inform instructional strategies and improve student outcomes. According to Hamilton et al. (2009), effective DDDM involves the collection, analysis, and interpretation of data to guide educational practices. This approach enables educators to identify areas of improvement and make informed decisions that enhance classroom instruction.

Challenges in Implementing Data Analytics

Despite the potential benefits, several challenges hinder the effective integration of data analytics in classroom instruction:

Data Overload Educators often face an overwhelming amount of data from various sources, including standardized tests, formative assessments, and attendance records. This data overload can lead to confusion and misinterpretation, making it difficult for teachers to extract actionable insights.

Lack of Training Many educators lack the necessary training to analyze and interpret data effectively. Without proper training, teachers may struggle to utilize data analytics tools, leading to underutilization of valuable resources.

Resistance to Change Some educators may resist adopting data-driven practices due to a fear of change or a belief that traditional teaching methods are sufficient. Overcoming this resistance requires a cultural shift within educational institutions that promotes data literacy and innovation.

Practical Examples of Enhancing Classroom Instruction

To illustrate the impact of data analytics on classroom instruction, several practical examples highlight successful implementations:

Personalized Learning Paths One notable example is the use of adaptive learning technologies, such as DreamBox Learning and Khan Academy. These platforms analyze student performance in real-time, adapting the curriculum to meet individual learning needs. For instance, if a student struggles with a specific mathematical concept, the platform will provide additional resources and practice problems tailored to that topic, ensuring mastery before progressing.

Formative Assessment Analysis Teachers can enhance instruction by analyzing formative assessment data to identify common misconceptions among students. For example, a middle school science teacher might use data from quizzes to determine that a significant number of students are struggling with the concept of photosynthesis. Armed with this knowledge, the teacher can adjust lesson plans to include more hands-on activities and visual aids that clarify the process, ultimately improving student understanding.

Collaborative Learning Environments Data analytics can also facilitate the creation of collaborative learning environments. Tools like Google Classroom and Microsoft Teams allow educators to track student engagement and participation in group activities. By analyzing this data, teachers can identify which students may need additional support in collaborative settings and adjust group compositions accordingly to enhance peer learning.

Equations and Models in Data Analytics

To quantify the impact of data analytics on classroom instruction, several equations and models can be employed. One common model is the Learning Analytics Framework, which can be represented as:

$$LA = f(D, A, I) \qquad (67)$$

Where:

- LA = Learning Analytics
- D = Data collected (e.g., assessments, attendance)
- A = Analysis methods (e.g., statistical analysis, machine learning)
- I = Instructional strategies implemented

This framework illustrates how data and analysis methods converge to inform instructional strategies, ultimately enhancing the learning experience.

Conclusion

Enhancing classroom instruction through data analytics represents a transformative approach to education. By understanding the theoretical underpinnings, addressing implementation challenges, and exploring practical examples, educators can effectively utilize data to create a more engaging and personalized learning environment. The future of education lies in harnessing the power of data to empower both teachers and students, leading to improved educational outcomes and a more informed approach to teaching and learning.

Data-Driven School Management

In the realm of education, data-driven school management has emerged as a transformative approach that leverages data analytics to enhance decision-making processes and improve student outcomes. This section delves into the theoretical foundations, challenges, and practical applications of data-driven management in educational institutions.

Theoretical Foundations

Data-driven decision-making (DDDM) in education is grounded in the principles of evidence-based management and continuous improvement. According to [?], DDDM involves collecting, analyzing, and interpreting data to guide strategic planning and operational decisions. This approach is supported by several theories, including:

- **Systems Theory:** This theory posits that schools function as complex systems where various components interact dynamically. By analyzing data from different aspects of school operations, administrators can identify patterns and optimize processes.

- **Feedback Loop Theory:** Effective management relies on feedback mechanisms that allow for adjustments based on data insights. Schools can implement continuous feedback loops to assess the impact of interventions and refine strategies accordingly.

- **Theory of Change:** This framework helps schools articulate their goals, assumptions, and pathways to achieve desired outcomes. Data serves as a critical component in evaluating progress and making necessary adjustments.

Challenges in Implementation

While the potential benefits of data-driven school management are significant, several challenges hinder its effective implementation:

- **Data Quality and Accessibility:** Schools often struggle with inconsistent data quality and fragmented data sources. Ensuring that data is accurate, timely, and accessible is crucial for informed decision-making.

- **Resistance to Change:** Educators and administrators may be resistant to adopting data-driven practices due to a lack of understanding or fear of accountability. Building a culture that values data-driven insights is essential for overcoming this resistance.

- **Privacy and Ethical Concerns:** The collection and analysis of student data raise privacy issues. Schools must navigate ethical considerations while ensuring compliance with regulations such as FERPA (Family Educational Rights and Privacy Act).

- **Training and Capacity Building:** Effective data-driven management requires skills in data analysis and interpretation. Professional development programs must be established to equip educators and administrators with the necessary competencies.

Practical Applications

Data-driven school management manifests in various practical applications that enhance operational efficiency and student achievement:

1. Resource Allocation Data analytics can inform resource allocation decisions by identifying areas of need within the school. For instance, by analyzing student performance data, administrators can allocate additional tutoring resources to subjects where students are struggling. This targeted approach ensures that resources are used effectively to address specific challenges.

2. Performance Monitoring Schools can implement data dashboards that provide real-time insights into student performance, attendance, and behavior. For example, a school might use a dashboard to track student grades across subjects, enabling educators to identify at-risk students early and intervene proactively.

3. Curriculum Development Data-driven insights can guide curriculum development by identifying trends in student learning outcomes. For example, if data shows that students consistently perform poorly in a particular area, educators can adjust the curriculum to include more targeted instruction and resources in that subject.

4. Stakeholder Engagement Data can facilitate communication and engagement with stakeholders, including parents and the community. Schools can share data on student progress and school performance through newsletters or online platforms, fostering transparency and collaboration.

5. Predictive Analytics Advanced analytics techniques, such as predictive modeling, can forecast student outcomes based on historical data. For instance, schools can use predictive analytics to identify students at risk of dropping out and implement targeted interventions to support them.

Examples of Successful Implementation

Several schools and districts have successfully implemented data-driven management practices:

Case Study 1: The New York City Department of Education The NYC Department of Education has developed a comprehensive data system known as ARIS (Achievement Reporting and Innovation System). This platform allows educators to access student performance data, attendance records, and other metrics to inform their teaching practices. As a result, schools using ARIS have reported improved student outcomes and enhanced collaboration among educators.

Case Study 2: The Houston Independent School District Houston ISD has embraced data-driven decision-making to improve student performance. By utilizing data analytics to identify trends and gaps in student achievement, the district has implemented targeted interventions, such as after-school tutoring programs, that have led to significant increases in student test scores.

Conclusion

Data-driven school management represents a paradigm shift in how educational institutions operate. By harnessing the power of data, schools can make informed decisions that enhance student learning, optimize resource allocation, and foster a culture of continuous improvement. However, successful implementation requires overcoming challenges related to data quality, resistance to change, and ethical considerations. As schools continue to embrace data-driven practices, they pave the way for a more effective and equitable education system.

Empowering Educators with Data

The advent of data analytics in education has transformed the landscape of teaching and learning. By harnessing the power of data, educators can make informed decisions that enhance student outcomes, tailor instruction to individual needs, and foster an environment of continuous improvement. This subsection explores the multifaceted ways in which data empowers educators, the theoretical frameworks supporting these practices, the challenges faced, and illustrative examples from the field.

Theoretical Foundations

The use of data in education is grounded in several key theories, including Constructivism and Data-Informed Decision Making (DIDM). Constructivism posits that learners construct their own understanding and knowledge of the world through experiences and reflecting on those experiences. Data analytics provides educators with insights into student performance, enabling them to adapt their teaching strategies accordingly.

Data-Informed Decision Making (DIDM) emphasizes the importance of using data to guide instructional practices. According to [Hattie(2009)], effective teaching is influenced by the feedback loop created through data analysis, which allows educators to assess the impact of their methods and make necessary adjustments. The integration of data into pedagogical practices aligns with the principles of formative assessment, where ongoing feedback is used to improve learning outcomes.

Challenges in Data Utilization

Despite the potential benefits, several challenges hinder the effective use of data in educational settings:

- **Data Overload:** Educators often face an overwhelming amount of data, making it difficult to identify relevant insights. The challenge lies in filtering through vast datasets to find actionable information.

- **Lack of Training:** Many educators lack the necessary training to interpret and utilize data effectively. Professional development programs must be implemented to equip teachers with data literacy skills.

- **Privacy Concerns:** The collection and analysis of student data raise ethical concerns regarding privacy and security. Educators must navigate these issues while ensuring compliance with regulations such as FERPA (Family Educational Rights and Privacy Act).

- **Resistance to Change:** Some educators may be resistant to adopting data-driven practices due to a lack of understanding of its benefits or fear of being evaluated based on data metrics.

Empowering Educators: Practical Examples

Numerous educational institutions have successfully implemented data-driven strategies to empower educators. Here are a few notable examples:

1. **Personalized Learning at Summit Public Schools:** Summit Public Schools utilizes a personalized learning platform that collects data on student performance and engagement. Educators receive real-time analytics that inform their instructional decisions, allowing them to tailor lessons to meet individual student needs. This approach has led to improved academic outcomes and increased student engagement.

2. **Data-Driven Instruction at Chicago Public Schools:** Chicago Public Schools implemented a data-driven instructional model where teachers analyze student data weekly. This practice enables educators to identify learning gaps and adjust their teaching strategies accordingly. The initiative has resulted in significant improvements in student achievement across various subjects.

3. **Using Learning Management Systems (LMS):** Many institutions employ LMS platforms that track student interactions, assessments, and progress. For example, platforms like Canvas and Moodle provide educators with dashboards that visualize student data, helping them identify at-risk students and intervene promptly.

4. **Formative Assessment Tools:** Tools such as Kahoot! and Socrative allow educators to gather real-time feedback from students during lessons. By analyzing this data, teachers can adjust their instruction on-the-fly, ensuring that they address student misconceptions immediately.

Conclusion

Empowering educators with data is a transformative endeavor that requires a commitment to professional development, ethical considerations, and a culture of collaboration. By leveraging data analytics, educators can enhance their instructional practices, personalize learning experiences, and ultimately improve student outcomes. As the education sector continues to evolve, it is imperative that educators embrace data as a tool for empowerment, fostering a data-driven culture that prioritizes student success.

Bibliography

[Hattie(2009)] Hattie, J. (2009). *Visible Learning: A Synthesis of Over 800 Meta-Analyses Relating to Achievement*. Routledge.

Innovating in Entertainment and Media

Recommender Systems and Content Curation

Recommender systems have become an integral part of the digital experience, influencing how users discover content across various platforms, from streaming services to e-commerce websites. These systems leverage algorithms to analyze user behavior and preferences, providing tailored recommendations that enhance user engagement and satisfaction.

Overview of Recommender Systems

Recommender systems can be broadly categorized into three main types: collaborative filtering, content-based filtering, and hybrid methods. Each method employs different techniques to generate recommendations.

Collaborative Filtering Collaborative filtering relies on user interactions and preferences to recommend items. This approach assumes that if two users share similar tastes, they are likely to enjoy the same items. The two primary techniques within collaborative filtering are:

- **User-based Collaborative Filtering:** This technique identifies users with similar preferences and recommends items that those similar users have liked. Mathematically, the similarity between users can be computed using cosine similarity:

$$\text{sim}(u, v) = \frac{\sum_{i \in I} r_{ui} \cdot r_{vi}}{\sqrt{\sum_{i \in I} r_{ui}^2} \cdot \sqrt{\sum_{i \in I} r_{vi}^2}}$$

where r_{ui} is the rating given by user u to item i, and I is the set of items rated by both users u and v.

- **Item-based Collaborative Filtering:** This method focuses on finding similarities between items rather than users. The recommendation is based on the similarity of items that a user has previously liked. The similarity between items can be computed similarly to user-based filtering.

Content-Based Filtering Content-based filtering recommends items based on the characteristics of the items themselves and the preferences of the user. For instance, if a user enjoys action movies, the system will recommend other movies in the action genre. The recommendation can be modeled using a feature vector representation of items and users. The cosine similarity can also be applied here:

$$\text{sim}(i, j) = \frac{F_i \cdot F_j}{\|F_i\| \|F_j\|}$$

where F_i and F_j are the feature vectors of items i and j, respectively.

Hybrid Methods Hybrid recommender systems combine multiple recommendation strategies to improve accuracy and overcome limitations associated with individual methods. For example, Netflix employs a hybrid approach that combines collaborative filtering with content-based filtering to provide a more robust recommendation system.

Challenges in Recommender Systems

Despite their widespread use, recommender systems face several challenges:

Cold Start Problem The cold start problem occurs when the system lacks sufficient data to make accurate recommendations. This can happen with new users who have not rated enough items or with new items that have not been rated by any users. Solutions to this problem include:

- **User Profiling:** Gathering demographic or contextual information about users to make initial recommendations.

- **Popularity-Based Recommendations:** Suggesting popular items until sufficient data is collected.

Data Sparsity In many cases, user-item interaction matrices are sparse, meaning that most users have not rated most items. This sparsity can lead to inaccurate recommendations. Techniques to mitigate this issue include:

- **Matrix Factorization:** Decomposing the user-item matrix into lower-dimensional matrices to capture latent factors.
- **Neighborhood Methods:** Leveraging the relationships between users and items to enhance recommendations.

Scalability As the volume of data grows, recommender systems must efficiently process and analyze vast amounts of information. Techniques such as:

- **Distributed Computing:** Utilizing frameworks like Apache Spark to handle large datasets.
- **Approximate Nearest Neighbors (ANN):** Implementing algorithms that quickly find similar items without exhaustive searches.

Applications of Recommender Systems

Recommender systems are employed across various industries, enhancing user experiences and driving engagement:

E-commerce Platforms like Amazon use recommender systems to suggest products based on user behavior, leading to increased sales. For instance, the "Customers who bought this item also bought" feature is a classic example of collaborative filtering in action.

Streaming Services Netflix and Spotify utilize recommender systems to personalize content suggestions, improving user retention. For example, Netflix's "Top Picks for You" leverages user viewing history and preferences to recommend shows and movies.

Social Media Social media platforms like Facebook and Instagram recommend posts and friends based on user interactions. These systems analyze likes, shares, and comments to curate a personalized feed.

News and Content Platforms Websites like Medium and Flipboard employ recommender systems to suggest articles based on user interests and reading habits, enhancing content discovery.

Future Directions in Recommender Systems

The future of recommender systems lies in addressing current challenges and leveraging emerging technologies:

Incorporating Contextual Information Future systems may integrate contextual data, such as location, time, and user mood, to provide more relevant recommendations. For example, a user searching for restaurants may receive different suggestions based on their current location or the time of day.

Utilizing Deep Learning Deep learning techniques, such as neural collaborative filtering and recurrent neural networks, are being explored to capture complex patterns in user behavior and item characteristics, leading to improved recommendations.

Enhancing Explainability As recommender systems become more complex, there is a growing need for transparency. Developing methods to explain recommendations can enhance user trust and satisfaction.

Addressing Ethical Concerns Recommender systems must navigate ethical challenges, such as filter bubbles and algorithmic bias. Future developments should prioritize fairness and inclusivity, ensuring diverse content exposure.

In conclusion, recommender systems play a pivotal role in content curation across various platforms, shaping user experiences and influencing decisions. By understanding the underlying theories, challenges, and applications, we can appreciate the significance of these systems in the data-driven landscape of the future.

Audience Insights and Targeted Advertising

In the digital age, understanding audience insights has become paramount for businesses aiming to maximize their advertising effectiveness. Targeted advertising leverages data analytics to deliver personalized content to specific user segments, enhancing engagement and conversion rates. This subsection explores the theoretical foundations of audience insights, the challenges associated with targeted advertising, and real-world examples that illustrate its impact.

Theoretical Foundations

Audience insights refer to the understanding of consumer behaviors, preferences, and demographics derived from data analysis. The primary theories underpinning audience insights include:

- **Consumer Behavior Theory:** This theory examines how individuals make purchasing decisions based on psychological, social, and emotional factors. Understanding these factors allows marketers to tailor their messages to resonate with specific audiences.

- **Segmentation Theory:** Segmentation involves dividing a broad target market into subsets of consumers with common needs or characteristics. The most common segmentation bases include demographics, psychographics, geographic location, and behavioral traits. The formula for calculating the size of a segment can be expressed as:

$$S = \frac{N}{T} \times 100$$

    where S is the segment size percentage, N is the number of individuals in the segment, and T is the total population size.

- **Data-Driven Marketing Theory:** This theory posits that decisions regarding marketing strategies should be based on data analysis rather than intuition. By analyzing data from various sources, marketers can gain insights into consumer behavior, leading to more effective advertising strategies.

Challenges in Targeted Advertising

Despite the advantages of targeted advertising, several challenges must be addressed:

- **Data Privacy Concerns:** With increasing scrutiny over data privacy regulations (e.g., GDPR, CCPA), companies must navigate the delicate balance between personalization and privacy. Mismanagement of consumer data can lead to legal repercussions and damage to brand reputation.

- **Ad Fatigue:** Overexposure to targeted ads can lead to ad fatigue, where consumers become desensitized to marketing messages. To combat this, advertisers need to rotate their ads and refresh content regularly to maintain engagement.

- **Algorithm Bias:** Algorithms used in targeted advertising can inadvertently reinforce biases present in the data. This can lead to discriminatory practices and alienate certain consumer groups. Continuous monitoring and adjustment of algorithms are necessary to mitigate bias.

Real-World Examples

Several companies have successfully harnessed audience insights for targeted advertising, leading to significant business outcomes:

- **Netflix:** By analyzing viewer data, Netflix personalizes recommendations, which has proven to be a key driver of user engagement. Their algorithm considers factors such as viewing history, ratings, and even the time of day when suggesting content. This targeted approach has resulted in increased viewer retention and satisfaction.

- **Amazon:** Amazon employs sophisticated algorithms to analyze consumer behavior and preferences, enabling them to present personalized product recommendations. The effectiveness of this strategy is evident in the statistic that approximately 35% of Amazon's revenue comes from its recommendation engine.

- **Facebook:** Facebook's advertising platform allows businesses to target users based on detailed demographic and behavioral data. Advertisers can create highly specific audience segments, leading to improved ad performance. For instance, a study showed that targeted ads on Facebook had a 30% higher click-through rate compared to non-targeted ads.

Conclusion

Audience insights and targeted advertising represent a powerful combination that can drive marketing success. By leveraging data analytics, businesses can create personalized advertising experiences that resonate with consumers. However, it is crucial to navigate the challenges associated with data privacy, ad fatigue, and algorithm bias to ensure sustainable success. As technology continues to evolve, the ability to harness audience insights will remain a vital aspect of effective advertising strategies.

Content Creation and Production

In the rapidly evolving landscape of entertainment and media, data analytics has emerged as a transformative force in content creation and production. This subsection explores the integration of data-driven methodologies in the creative process, the challenges faced by content creators, and successful examples of data-informed production strategies.

The Role of Data in Content Creation

Data analytics plays a pivotal role in understanding audience preferences, predicting trends, and optimizing content for various platforms. The use of data allows creators to tailor their work to meet the specific desires of their target demographics. For instance, streaming services like Netflix utilize sophisticated algorithms to analyze viewing habits, which inform decisions on what shows to produce or renew.

The fundamental equation guiding this process can be expressed as:

$$C = f(A, T, D) \qquad (68)$$

where C represents content creation, A is audience preferences, T denotes trends in the media landscape, and D signifies data analytics insights. This equation underscores the interconnectedness of audience insights, market trends, and data analysis in shaping successful content.

Challenges in Data-Driven Content Production

While the benefits of data-driven content creation are apparent, several challenges persist. One significant issue is the potential for data overload. Creators may find themselves inundated with vast amounts of data, making it difficult to extract actionable insights. The complexity of analyzing unstructured data, such as social media interactions or viewer comments, can further complicate the creative process.

Additionally, there is the risk of homogenization in content. Relying heavily on data analytics may lead to formulaic productions that prioritize proven formulas over innovative storytelling. This phenomenon can stifle creativity and result in a lack of diversity in content offerings.

Successful Examples of Data-Driven Content Creation

Despite these challenges, many organizations have successfully integrated data analytics into their content creation processes. A notable example is Netflix's original programming strategy. By analyzing viewing patterns, Netflix identified a demand for specific genres and themes, such as the success of shows like *Stranger Things*, which combined elements of nostalgia and supernatural thrillers. The data-driven approach not only informed the decision to produce the show but also shaped its marketing strategy, targeting audiences who had shown interest in similar content.

Another example is the music industry, where platforms like Spotify leverage data to curate personalized playlists and recommend new artists to listeners. By analyzing user behavior, Spotify can identify emerging trends and promote content that aligns with listener preferences, thereby enhancing user engagement.

The Future of Content Creation with Data Analytics

As technology advances, the integration of data analytics in content creation is expected to deepen. The rise of artificial intelligence (AI) and machine learning (ML) will enable even more sophisticated analysis of audience behavior and preferences. For instance, AI algorithms can generate insights from complex datasets, uncovering patterns that may not be immediately apparent to human analysts.

Moreover, the use of predictive analytics will allow creators to anticipate audience reactions to new content before its release. This capability could lead to more strategic decision-making in production, reducing the risk of failure and maximizing audience engagement.

The equation that could represent this future landscape is:

$$I = g(P, A, E) \qquad (69)$$

where I is the innovation in content, P represents predictive analytics, A denotes audience engagement metrics, and E signifies emerging technologies. This equation illustrates how innovation in content will increasingly rely on predictive insights, audience interaction data, and technological advancements.

Conclusion

In conclusion, the intersection of data analytics and content creation presents both opportunities and challenges. While data-driven insights can enhance the creative process and lead to more engaging content, it is essential for creators to balance data reliance with artistic intuition. As the media landscape continues to evolve, embracing innovative data practices while fostering creativity will be crucial for the future of content production. By navigating these complexities, content creators can harness the power of data to produce compelling narratives that resonate with audiences worldwide.

Data Journalism and Fact-Checking

Data journalism is an evolving field that leverages data analysis to tell compelling stories, uncover truths, and provide insights into complex issues. In an age where information is abundant yet often misleading, the role of data journalism becomes paramount in promoting transparency, accountability, and informed public discourse. This subsection explores the theoretical foundations, challenges, and practical examples of data journalism and fact-checking.

Theoretical Foundations of Data Journalism

Data journalism merges traditional journalism practices with data analysis techniques. According to [Cohen(2015)], it is defined as "the practice of using data as a primary source for reporting and storytelling." The theoretical underpinnings of data journalism can be traced back to several key concepts:

- **Information Hierarchy:** The idea that data can be organized and presented in a way that enhances understanding. The *Information Hierarchy* model, as proposed by [Shannon(1948)], emphasizes the importance of clarity and accessibility in data presentation.

- **Data Visualization:** The use of visual representations to communicate data findings effectively. [Tufte(2006)] argues that well-designed visualizations can reveal patterns and insights that are not immediately apparent in raw data.

- **Narrative Construction:** The art of weaving data into a compelling story. [Bamford(2017)] highlights that a strong narrative can contextualize data, making it relatable to audiences.

Challenges in Data Journalism

While data journalism holds significant potential, it also faces numerous challenges:

- **Data Quality and Reliability:** Journalists often encounter datasets that are incomplete, outdated, or biased. This raises concerns about the validity of the conclusions drawn. For instance, a study by [Lazer(2018)] emphasizes the importance of scrutinizing data sources to avoid perpetuating misinformation.

- **Technical Skills Gap:** Many journalists lack the technical skills required for data analysis and visualization. A report by [Pew(2019)] found that only 27% of journalists feel comfortable working with data, underscoring the need for training in data literacy.

- **Ethical Considerations:** The use of data in journalism raises ethical questions, particularly regarding privacy and consent. [O'Sullivan(2020)] warns that journalists must navigate these issues carefully to maintain public trust.

The Role of Fact-Checking in Data Journalism

Fact-checking is an essential component of data journalism, serving as a mechanism to verify claims and ensure accuracy. The process of fact-checking involves several steps:

1. **Source Verification:** Confirming the credibility of data sources. This includes checking the origin of the data and the methodology used to collect it.

2. **Data Analysis:** Analyzing the data to identify patterns or discrepancies. Statistical techniques such as regression analysis can be employed to determine the significance of findings.

3. **Contextualization:** Providing context to data points to avoid misinterpretation. For example, stating that "unemployment rates have increased by 5%" without context can mislead readers about the overall economic situation.

4. **Transparency:** Disclosing the data sources and methodologies used in reporting. [Graves(2016)] emphasizes that transparency builds trust with audiences and allows for independent verification.

Examples of Data Journalism and Fact-Checking

Several notable examples illustrate the impact of data journalism and fact-checking:

- **The New York Times' COVID-19 Tracker:** During the pandemic, The New York Times created a comprehensive COVID-19 tracker that provided real-time data on infections, deaths, and vaccinations. This initiative showcased how data journalism can inform the public and guide policy decisions.

- **PolitiFact:** An independent fact-checking organization, PolitiFact uses a rigorous methodology to evaluate the accuracy of political statements. Their "Truth-O-Meter" visually represents the veracity of claims, making it accessible to a broad audience.

- **The Guardian's Data Stories:** The Guardian has produced several data-driven stories that reveal social issues, such as income inequality and climate change. Their use of interactive visualizations allows readers to engage with the data meaningfully.

Conclusion

Data journalism and fact-checking are vital in today's information landscape, where misinformation can spread rapidly. By harnessing the power of data, journalists can uncover truths, inform the public, and hold institutions accountable. However, the challenges of data quality, technical skills, and ethical considerations must be addressed to maximize the potential of this field. As we move forward, the collaboration between data scientists and journalists will be crucial in shaping a more informed society.

Bibliography

[Cohen(2015)] Cohen, A. (2015). *Data Journalism: A Handbook for Freelancers.* London: Routledge.

[Shannon(1948)] Shannon, C. E. (1948). A Mathematical Theory of Communication. *Bell System Technical Journal*, 27(3), 379–423.

[Tufte(2006)] Tufte, E. R. (2006). *The Visual Display of Quantitative Information.* Cheshire, CT: Graphics Press.

[Bamford(2017)] Bamford, A. (2017). *The Art of Data Storytelling.* New York: HarperCollins.

[Lazer(2018)] Lazer, D. M. J., et al. (2018). The Science of Fake News. *Science*, 359(6380), 1094–1096.

[Pew(2019)] Pew Research Center. (2019). The Future of News: A Survey of Journalists. Retrieved from https://www.pewresearch.org/journalism/2019/05/20/the-future-of-news/

[O'Sullivan(2020)] O'Sullivan, D. (2020). Data Journalism Ethics: A Framework for Reporting. *Journalism Ethics*, 15(1), 1-15.

[Graves(2016)] Graves, L. (2016). *Deciding What's True: The Rise of Political Fact-Checking in American Journalism.* New York: Columbia University Press.

Shaping the Future of Entertainment

The entertainment industry is undergoing a seismic shift, driven by advancements in data analytics and artificial intelligence (AI). As we delve into this transformation, it is essential to understand the theories, challenges, and real-world applications that are shaping the future of how we consume and create entertainment content.

Theoretical Frameworks

At the heart of this revolution is the theory of **user engagement**, which posits that understanding audience behavior can lead to more personalized and impactful content. The *Uses and Gratifications Theory* suggests that audiences actively seek out media that fulfills their specific needs—be it entertainment, information, or social interaction. With the advent of big data, entertainment companies can analyze vast amounts of viewer data to identify these needs and tailor content accordingly.

Additionally, the **Cognitive Load Theory** plays a crucial role in content creation. This theory emphasizes that the amount of information presented should not overwhelm the audience's cognitive capacity. By leveraging data analytics, creators can optimize the pacing, complexity, and structure of narratives to enhance viewer retention and satisfaction.

Challenges in the Entertainment Landscape

While the integration of data analytics in entertainment offers numerous benefits, it also presents significant challenges:

- **Data Privacy Concerns:** With the collection of user data comes the responsibility to protect it. The entertainment industry must navigate complex regulations such as the General Data Protection Regulation (GDPR) to ensure user privacy while leveraging data for personalization.

- **Content Saturation:** As platforms like Netflix and Hulu flood the market with content, distinguishing oneself becomes increasingly difficult. Data analytics can help identify niche markets and underrepresented genres, but the sheer volume of content can lead to viewer fatigue.

- **Algorithmic Bias:** Algorithms that dictate content recommendations can inadvertently promote bias. If not carefully monitored, these algorithms may reinforce existing stereotypes or limit exposure to diverse narratives.

Real-World Applications

The integration of data analytics in entertainment is not merely theoretical; it is being actively applied across various facets of the industry:

Recommender Systems One of the most prominent applications of data analytics is in recommender systems. Platforms like Netflix utilize collaborative filtering algorithms to suggest content based on user preferences and viewing history. The basic equation governing collaborative filtering can be represented as follows:

$$R_{ij} = \frac{\sum_{k \in N(i)} (R_{kj} - \bar{R}_k)}{|N(i)|} + \bar{R}_i$$

Where: - R_{ij} is the predicted rating for item j by user i, - $N(i)$ is the set of users similar to i, - $\bar{R}_k$ is the average rating of user k, - $|N(i)|$ is the number of similar users, - $\bar{R}_i$ is the average rating of user i.

This algorithm allows platforms to create highly personalized viewing experiences, significantly enhancing user engagement.

Content Creation Data analytics is also transforming content creation. Studios like Disney use predictive analytics to gauge audience interest in potential projects before greenlighting them. By analyzing social media trends, search queries, and demographic data, they can identify what types of stories resonate with specific audiences. For instance, the success of the Marvel Cinematic Universe can be attributed to its data-driven approach in understanding audience preferences for superhero narratives.

Interactive Storytelling Furthermore, the rise of interactive storytelling—exemplified by Netflix's *Black Mirror: Bandersnatch*—highlights how data can shape narrative structures. By allowing viewers to make choices that influence the storyline, creators can collect data on user preferences and engagement levels, leading to more refined and engaging experiences in future projects.

Future Directions

Looking ahead, the future of entertainment will likely be characterized by:

- **Augmented and Virtual Reality (AR/VR):** As AR and VR technologies evolve, data analytics will play a crucial role in creating immersive experiences tailored to individual user preferences.

- **AI-Generated Content:** The use of AI in scriptwriting and content creation is on the rise. Tools like OpenAI's GPT-3 can assist writers by generating story ideas or dialogue based on data-driven insights into audience preferences.

- **Enhanced Audience Interaction:** Future platforms may incorporate real-time feedback mechanisms, allowing viewers to influence content dynamically, further blurring the lines between creators and consumers.

In conclusion, the intersection of data analytics and entertainment is reshaping the landscape in profound ways. By harnessing the power of data, creators can produce content that not only entertains but also resonates deeply with audiences, paving the way for a more engaging and personalized entertainment experience. As we continue to explore this evolving field, it is crucial to address the ethical implications and strive for inclusivity, ensuring that the future of entertainment reflects the diverse voices and stories of our global society.

Empowering Individuals and Communities

Leveraging Data for Social Good

Addressing Global Health Issues

The intersection of data analytics and global health has emerged as a critical area of focus, particularly in addressing pressing health challenges that affect populations worldwide. As the world becomes increasingly interconnected, understanding and managing health issues through data-driven approaches is essential for improving health outcomes and ensuring equitable access to healthcare resources.

The Role of Data in Global Health

Data plays a pivotal role in understanding the complex dynamics of global health issues. By collecting, analyzing, and interpreting health data, researchers and policymakers can identify trends, assess risks, and develop targeted interventions. The World Health Organization (WHO) emphasizes that data is crucial for monitoring health systems, evaluating health policies, and guiding resource allocation.

$$\text{Health Outcome} = f(\text{Socioeconomic Factors}, \text{Environmental Factors}, \text{Healthcare Access}) \tag{70}$$

This equation illustrates the multifactorial nature of health outcomes, where various determinants interact to influence overall health status.

Key Global Health Issues Addressed by Data Analytics

Several global health issues can be significantly impacted by data analytics, including:

A. Infectious Diseases Infectious diseases such as HIV/AIDS, malaria, and tuberculosis continue to pose significant challenges to public health. Data analytics enables the identification of outbreak patterns and the effectiveness of interventions. For example, the use of geographic information systems (GIS) has been instrumental in tracking the spread of diseases and targeting vaccination campaigns.

$$R_0 = \frac{\beta}{\gamma} \tag{71}$$

Where R_0 is the basic reproduction number, β is the transmission rate, and γ is the recovery rate. Understanding R_0 helps public health officials determine the necessary vaccination coverage to achieve herd immunity.

B. Non-Communicable Diseases (NCDs) NCDs, such as diabetes and cardiovascular diseases, are on the rise globally, particularly in low- and middle-income countries. Data analytics facilitates the identification of risk factors and the development of preventive strategies. For instance, machine learning algorithms can analyze electronic health records to predict which patients are at higher risk of developing NCDs.

$$\text{Risk Score} = \alpha + \beta_1 \cdot \text{Age} + \beta_2 \cdot \text{BMI} + \beta_3 \cdot \text{Cholesterol} \tag{72}$$

In this linear regression model, the risk score is calculated based on age, body mass index (BMI), and cholesterol levels, allowing healthcare providers to implement early interventions.

C. Mental Health Mental health issues are increasingly recognized as a global health priority. Data analytics can help identify trends in mental health disorders and assess the effectiveness of treatment programs. For example, sentiment analysis of social media data can provide insights into community mental health trends, enabling targeted outreach and support.

Challenges in Utilizing Data for Global Health

Despite the potential of data analytics to address global health issues, several challenges remain:

A. **Data Quality and Availability** The quality and availability of health data can vary significantly across regions. In many low-resource settings, data collection systems are underdeveloped, leading to gaps in information. This can hinder the ability to make informed decisions based on accurate data.

B. **Privacy and Ethical Concerns** As health data becomes increasingly digitized, concerns regarding privacy and ethical use arise. Ensuring that data is collected, stored, and analyzed in a manner that protects individual privacy is paramount. Data breaches can undermine public trust and deter individuals from seeking care.

C. **Interoperability of Health Systems** The lack of interoperability among health information systems can pose significant barriers to effective data sharing and analysis. Standardizing data formats and protocols is essential for enabling seamless integration and collaboration across different health systems.

Case Studies of Data-Driven Approaches in Global Health

A. **The Global Polio Eradication Initiative** The Global Polio Eradication Initiative (GPEI) utilizes data analytics to track polio outbreaks and vaccination coverage. By employing real-time data collection and analysis, GPEI has successfully reduced polio cases by over 99% since its inception in 1988. The initiative employs a robust surveillance system that integrates data from health facilities, community reports, and environmental samples to monitor transmission dynamics.

B. **The COVID-19 Pandemic** The COVID-19 pandemic highlighted the critical role of data analytics in managing global health crises. Governments and health organizations utilized data to model the spread of the virus, allocate resources, and inform public health responses. For instance, the use of contact tracing apps and predictive modeling played a vital role in controlling outbreaks and informing vaccination strategies.

Conclusion

Addressing global health issues through data analytics presents both opportunities and challenges. By leveraging data-driven approaches, stakeholders can develop effective interventions, improve health outcomes, and ensure that healthcare resources are allocated equitably. However, overcoming challenges related to data quality, privacy, and interoperability is essential for maximizing the potential of data in global health. As we move forward, fostering collaboration among researchers, policymakers, and communities will be crucial in harnessing the power of data to address the world's most pressing health challenges.

Poverty Alleviation and Economic Empowerment

Poverty is a persistent global challenge that affects millions of individuals and families, often leading to a cycle of disadvantage that is difficult to break. This section explores how data analytics can play a transformative role in poverty alleviation and economic empowerment by providing insights that drive effective interventions, inform policy decisions, and foster inclusive growth.

Understanding Poverty through Data

To effectively address poverty, it is crucial to understand its multidimensional nature. The World Bank defines poverty as the inability to attain a minimum standard of living, which encompasses not only income but also access to basic services such as education, healthcare, and clean water. The multidimensional poverty index (MPI) incorporates various indicators to measure poverty, including:

$$\text{MPI} = \frac{1}{N} \sum_{i=1}^{N} (\text{Weighted Deprivation Score})_i \quad (73)$$

Where N is the total number of individuals assessed, and the Weighted Deprivation Score reflects the number of deprivations experienced by each individual.

Data analytics can provide a nuanced understanding of poverty by identifying patterns and correlations within these indicators. For instance, through the analysis of large datasets, researchers can uncover the relationships between education levels, employment opportunities, and income variability, leading to targeted interventions.

Challenges in Poverty Alleviation

Despite the potential of data analytics, several challenges persist in effectively leveraging data for poverty alleviation:

- **Data Availability and Quality:** Many regions, particularly in developing countries, lack comprehensive and reliable data. Inconsistent data collection methods and a lack of infrastructure can hinder effective analysis.

- **Contextual Factors:** Poverty is influenced by a multitude of contextual factors, including cultural, social, and political dynamics. Data-driven solutions must be adaptable to local conditions to be effective.

- **Digital Divide:** Access to technology and the internet remains unequal, particularly in rural and marginalized communities. This digital divide can limit the reach of data-driven initiatives.

Data-Driven Interventions for Economic Empowerment

Data analytics can empower individuals and communities by informing targeted interventions that address the root causes of poverty. Some effective strategies include:

- **Microfinance and Credit Scoring:** Data analytics can enhance microfinance initiatives by developing more accurate credit scoring models that assess the creditworthiness of low-income individuals. For example, using alternative data sources such as mobile phone usage patterns or transaction histories can help financial institutions provide loans to those who would otherwise be excluded from traditional banking systems.

- **Skill Development Programs:** By analyzing labor market trends and skill gaps, organizations can design training programs that equip individuals with the skills needed for in-demand jobs. For instance, data analytics can identify sectors experiencing growth and tailor educational programs to meet those needs, thus enhancing employability and income potential.

- **Targeted Social Programs:** Data can be used to identify vulnerable populations and tailor social programs to meet their specific needs. For example, geographic information systems (GIS) can map areas with high poverty rates and assess the accessibility of social services, allowing for more strategic resource allocation.

Case Studies of Success

Several successful initiatives illustrate the potential of data analytics in poverty alleviation and economic empowerment:

- **The Grameen Bank Model:** Founded by Muhammad Yunus in Bangladesh, the Grameen Bank utilizes data analytics to assess the needs of low-income individuals and provide microloans. By analyzing repayment patterns and borrower profiles, the bank has successfully empowered millions of women to start their own businesses, leading to increased household income and improved living standards.

- **The World Bank's Poverty Mapping:** The World Bank employs data analytics to create poverty maps that visualize poverty levels across different regions. These maps enable policymakers to identify areas in need of intervention and allocate resources effectively. The use of satellite imagery and demographic data has proven invaluable in targeting aid and development programs.

- **Data-Driven Agricultural Initiatives:** In various African countries, organizations have harnessed data analytics to improve agricultural productivity among smallholder farmers. By analyzing weather patterns, soil conditions, and market prices, farmers can make informed decisions about crop selection and resource allocation, ultimately increasing yields and income.

Conclusion

The integration of data analytics in poverty alleviation and economic empowerment presents a significant opportunity to create lasting change. By leveraging data to inform interventions, policymakers and organizations can develop targeted solutions that address the root causes of poverty. However, it is essential to remain mindful of the challenges associated with data accessibility, quality, and contextual relevance.

As we move forward, fostering collaboration between data scientists, policymakers, and community leaders will be crucial in ensuring that data-driven initiatives effectively empower individuals and communities, ultimately contributing to a more equitable and prosperous future.

Environmental Conservation and Sustainability

The interplay between data analytics and environmental conservation has emerged as a critical area of study and application. As the world grapples with the challenges posed by climate change, biodiversity loss, and resource depletion, the role of data in fostering sustainable practices and informing policy decisions cannot be overstated. This subsection explores the theoretical foundations, prevalent challenges, and practical examples of how data analytics is revolutionizing environmental conservation and sustainability efforts.

Theoretical Foundations

At the heart of environmental conservation is the concept of sustainability, which can be defined as the ability to meet the needs of the present without compromising the ability of future generations to meet their own needs [?]. This principle encompasses three pillars: environmental protection, economic viability, and social equity. Data analytics serves as a bridge connecting these pillars by providing insights that facilitate informed decision-making.

The theory of ecological footprinting, introduced by Wackernagel and Rees [?], quantifies the demand placed on Earth's ecosystems. It compares human consumption against the planet's ability to regenerate resources. The equation for calculating an ecological footprint is given by:

$$EF = \frac{C}{Y} \qquad (74)$$

where EF is the ecological footprint, C is the total consumption of resources, and Y is the yield of those resources per unit area. Data analytics enables the continuous monitoring of these variables, allowing for timely interventions to reduce ecological impacts.

Challenges in Environmental Data Analytics

Despite the potential benefits, several challenges hinder the effective use of data analytics in environmental conservation:

- **Data Availability and Quality:** Access to high-quality, comprehensive environmental data is often limited. Many regions lack the infrastructure to collect and manage data effectively, leading to gaps in knowledge.

- **Complexity of Environmental Systems:** Ecosystems are inherently complex, with numerous interdependent factors influencing their health. This complexity makes it challenging to develop predictive models that accurately reflect ecological dynamics.

- **Bias and Misinterpretation:** Data can be subject to biases, whether through collection methods or analysis techniques. Misinterpretation of data can lead to misguided conservation efforts, potentially exacerbating existing problems.

- **Stakeholder Engagement:** Effective conservation requires collaboration among various stakeholders, including governments, NGOs, and local communities. Data analytics must be communicated in an accessible manner to facilitate engagement and collective action.

Practical Applications of Data Analytics in Environmental Conservation

Data analytics has been successfully applied in various domains of environmental conservation, yielding significant benefits. Here are some notable examples:

1. **Wildlife Conservation** Data-driven approaches have transformed wildlife conservation strategies. For instance, the use of satellite telemetry and GPS tracking allows researchers to monitor animal movements and behaviors in real-time. This data can be analyzed to identify critical habitats, migration patterns, and potential threats, enabling targeted conservation actions. The work of the *Wildlife Conservation Society* exemplifies this approach, employing advanced analytics to protect endangered species such as the African elephant (*Loxodonta africana*) and the Amur leopard (*Panthera pardus orientalis*) [?].

2. **Climate Change Mitigation** Data analytics plays a vital role in climate change mitigation by enabling the assessment of greenhouse gas emissions and the effectiveness of reduction strategies. The Global Carbon Project utilizes extensive datasets to model carbon emissions across different sectors. By analyzing trends, policymakers can identify key areas for intervention, such as transitioning to renewable energy sources and improving energy efficiency [?].

3. **Sustainable Agriculture** In agriculture, data analytics is being harnessed to promote sustainable practices. Precision agriculture employs sensors, drones, and satellite imagery to collect data on soil health, crop growth, and weather patterns. This information is analyzed to optimize resource use, reduce waste, and enhance productivity. For example, the use of data analytics in precision irrigation has been shown to reduce water consumption by up to 30% while maintaining crop yields [?].

4. **Urban Sustainability** Data analytics is also pivotal in creating sustainable urban environments. Smart city initiatives leverage data from various sources, including traffic patterns, energy consumption, and waste management systems, to enhance urban planning and resource allocation. The city of Barcelona, for instance, employs data analytics to optimize public transportation routes, reduce traffic congestion, and improve air quality [?].

Conclusion

The integration of data analytics into environmental conservation and sustainability efforts presents a promising pathway toward addressing some of the most pressing challenges of our time. By harnessing the power of data, stakeholders can make informed decisions that promote ecological health, enhance resource efficiency, and foster social equity. However, overcoming the inherent challenges of data availability, complexity, and stakeholder engagement remains crucial for maximizing the potential of analytics in driving meaningful change. As we move forward, it is imperative to continue exploring innovative data-driven solutions that support a sustainable future for all.

Disaster Response and Preparedness

In an increasingly unpredictable world, the importance of effective disaster response and preparedness cannot be overstated. Fatima Wang's analytics breakthroughs have significantly transformed how we approach disaster management, leveraging data to enhance our preparedness and response strategies. This subsection explores the theoretical frameworks, prevalent challenges, and real-world applications of data analytics in disaster response.

Theoretical Frameworks

Disaster response and preparedness can be understood through various theoretical lenses, including systems theory, complexity theory, and decision theory. Systems theory emphasizes the interconnectivity of various components within disaster management, highlighting that effective response requires coordination among multiple stakeholders, including government agencies, non-profits, and local communities. Complexity theory acknowledges that disasters are inherently unpredictable and dynamic, necessitating adaptive responses that can evolve as situations change. Decision theory provides a structured approach to making choices under uncertainty, which is crucial in high-stakes scenarios where timely decisions can save lives.

Challenges in Disaster Management

Despite advancements in data analytics, several challenges persist in disaster response:

- **Data Availability and Quality:** Often, critical data may be incomplete, outdated, or not collected in real-time. The lack of high-quality data can hinder effective decision-making.

- **Interoperability of Systems:** Different agencies may use disparate systems that do not communicate effectively, leading to fragmented information and delayed responses.

- **Public Trust and Engagement:** Communities may be skeptical of data-driven approaches, especially if past experiences with authorities have been negative. Building trust is essential for effective collaboration.

- **Resource Allocation:** Limited resources can complicate the deployment of analytics tools. Prioritizing which technologies to invest in is a critical challenge for many organizations.

Applications of Data Analytics in Disaster Response

Fatima's work has led to innovative applications of data analytics that address these challenges. Here are some notable examples:

Predictive Modeling for Disaster Forecasting Predictive analytics can significantly enhance disaster preparedness by forecasting potential disasters before they occur. For example, machine learning algorithms analyze historical data on natural disasters, such as hurricanes or floods, to predict their likelihood and potential impact. The equation for a basic predictive model can be expressed as:

$$P(Y|X) = \frac{P(X|Y) \cdot P(Y)}{P(X)} \tag{75}$$

where $P(Y|X)$ is the probability of a disaster occurring given certain conditions X, $P(X|Y)$ is the likelihood of observing those conditions given a disaster Y, $P(Y)$ is the prior probability of the disaster, and $P(X)$ is the overall probability of the observed conditions.

Real-Time Data Analytics for Situational Awareness During a disaster, real-time data analytics play a crucial role in maintaining situational awareness. For instance, social media platforms can be monitored to gauge public sentiment and gather information on unfolding events. Natural language processing (NLP) techniques can analyze tweets or posts to identify areas in need of urgent assistance. An example of a sentiment analysis algorithm can be represented as follows:

$$S = \sum_{i=1}^{n} w_i \cdot t_i \tag{76}$$

where S is the overall sentiment score, w_i represents the weight of each term i based on its importance, and t_i is the term frequency of each sentiment-bearing word.

Resource Optimization Using Geographic Information Systems (GIS)   GIS technology allows for the visualization and analysis of spatial data, which is invaluable in disaster response. By mapping resources and affected areas, responders can optimize their deployment strategies. For example, the equation for calculating the optimal location for resource allocation can be modeled as:

$$\text{Minimize} \quad Z = \sum_{i=1}^{m} \sum_{j=1}^{n} c_{ij} x_{ij} \tag{77}$$

subject to:

$$\sum_{j=1}^{n} x_{ij} \leq b_i \quad \forall i \tag{78}$$

$$x_{ij} \geq 0 \quad \forall i,j \tag{79}$$

where c_{ij} is the cost of assigning resources from location i to area j, x_{ij} is the quantity of resources allocated, and b_i is the total available resources at location i.

Case Studies and Real-World Examples

Several case studies illustrate the impact of data analytics on disaster response:

Hurricane Harvey (2017)   During Hurricane Harvey, data analytics played a pivotal role in coordinating rescue efforts. The Federal Emergency Management Agency (FEMA) utilized predictive modeling to forecast flood zones, enabling timely evacuations and resource allocation. Social media analytics helped identify areas with urgent needs, allowing responders to prioritize their efforts effectively.

COVID-19 Pandemic Response   In the context of the COVID-19 pandemic, data analytics was crucial for tracking infection rates and resource allocation. Governments worldwide used data dashboards to visualize the spread of the virus and allocate medical resources efficiently. The use of machine learning models to predict outbreaks and assess healthcare capacity exemplifies the power of analytics in crisis management.

Conclusion

Fatima Wang's contributions to data analytics have revolutionized disaster response and preparedness, providing innovative solutions to longstanding challenges. By leveraging predictive modeling, real-time data analytics, and GIS technology, responders can enhance situational awareness, optimize resource allocation, and ultimately save lives. As we look to the future, continued advancements in data analytics will be essential in building resilient communities capable of effectively responding to disasters.

Data-Driven Advocacy and Policymaking

In an era where data plays an increasingly critical role in shaping societal outcomes, data-driven advocacy and policymaking have emerged as essential tools for promoting social justice, equality, and effective governance. The integration of data analytics into advocacy efforts allows organizations and policymakers to make informed decisions, align resources with pressing needs, and evaluate the effectiveness of their initiatives. This subsection explores the theoretical foundations, challenges, and practical examples of data-driven advocacy and policymaking.

Theoretical Foundations

The theoretical underpinnings of data-driven advocacy and policymaking can be traced to several key concepts in public policy and social science. One of the foundational theories is the **Evidence-Based Policy Making (EBPM)** framework, which posits that policies should be informed by the best available evidence derived from data. EBPM emphasizes the importance of utilizing empirical research and data analytics to inform decisions and evaluate outcomes.

Another relevant theory is the **Theory of Change**, which outlines the causal pathways through which specific interventions lead to desired outcomes. By employing data analytics to map these pathways, advocates can identify critical leverage points and measure the impact of their initiatives. The use of data in this context not only enhances the credibility of advocacy efforts but also fosters transparency and accountability.

Challenges in Data-Driven Advocacy

Despite the potential benefits, several challenges hinder the effective implementation of data-driven advocacy and policymaking:

- **Data Accessibility:** Access to high-quality data remains a significant barrier for many advocacy organizations. Publicly available datasets may be outdated, incomplete, or biased, limiting the ability to draw accurate conclusions.

- **Data Literacy:** A lack of data literacy among advocates and policymakers can impede the effective use of data. Organizations may struggle to interpret complex data analyses or may lack the technical skills required to leverage advanced analytics.

- **Ethical Considerations:** The use of data in advocacy raises ethical concerns, particularly regarding privacy and consent. Advocates must navigate the fine line between utilizing data for social good and respecting individuals' rights to privacy.

- **Resistance to Change:** Traditional policymaking processes can be resistant to data-driven approaches. Policymakers may be hesitant to adopt new methodologies that challenge established norms or practices.

Examples of Data-Driven Advocacy

Several organizations and initiatives exemplify the successful application of data-driven advocacy and policymaking:

- **The Urban Institute:** This research organization utilizes data analytics to inform policies related to urban development, poverty alleviation, and social equity. By analyzing large datasets, the Urban Institute provides policymakers with actionable insights that drive evidence-based decision-making.

- **DataKind:** This nonprofit organization connects data scientists with social sector organizations to tackle pressing social issues. Through data analysis and visualization, DataKind empowers organizations to leverage data in their advocacy efforts, enhancing their ability to drive change.

- **The Center for Disease Control and Prevention (CDC):** The CDC employs data analytics to inform public health policies and initiatives. By analyzing health data trends, the CDC identifies emerging health threats and develops targeted interventions, ultimately improving health outcomes in communities.

- **The World Bank:** The World Bank utilizes data-driven approaches to inform its development policies. By analyzing economic and social data, the organization identifies key areas for investment and intervention, helping to alleviate poverty and promote sustainable development globally.

The Role of Technology in Data-Driven Advocacy

Advancements in technology have significantly enhanced the capabilities of data-driven advocacy. The proliferation of **big data** and **machine learning** has enabled organizations to analyze vast amounts of information, uncover patterns, and derive insights that were previously unattainable. Furthermore, the rise of **data visualization tools** allows advocates to present complex data in accessible formats, making it easier to communicate findings to stakeholders and the general public.

$$\text{Impact} = \frac{\text{Outcome}}{\text{Input}} \quad \text{(Measuring the effectiveness of advocacy initiatives)} \quad (80)$$

This equation illustrates the relationship between the outcomes achieved through advocacy efforts and the resources invested. By employing data analytics, advocates can optimize their strategies, ensuring that their initiatives yield the maximum impact.

Future Directions

Looking ahead, the future of data-driven advocacy and policymaking will likely be shaped by several key trends:

- **Increased Collaboration:** Advocacy organizations will increasingly collaborate with data scientists, tech companies, and academic institutions to leverage expertise and resources in data analytics.

- **Focus on Equity:** As data-driven approaches become more prevalent, advocates will need to prioritize equity in data collection and analysis, ensuring that marginalized communities are represented and their voices are heard.

- **Policy Innovation:** Data-driven insights will drive innovative policy solutions, enabling governments to address complex social issues more effectively and efficiently.

- **Enhanced Public Engagement:** As data becomes more accessible, advocacy organizations will engage the public in data-driven discussions, fostering a culture of informed civic participation.

In conclusion, data-driven advocacy and policymaking represent a transformative approach to addressing societal challenges. By harnessing the power of data, advocates can enhance their effectiveness, promote accountability, and ultimately drive meaningful change in their communities and beyond. The journey toward a data-driven future requires overcoming challenges, embracing ethical considerations, and fostering collaboration across sectors. As we continue to navigate this landscape, the potential for data to empower advocacy efforts remains boundless.

Transforming Workspaces

Data-Driven Decision-Making in Organizations

Data-driven decision-making (DDDM) has emerged as a cornerstone of modern organizational strategy, enabling companies to leverage vast amounts of data to inform their choices and enhance operational efficiency. This approach contrasts sharply with traditional decision-making, which often relies on intuition or anecdotal evidence. DDDM is predicated on the belief that data, when analyzed appropriately, can provide insights that lead to better business outcomes.

Theoretical Framework

The theoretical underpinnings of data-driven decision-making can be traced to several key concepts in management and information systems. One prominent theory is the **Data-Information-Knowledge-Wisdom (DIKW)** hierarchy, which illustrates the transformation of raw data into actionable insights:

$$\text{Data} \rightarrow \text{Information} \rightarrow \text{Knowledge} \rightarrow \text{Wisdom} \qquad (81)$$

In this hierarchy, data is the raw, unprocessed facts. When contextualized, it becomes information. Knowledge arises when information is processed and understood, while wisdom involves the application of knowledge in decision-making.

Another relevant theory is the **Decision Theory**, which focuses on the reasoning underlying an agent's choices. Decision theory can be mathematically formulated, often using utility functions to represent preferences. A common expression for expected utility is:

$$EU = \sum_{i=1}^{n} p_i \cdot u(x_i) \qquad (82)$$

where EU is the expected utility, p_i is the probability of outcome i, and $u(x_i)$ is the utility of outcome x_i.

Challenges in Data-Driven Decision-Making

Despite its advantages, organizations face several challenges when implementing data-driven decision-making:

- **Data Quality:** Poor data quality can lead to incorrect conclusions. Organizations must ensure that the data collected is accurate, complete, and relevant.

- **Data Overload:** The sheer volume of data can overwhelm decision-makers. Identifying which data points are pertinent to specific decisions is crucial.

- **Cultural Resistance:** Employees may be resistant to adopting a data-driven approach, especially if they are accustomed to traditional decision-making methods. Overcoming this resistance requires a cultural shift within the organization.

- **Skills Gap:** There is often a lack of skilled personnel who can analyze data effectively. Organizations must invest in training or hire data professionals to bridge this gap.

- **Ethical Considerations:** The use of data raises ethical issues, particularly concerning privacy and consent. Organizations must navigate these concerns while still leveraging data for decision-making.

Examples of Data-Driven Decision-Making

Numerous organizations have successfully implemented data-driven decision-making strategies, demonstrating its potential benefits:

Example 1: Amazon   Amazon utilizes data analytics to personalize customer experiences. By analyzing purchasing patterns and browsing history, Amazon can recommend products tailored to individual preferences. This approach has significantly increased customer engagement and sales.

Example 2: Netflix   Netflix employs data-driven decision-making to inform content creation and recommendation algorithms. By analyzing viewer preferences and viewing habits, Netflix can predict which genres or types of shows will resonate with audiences, leading to successful original content productions.

Example 3: Target   Target has famously used data analytics to predict customer behavior, such as identifying when customers are likely to be pregnant based on purchasing patterns. This insight allows Target to tailor marketing strategies and product offerings to meet the needs of specific customer segments.

Conclusion

Data-driven decision-making represents a paradigm shift in how organizations approach strategic choices. By leveraging data analytics, organizations can enhance their decision-making processes, leading to improved outcomes and competitive advantages. However, to fully realize the benefits of DDDM, organizations must address challenges related to data quality, cultural resistance, and ethical considerations. As technology continues to evolve, the integration of data-driven strategies will likely become even more critical for organizational success.

Bibliography

[1] Rowley, J. (2007). The wisdom hierarchy: representations of the DIKW hierarchy. *Journal of Information Science*, 33(2), 163-180.

[2] von Neumann, J., & Morgenstern, O. (1944). *Theory of Games and Economic Behavior*. Princeton University Press.

[3] Dholakia, U. M., & Kshetri, N. (2004). The impact of data analytics on customer satisfaction in e-commerce: A case study of Amazon.com. *Journal of Electronic Commerce Research*, 5(3), 157-169.

[4] Gans, J. S., & Scott, E. (2013). The impact of data-driven decision making on the success of Netflix. *Harvard Business Review*, 91(6), 104-112.

[5] Duhigg, C. (2012). How companies learn your secrets. *The New York Times Magazine*.

Employee Productivity and Well-being

Employee productivity and well-being are critical components of organizational success, especially in a data-driven environment. Organizations are increasingly recognizing that a healthy and engaged workforce is not only more productive but also contributes to a positive organizational culture and better overall performance. This section explores the interplay between data analytics, employee productivity, and well-being, drawing on relevant theories, problems, and practical examples.

Theoretical Framework

The relationship between employee productivity and well-being can be understood through various theoretical frameworks. One prominent theory is the **Job Demands-Resources (JD-R) model**, which posits that job characteristics can be categorized into two groups: demands and resources.

$$\text{Job Demands} + \text{Job Resources} \rightarrow \text{Employee Well-being} \quad (83)$$

According to this model, high job demands (e.g., workload, time pressure) can lead to stress and burnout, while adequate job resources (e.g., support, autonomy) can enhance motivation and engagement. Thus, organizations should aim to balance demands and resources to foster well-being and productivity.

Challenges in Measuring Productivity and Well-being

Despite the clear link between productivity and well-being, measuring these constructs poses significant challenges. Traditional metrics of productivity, such as output per hour worked, often fail to account for qualitative aspects of work, such as employee morale and job satisfaction. Furthermore, well-being is a multifaceted construct that encompasses physical, mental, and emotional health.

To address these challenges, organizations can employ data analytics to gain insights into employee productivity and well-being. For instance, using surveys and feedback tools can help capture employee sentiments and identify areas for improvement. However, organizations must also be mindful of the potential biases in self-reported data and ensure that measures are valid and reliable.

Data-Driven Approaches to Enhance Productivity and Well-being

1. **Predictive Analytics:** Organizations can utilize predictive analytics to identify patterns and trends in employee behavior. By analyzing data from various sources, such as performance reviews and attendance records, organizations can predict potential declines in productivity and intervene proactively. For example, if data indicates a drop in performance among a specific team, management can investigate the underlying causes and provide additional support or resources.

$$\text{Productivity Score} = f(\text{Performance Metrics}, \text{Engagement Levels}, \text{Well-being Indicators}) \quad (84)$$

2. **Personalized Employee Programs:** Leveraging data analytics allows organizations to tailor employee wellness programs to meet individual needs. For instance, organizations can analyze employee demographics and preferences to design targeted initiatives, such as mental health resources, flexible work arrangements, or professional development opportunities. This personalized approach can significantly enhance employee engagement and satisfaction.

3. **Real-time Feedback Mechanisms:** Implementing real-time feedback tools can help organizations monitor employee well-being continuously. Tools such as pulse surveys and sentiment analysis can provide immediate insights into employee morale, enabling management to make timely adjustments. For example, if feedback indicates that employees are feeling overwhelmed, management can implement measures to alleviate workload and enhance support.

Case Studies and Examples

1. **Google's People Analytics:** Google is renowned for its data-driven approach to employee productivity and well-being. Through its People Analytics team, the company analyzes vast amounts of employee data to understand factors that contribute to high performance and job satisfaction. For example, Google found that employees who felt a sense of belonging were more productive. As a result, the company initiated programs focused on inclusion and team-building, leading to improved employee engagement and productivity.

2. **IBM's Well-being Initiatives:** IBM has implemented various data-driven initiatives to enhance employee well-being. The company uses analytics to assess employee engagement levels and identify trends related to burnout and stress. By providing tailored wellness programs and resources based on data insights, IBM has seen a significant increase in employee satisfaction and a decrease in turnover rates.

3. **Salesforce's Ohana Culture:** Salesforce emphasizes a strong company culture centered around employee well-being, known as the "Ohana" culture. The organization uses data analytics to measure employee engagement and satisfaction regularly. By continuously monitoring these metrics, Salesforce can adapt its policies and programs to ensure that employees feel valued and supported, ultimately driving productivity.

Conclusion

In conclusion, the integration of data analytics into employee productivity and well-being initiatives is essential for organizations seeking to thrive in a competitive landscape. By leveraging predictive analytics, personalized programs, and real-time feedback mechanisms, organizations can create a supportive environment that fosters both productivity and well-being. As the workforce continues to evolve, prioritizing employee well-being will be crucial for ensuring long-term success and sustainability.

Talent Acquisition and Workforce Planning

In the contemporary landscape of business, talent acquisition and workforce planning have emerged as critical components for organizational success. The effective alignment of human resources with strategic goals not only enhances productivity but also fosters innovation. This section delves into the integration of data analytics in talent acquisition and workforce planning, exploring relevant theories, prevalent challenges, and practical examples.

Theoretical Framework

The theoretical underpinnings of talent acquisition and workforce planning can be traced back to several key concepts in human resource management (HRM). One prominent theory is the **Resource-Based View (RBV)** of the firm, which posits that human capital is a vital resource that can provide a competitive advantage. According to [1], organizations that effectively manage their human resources are more likely to achieve superior performance.

$$\text{Competitive Advantage} = \text{Value} + \text{Rarity} + \text{Imitability} + \text{Organization} \quad (85)$$

This equation highlights that a firm's competitive advantage hinges on its ability to leverage valuable, rare, and inimitable resources, with human capital being a cornerstone of this framework.

Additionally, the **Human Capital Theory** emphasizes the value of investing in employee skills and knowledge as a means to enhance productivity and organizational performance [2]. This theory underscores the importance of strategic workforce planning, where organizations must identify the skills needed for future success and align their talent acquisition strategies accordingly.

Challenges in Talent Acquisition and Workforce Planning

Despite the theoretical advantages, organizations face several challenges in the realm of talent acquisition and workforce planning:

1. **Skill Shortages**: The rapid evolution of technology has led to a skills gap in many industries. According to a report by the World Economic Forum, 54% of employees will require significant reskilling by 2022 [5]. This gap complicates the talent acquisition process as organizations struggle to find candidates with the necessary skills.

2. **Bias in Recruitment**: Unconscious biases can influence hiring decisions, leading to a lack of diversity within organizations. Research indicates that diverse

teams outperform homogeneous ones, making it essential for organizations to implement data-driven recruitment strategies that minimize bias [3].

3. **Retention Issues**: High turnover rates can disrupt workforce planning and incur significant costs. The cost of employee turnover can range from 50% to 200% of an employee's annual salary, depending on the role [4]. Organizations must not only attract talent but also create an environment conducive to retention.

Data-Driven Approaches to Talent Acquisition

The integration of data analytics into talent acquisition offers a pathway to address these challenges effectively. Organizations can leverage various data sources to enhance their recruitment strategies:

1. **Predictive Analytics**: By analyzing historical hiring data, organizations can identify patterns that lead to successful hires. Predictive analytics can help forecast candidate success based on various factors, such as education, experience, and cultural fit. For instance, a study by [6] demonstrated that companies using predictive analytics in their hiring processes saw a 30% increase in employee retention.

2. **Job Market Analysis**: Utilizing data analytics tools to analyze job market trends can help organizations understand the availability of talent in specific regions or industries. This information allows for strategic workforce planning, enabling organizations to target their recruitment efforts effectively.

3. **Employee Referral Programs**: Data-driven employee referral programs can enhance talent acquisition by tapping into existing employees' networks. Research shows that referred candidates are 55% faster to hire and have a 25% higher retention rate than non-referred candidates [7].

Case Study: Google

A prime example of successful talent acquisition and workforce planning through data analytics is Google. The tech giant employs a data-driven approach to recruitment, using algorithms to analyze candidate data and predict job performance. Google's hiring process includes structured interviews and assessments designed to minimize bias and focus on skills and potential rather than pedigree.

Additionally, Google has implemented workforce planning models that utilize data analytics to predict future hiring needs based on business growth projections. This proactive approach allows them to maintain a competitive edge in the fast-paced tech industry.

Conclusion

In conclusion, talent acquisition and workforce planning are essential for organizations aiming to thrive in a data-driven world. By leveraging data analytics, organizations can overcome challenges such as skill shortages, bias, and retention issues. The integration of theoretical frameworks, such as the Resource-Based View and Human Capital Theory, further underscores the importance of strategic human resource management. As demonstrated by industry leaders like Google, a data-driven approach can lead to more effective recruitment processes and a more engaged workforce, ultimately driving innovation and success.

Bibliography

[1] Barney, J. B. (1991). Firm Resources and Sustained Competitive Advantage. *Journal of Management*, 17(1), 99-120.

[2] Becker, G. S. (1993). *Human Capital: A Theoretical and Empirical Analysis, with Special Reference to Education*. University of Chicago Press.

[3] Herring, C. (2009). Does Diversity Pay?: Race, Gender, and the Business Case for Diversity. *American Sociological Review*, 74(2), 208-224.

[4] Society for Human Resource Management. (2016). The Cost of Turnover. Retrieved from https://www.shrm.org/resourcesandtools/tools-and-samples/toolkits/pages/costofturnover.aspx

[5] World Economic Forum. (2020). The Future of Jobs Report 2020. Retrieved from https://www.weforum.org/reports/the-future-of-jobs-report-2020

[6] Baker, M. (2019). Predictive Analytics in Talent Acquisition: A Case Study. *Journal of Business Research*, 102, 123-134.

[7] Baker, M. (2020). The Impact of Employee Referral Programs on Talent Acquisition. *Human Resource Management Review*, 30(3), 100-115.

Diversity and Inclusion Initiatives

Diversity and inclusion (D&I) initiatives are essential components in the modern workplace, particularly in the field of data science. Fatima Wang recognized early on that a diverse workforce leads to enhanced creativity, improved problem-solving, and better decision-making. This section explores the theoretical foundations of diversity and inclusion, the challenges faced in implementing these initiatives, and examples of successful D&I strategies in organizations.

Theoretical Foundations of Diversity and Inclusion

Diversity encompasses various dimensions, including race, gender, ethnicity, age, sexual orientation, disability, and socio-economic background. Inclusion, on the other hand, refers to the practices and policies that create a welcoming environment for all individuals, allowing them to contribute fully and feel valued.

The **Social Identity Theory** (Tajfel & Turner, 1979) posits that individuals categorize themselves and others into social groups, which can lead to in-group favoritism and out-group discrimination. This theory highlights the importance of understanding how social identities affect workplace dynamics and the necessity of fostering an inclusive culture to mitigate biases.

Moreover, the **Business Case for Diversity** suggests that diverse teams are more innovative and perform better. A McKinsey report (2020) found that companies in the top quartile for gender diversity on executive teams were 25% more likely to experience above-average profitability compared to those in the bottom quartile. This correlation emphasizes the value of D&I initiatives not just as ethical imperatives but as strategic advantages.

Challenges in Implementing Diversity and Inclusion Initiatives

Despite the clear benefits, organizations face several challenges in implementing effective D&I initiatives:

- **Unconscious Bias:** Many individuals are unaware of their biases, which can influence hiring, promotion, and team dynamics. For instance, a study by the National Bureau of Economic Research (2019) revealed that resumes with names perceived as "ethnic" received fewer callbacks than those with traditionally Anglo-Saxon names, highlighting the impact of unconscious bias in recruitment.

- **Resistance to Change:** Employees may resist D&I initiatives due to a lack of understanding or fear of the unknown. This resistance can stem from a belief that diversity efforts threaten existing power structures or lead to reverse discrimination.

- **Tokenism:** Organizations may adopt D&I initiatives superficially, hiring diverse individuals without providing them with the necessary support or opportunities for advancement. This can lead to feelings of isolation and disillusionment among underrepresented groups.

BIBLIOGRAPHY

Successful Examples of Diversity and Inclusion Initiatives

Fatima Wang's work in data science highlights several successful D&I initiatives that can serve as models for organizations:

1. **Comprehensive Training Programs:** Companies like Google and Microsoft have implemented extensive training programs aimed at raising awareness of unconscious bias. These programs often include workshops, seminars, and online courses that educate employees about the importance of diversity and how to foster an inclusive environment.

2. **Diverse Hiring Practices:** Initiatives such as blind recruitment, where identifying information is removed from resumes, have been adopted by firms like Deloitte. This practice helps minimize bias in the hiring process, allowing candidates to be evaluated solely based on their skills and qualifications.

3. **Employee Resource Groups (ERGs):** Organizations like Accenture have established ERGs to support underrepresented employees. These groups provide a platform for networking, mentorship, and advocacy, creating a sense of community and belonging within the organization.

4. **Accountability Metrics:** Companies such as Salesforce have set measurable diversity goals and regularly report on their progress. By holding leadership accountable for diversity outcomes, organizations can ensure that D&I initiatives are taken seriously and integrated into the company culture.

Conclusion

In conclusion, diversity and inclusion initiatives are vital for fostering a culture of innovation and collaboration in data science and other fields. By addressing unconscious bias, overcoming resistance to change, and implementing successful strategies, organizations can create an environment where all employees feel valued and empowered to contribute. Fatima Wang's commitment to D&I not only enhances her work but also sets a precedent for future innovators to prioritize these initiatives in their organizations. As the data revolution continues, embracing diversity will be essential for driving sustainable growth and innovation.

Redefining the Future of Work

The future of work is undergoing a profound transformation, driven by advancements in data analytics, artificial intelligence (AI), and changing societal expectations. This section delves into how Fatima Wang's contributions to data science are reshaping the workplace, enhancing productivity, fostering employee well-being, and redefining organizational structures.

The Role of Data in Workplace Transformation

Data is increasingly becoming the backbone of decision-making processes in organizations. By leveraging data analytics, businesses can gain insights into employee performance, engagement, and productivity. For instance, the application of predictive analytics allows companies to forecast employee turnover rates, enabling proactive measures to retain talent.

$$\text{Turnover Rate} = \frac{\text{Number of Departures}}{\text{Average Number of Employees}} \times 100 \qquad (86)$$

This formula illustrates how organizations can quantify turnover and make data-driven decisions to improve retention strategies.

Enhancing Employee Productivity and Well-being

Fatima's work emphasizes the importance of creating a data-driven culture that prioritizes employee well-being. Organizations are now using analytics to assess the factors that contribute to employee satisfaction and productivity. For example, companies can analyze survey data to identify correlations between workplace conditions and employee performance.

Research indicates that organizations that invest in employee well-being see a significant return on investment. According to a study by the Gallup Organization, businesses with high employee engagement outperform their competitors by 147% in earnings per share (EPS). This correlation underscores the necessity of using data to create a conducive work environment.

Talent Acquisition and Workforce Planning

Data analytics revolutionizes talent acquisition processes. By utilizing algorithms that analyze resumes and applicant data, organizations can streamline recruitment, ensuring a better fit between candidates and company culture. For instance, companies like Unilever have implemented AI-driven assessments that analyze candidates' video interviews to predict their suitability for specific roles.

Moreover, workforce planning is enhanced through data analytics, allowing organizations to identify skill gaps and forecast future hiring needs. This proactive approach ensures that businesses remain agile in a rapidly changing market landscape.

Diversity and Inclusion Initiatives

Fatima's insights into data ethics highlight the need for organizations to use data responsibly, especially concerning diversity and inclusion (D&I) initiatives. By analyzing workforce demographics, organizations can identify areas where diversity is lacking and implement targeted strategies to promote inclusivity.

For example, companies can use data analytics to track the representation of various demographics within their workforce and assess the effectiveness of their D&I programs. This data-driven approach not only fosters a more inclusive workplace but also enhances creativity and innovation, as diverse teams are known to produce better outcomes.

Redefining Organizational Structures

The traditional hierarchical organizational structure is evolving into more flexible, team-based models that emphasize collaboration and innovation. Fatima's research advocates for using data to understand team dynamics and optimize collaboration.

For example, organizations can employ network analysis to visualize collaboration patterns among employees. By identifying key influencers and communication bottlenecks, companies can restructure teams for optimal performance.

The equation below illustrates the concept of centrality in network analysis, which helps organizations identify influential team members:

$$C(v) = \sum_{u \in G} \frac{1}{d(u,v)} \tag{87}$$

Where $C(v)$ is the centrality of node v, G is the graph representing the organization's network, and $d(u,v)$ is the distance between nodes u and v.

The Future of Work: A Data-Driven Perspective

The future of work will be characterized by an increased reliance on data analytics to inform every aspect of organizational operations. As businesses embrace digital transformation, the integration of AI and machine learning will further enhance decision-making processes.

Fatima Wang's vision for the future of work emphasizes the importance of continuous learning and adaptability. Organizations that prioritize data literacy among their employees will be better positioned to navigate the complexities of the modern workplace.

In conclusion, the future of work is being redefined through the lens of data analytics. By embracing a data-driven approach, organizations can enhance productivity, foster employee well-being, promote diversity and inclusion, and create more agile structures. Fatima Wang's contributions to this field not only illuminate the path forward but also inspire future innovators to harness the power of data in reshaping the workplace for the better.

Data Privacy and Ethics

Navigating the Ethical Challenges of Data

In the rapidly evolving landscape of data science, ethical challenges have emerged as a central concern for practitioners, researchers, and policymakers alike. As data becomes increasingly integral to decision-making processes across various sectors, the imperative to navigate these ethical challenges has never been more critical. This section explores the fundamental ethical dilemmas associated with data collection, analysis, and application, alongside theoretical frameworks and practical examples that illustrate these challenges.

Defining Ethical Challenges in Data Science

Ethics in data science encompasses a range of issues, including privacy, consent, bias, and accountability. These challenges stem from the vast amounts of data generated daily, often without the explicit consent of individuals. The primary ethical concerns can be categorized as follows:

- **Privacy:** The collection and storage of personal data raise significant privacy concerns. Individuals may not be aware of how their data is being used, leading to potential violations of their privacy rights.

- **Informed Consent:** Obtaining informed consent is a cornerstone of ethical data practices. However, the complexities of data usage and the often vague terms of service agreements can obscure true consent.

- **Bias and Discrimination:** Algorithms trained on biased data can perpetuate and amplify existing inequalities, leading to discriminatory outcomes in areas such as hiring, lending, and law enforcement.
- **Accountability:** Determining accountability for decisions made by algorithms poses a significant challenge. If an algorithm causes harm, it can be difficult to ascertain who is responsible—the developer, the organization, or the algorithm itself.

Theoretical Frameworks for Ethical Data Practices

Several theoretical frameworks can guide ethical decision-making in data science. These frameworks provide a foundation for understanding the implications of data practices and help identify ethical responsibilities.

- **Utilitarianism:** This ethical theory suggests that actions should be evaluated based on their consequences, aiming for the greatest good for the greatest number. In data science, this could involve weighing the benefits of data usage against potential harms to individuals or communities.
- **Deontological Ethics:** This framework emphasizes the importance of rules and duties. In the context of data ethics, it underscores the necessity of adhering to ethical guidelines and regulations, regardless of the outcomes.
- **Virtue Ethics:** Focusing on the character of the decision-makers, virtue ethics encourages data scientists to cultivate virtues such as honesty, fairness, and integrity in their work.

Identifying Ethical Problems in Data Practices

To effectively navigate ethical challenges, it is crucial to identify specific problems that arise in data practices. Some prominent ethical issues include:

1. **Data Breaches:** Unauthorized access to sensitive data can lead to significant harm, including identity theft and financial loss. For instance, the Equifax data breach in 2017 exposed the personal information of approximately 147 million individuals, highlighting the need for robust data security measures.
2. **Surveillance:** The use of data for surveillance purposes raises ethical concerns about autonomy and privacy. Governments and corporations may monitor individuals without their consent, leading to a chilling effect on free expression.

3. **Algorithmic Bias:** Algorithms can inadvertently discriminate against certain groups if trained on biased datasets. A notable example is the use of predictive policing algorithms, which have been criticized for disproportionately targeting minority communities based on historical crime data.

Case Studies Illustrating Ethical Challenges

Examining real-world examples can illuminate the ethical challenges faced by data scientists.

- **Cambridge Analytica:** The scandal involving Cambridge Analytica's misuse of Facebook data for political advertising raised profound ethical questions regarding consent, privacy, and the manipulation of public opinion. Millions of users' data was harvested without consent, leading to calls for stricter data protection regulations.

- **Facial Recognition Technology:** The deployment of facial recognition technology by law enforcement agencies has sparked debates over privacy and racial bias. Studies have shown that these systems often misidentify people of color at higher rates than white individuals, raising concerns about fairness and accountability in their use.

Strategies for Ethical Data Practices

To address these ethical challenges, several strategies can be implemented:

- **Establishing Clear Guidelines:** Organizations should develop comprehensive ethical guidelines for data collection and usage, ensuring that all stakeholders are aware of their responsibilities.

- **Conducting Ethical Audits:** Regular audits can help identify potential ethical issues in data practices, allowing organizations to address problems proactively.

- **Promoting Transparency:** Being transparent about data usage and decision-making processes can help build trust with stakeholders and mitigate ethical concerns.

- **Engaging Diverse Perspectives:** Involving a diverse group of stakeholders in the data science process can help identify and address potential biases and ethical issues.

Conclusion

Navigating the ethical challenges of data science is a complex but essential endeavor. As data continues to play a pivotal role in shaping our world, it is imperative for data scientists to prioritize ethical considerations in their work. By understanding the theoretical frameworks, identifying specific problems, and implementing effective strategies, practitioners can contribute to a more ethical and responsible data-driven future. The journey toward ethical data practices is ongoing, requiring vigilance, collaboration, and a commitment to doing what is right for individuals and society as a whole.

Ensuring Data Privacy and Security

In an increasingly data-driven world, ensuring data privacy and security has become a paramount concern for individuals, organizations, and governments alike. The rapid growth of data collection technologies, coupled with the rise of sophisticated cyber threats, necessitates a comprehensive understanding of privacy principles and security measures. This section delves into the theoretical foundations of data privacy and security, the challenges faced in safeguarding personal information, and practical examples of effective strategies employed to protect data.

Theoretical Foundations of Data Privacy

Data privacy is grounded in several key theories and principles that guide the ethical collection, storage, and use of personal information. One foundational theory is the **Fair Information Practices** (FIPs), which outlines a set of principles that govern how organizations should handle personal data. The FIPs include:

- **Notice/Awareness:** Individuals should be informed when their data is being collected and how it will be used.

- **Choice/Consent:** Individuals should have the option to consent to the collection and use of their data.

- **Access/Participation:** Individuals should have the right to access their data and correct inaccuracies.

- **Integrity/Security:** Organizations must ensure the accuracy and security of personal data.

- **Enforcement/Redress:** There should be mechanisms in place for individuals to seek redress in cases of data misuse.

These principles form the basis for various data protection regulations, such as the General Data Protection Regulation (GDPR) in the European Union, which emphasizes the importance of individual rights in data processing.

Challenges in Data Privacy and Security

Despite the theoretical frameworks in place, numerous challenges complicate the effective implementation of data privacy and security measures:

- **Data Breaches:** High-profile data breaches have become commonplace, exposing millions of records and leading to significant financial and reputational damage. For instance, the 2017 Equifax breach compromised the personal information of approximately 147 million individuals, highlighting vulnerabilities in data security practices.

- **Inadequate Security Measures:** Many organizations lack robust security protocols, making them susceptible to cyberattacks. The *Verizon Data Breach Investigations Report* consistently indicates that a significant percentage of breaches result from weak passwords, unpatched vulnerabilities, and social engineering attacks.

- **Evolving Threat Landscape:** Cyber threats are continually evolving, with attackers employing increasingly sophisticated techniques to bypass security measures. Ransomware attacks, such as the 2021 Colonial Pipeline incident, demonstrate how critical infrastructure can be targeted, resulting in widespread disruption and financial loss.

- **User Awareness and Behavior:** Individuals often underestimate the importance of data privacy, leading to risky online behaviors. A study by the Pew Research Center found that a substantial number of users share personal information without understanding the potential consequences, making them vulnerable to identity theft and fraud.

Strategies for Ensuring Data Privacy and Security

To mitigate the risks associated with data privacy and security, organizations and individuals can adopt several best practices:

- **Data Encryption:** Encrypting sensitive data ensures that even if it is intercepted, it remains unreadable without the appropriate decryption key. The use of strong encryption algorithms, such as **AES (Advanced Encryption Standard)**, is crucial in protecting data both in transit and at rest.

- **Access Controls:** Implementing strict access controls ensures that only authorized personnel can access sensitive data. Role-based access control (RBAC) and the principle of least privilege (PoLP) can help minimize exposure to data breaches.

- **Regular Security Audits:** Conducting regular security audits and vulnerability assessments can help organizations identify and address potential weaknesses in their systems. The *NIST Cybersecurity Framework* provides a structured approach for organizations to manage cybersecurity risks.

- **User Education and Awareness:** Educating users about data privacy best practices, such as recognizing phishing attempts and using strong, unique passwords, can significantly reduce the risk of data breaches. Organizations should implement ongoing training programs to keep employees informed about the latest threats.

- **Compliance with Regulations:** Adhering to data protection regulations, such as GDPR and the California Consumer Privacy Act (CCPA), not only helps organizations avoid legal penalties but also fosters trust with customers by demonstrating a commitment to data privacy.

Examples of Effective Data Privacy and Security Practices

Several organizations have successfully implemented data privacy and security measures that serve as models for others:

- **Apple Inc.:** Apple has positioned itself as a leader in data privacy, emphasizing its commitment to user privacy through features such as *App Tracking Transparency* and end-to-end encryption for iMessages. By prioritizing user privacy, Apple has built a strong reputation and gained customer trust.

- **Microsoft Azure:** Microsoft Azure provides a comprehensive set of security features, including advanced threat protection and compliance certifications.

The platform's *Security Center* offers tools for monitoring and managing security across cloud services, helping organizations maintain a secure environment.

- **ProtonMail:** ProtonMail is a secure email service that uses end-to-end encryption to protect user communications. By prioritizing privacy and security, ProtonMail has attracted users who are concerned about data breaches and surveillance.

- **GDPR Compliance:** Companies that have successfully navigated GDPR compliance, such as *Deloitte*, have established transparent data handling practices, ensuring that users are informed about their data rights and how their information is used.

Conclusion

Ensuring data privacy and security is a complex but essential endeavor in the digital age. By understanding the theoretical foundations of data privacy, recognizing the challenges posed by evolving cyber threats, and implementing effective strategies, individuals and organizations can better protect sensitive information. As data continues to play a pivotal role in our lives, fostering a culture of privacy and security will be crucial for building trust and safeguarding personal information in an interconnected world.

Responsible Use of Biometric Data

The advent of biometric data technologies has revolutionized the way individuals interact with systems, providing a unique and often more secure method of identification. Biometric data, which includes fingerprints, facial recognition, iris scans, and voice recognition, offers a range of applications from enhancing security protocols to streamlining user experiences. However, the responsible use of such sensitive data is paramount in ensuring ethical standards and protecting individual privacy.

Theoretical Framework

The responsible use of biometric data is grounded in several theoretical frameworks, including privacy theories, ethical considerations, and data protection regulations. Key theories include:

DATA PRIVACY AND ETHICS

- **Privacy as Contextual Integrity:** This theory posits that privacy is not merely about control over personal information but is also about the appropriateness of information flows in specific contexts. Biometric data must be collected and used in a manner that aligns with the expectations of individuals based on the context of its collection.

- **Utilitarianism:** This ethical framework evaluates actions based on their consequences. In the context of biometric data, the benefits of enhanced security and efficiency must be weighed against potential risks to individual privacy and autonomy.

- **Deontological Ethics:** This approach emphasizes the importance of following ethical rules and principles. It suggests that organizations must adhere to strict guidelines regarding consent, data storage, and usage to respect individual rights.

Problems in the Use of Biometric Data

Despite the advantages of biometric systems, several significant problems arise:

- **Privacy Concerns:** Biometric data is inherently personal and immutable. Unlike passwords, biometric traits cannot be changed if compromised. This raises concerns about long-term privacy implications, particularly if data is misused or leaked.

- **Informed Consent:** Obtaining informed consent can be challenging, as individuals may not fully understand how their biometric data will be used, stored, or shared. This lack of understanding can lead to consent being deemed invalid.

- **Data Security:** Biometric databases are attractive targets for cybercriminals. The security of stored biometric data is crucial, as breaches can lead to identity theft and other malicious activities.

- **Bias and Discrimination:** Biometric systems can exhibit biases, particularly in facial recognition technologies, which have been shown to have higher error rates for people of color and women. This raises ethical concerns regarding fairness and equality in technology deployment.

Examples of Responsible Use

Several organizations and initiatives exemplify the responsible use of biometric data:

- **Apple's Face ID:** Apple has implemented robust privacy measures in its Face ID technology. The facial recognition data is stored locally on the device and is not sent to external servers, minimizing the risk of data breaches. Additionally, Apple emphasizes user consent and transparency in its data handling practices.

- **Biometric Authentication in Banking:** Financial institutions are increasingly adopting biometric authentication methods, such as fingerprint and voice recognition, to enhance security. Banks typically implement strong encryption and strict access controls to protect biometric data, ensuring compliance with data protection regulations like GDPR.

- **Nonprofit Initiatives for Social Good:** Organizations like ClearView AI have faced criticism for their practices; however, some nonprofits use biometric data responsibly to aid in humanitarian efforts, such as identifying missing persons in disaster zones while ensuring transparency and ethical standards are upheld.

Regulatory Frameworks

To mitigate the risks associated with biometric data use, various regulatory frameworks have been established:

- **General Data Protection Regulation (GDPR):** In the European Union, GDPR provides comprehensive guidelines on the collection and processing of personal data, including biometric data. It mandates explicit consent, transparency, and the right to access and delete personal data.

- **Biometric Information Privacy Act (BIPA):** In the United States, Illinois enacted BIPA, which requires organizations to obtain informed consent before collecting biometric data. It also mandates secure storage and limits data retention periods.

- **California Consumer Privacy Act (CCPA):** CCPA enhances privacy rights and consumer protection for residents of California, including provisions for biometric data. It allows individuals to know what personal data is collected and to whom it is sold.

Conclusion

The responsible use of biometric data is essential in navigating the complexities of privacy, ethics, and technology. Organizations must prioritize transparency, informed consent, and data security to build trust with users and ensure compliance with legal frameworks. As biometric technologies continue to evolve, ongoing dialogue and collaboration among technologists, ethicists, and policymakers will be crucial in shaping a future where biometric data is used ethically and responsibly, ultimately benefiting society while protecting individual rights.

Transparency and Accountability in Data Science

In the rapidly evolving field of data science, the principles of transparency and accountability are paramount. As organizations increasingly rely on data-driven decision-making, the ethical implications of data usage become more pronounced. This subsection delves into the importance of these principles, the challenges faced in their implementation, and examples of best practices that can guide the future of data science.

The Importance of Transparency

Transparency in data science refers to the clarity with which data processes, methodologies, and outcomes are communicated. This transparency is essential for several reasons:

- **Trust Building:** Stakeholders, including consumers and regulatory bodies, are more likely to trust data-driven insights when they understand the underlying processes. Transparency fosters an environment of trust and collaboration.

- **Informed Decision-Making:** When data processes are transparent, decision-makers can better understand the implications of data analyses, leading to more informed choices.

- **Enhancing Reproducibility:** Transparent methodologies allow other researchers and practitioners to replicate studies, which is a cornerstone of scientific integrity.

Challenges to Transparency

Despite its importance, achieving transparency in data science is fraught with challenges:

- **Complexity of Algorithms:** Many data science techniques, particularly those involving machine learning, are inherently complex. The so-called "black box" nature of these algorithms makes it difficult to explain how decisions are made.

- **Data Privacy Concerns:** Organizations often face a dilemma between transparency and privacy. Disclosing too much information about data sources or methodologies can compromise sensitive data.

- **Lack of Standardization:** The absence of universally accepted standards for transparency in data science practices leads to inconsistencies across different organizations and industries.

Accountability in Data Science

Accountability refers to the responsibility of data scientists and organizations to ensure that their data practices are ethical and that they can justify their decisions. Key aspects of accountability include:

- **Ethical Guidelines:** Establishing ethical guidelines helps data scientists navigate the complexities of their work. These guidelines should address issues such as bias, fairness, and the potential societal impact of data analyses.

- **Clear Documentation:** Maintaining thorough documentation of data sources, methodologies, and decision-making processes is crucial for accountability. This documentation serves as a reference for stakeholders and aids in audits and reviews.

- **Stakeholder Engagement:** Engaging stakeholders in the data process ensures that diverse perspectives are considered, enhancing accountability and ethical considerations in data-driven decisions.

Examples of Best Practices

Several organizations have successfully implemented transparency and accountability measures in their data science practices:

- **Google's Model Cards:** Google has introduced Model Cards, which are documentation that provides information about machine learning models, including their intended use, performance metrics, and ethical considerations. This initiative promotes transparency and helps stakeholders understand the models' capabilities and limitations.

- **IBM's AI Fairness 360:** IBM has developed a toolkit called AI Fairness 360, which helps data scientists detect and mitigate bias in machine learning models. By providing tools for accountability, IBM empowers organizations to ensure that their AI systems are fair and ethical.

- **Open Data Initiatives:** Various governments and organizations have embraced open data initiatives, making datasets publicly available to promote transparency. For instance, the City of New York provides access to a wealth of datasets, allowing citizens to scrutinize city operations and hold officials accountable.

Conclusion

In conclusion, transparency and accountability are essential components of responsible data science practices. As the field continues to evolve, it is imperative for data scientists and organizations to prioritize these principles. By fostering a culture of transparency and accountability, the data science community can build trust, enhance decision-making, and contribute to a more ethical and equitable society. The future of data science lies not only in technological advancements but also in the commitment to ethical practices that respect the rights and dignity of all individuals.

$$\text{Accountability Score} = \frac{\text{Number of Ethical Guidelines Followed}}{\text{Total Number of Guidelines}} \times 100\% \quad (88)$$

This equation illustrates a simple metric for measuring accountability within an organization. By quantifying adherence to ethical guidelines, organizations can assess their commitment to accountability in data science practices.

Striking the Balance between Innovation and Ethics

In the rapidly evolving landscape of data science and analytics, the pursuit of innovation often collides with ethical considerations. Striking a balance between these two forces is crucial for fostering a sustainable and responsible approach to technology. This section explores the theoretical frameworks, challenges, and practical examples that illustrate the delicate interplay between innovation and ethics in the realm of data science.

Theoretical Frameworks

To understand the balance between innovation and ethics, it is essential to consider several theoretical frameworks that guide ethical decision-making in technology. One prominent framework is the **Utilitarianism** theory, which posits that the best action is the one that maximizes utility, typically defined as that which produces the greatest well-being of the greatest number of people. In the context of data science, this theory advocates for innovations that yield significant societal benefits, such as improved healthcare outcomes or enhanced public safety.

However, utilitarianism can lead to ethical dilemmas, particularly when the benefits to the majority come at the expense of a minority. For instance, the deployment of predictive policing algorithms may reduce crime rates in certain neighborhoods but disproportionately target marginalized communities, raising serious ethical concerns about fairness and justice.

Another critical framework is **Deontological ethics**, which emphasizes the importance of adhering to moral rules and duties. This approach argues that certain actions are inherently right or wrong, regardless of their consequences. In data science, this perspective underscores the necessity of respecting individual privacy rights and ensuring informed consent when collecting and analyzing personal data.

A third framework is **Virtue ethics**, which focuses on the character and intentions of the individuals involved in the innovation process. This approach encourages data scientists and technologists to cultivate virtues such as honesty, integrity, and empathy, guiding them to consider the broader implications of their work on society.

Challenges in Balancing Innovation and Ethics

Despite the existence of these frameworks, several challenges complicate the balance between innovation and ethics in data science. One significant challenge is the **rapid pace of technological advancement**. The speed at which new technologies emerge often outpaces the development of ethical guidelines and regulatory frameworks. For example, the rise of artificial intelligence (AI) and machine learning has led to innovations that can analyze vast amounts of data and make decisions with minimal human intervention. However, the lack of established ethical standards for AI deployment raises concerns about accountability, bias, and transparency.

Another challenge is the **data privacy crisis**. With the proliferation of data collection practices, individuals' personal information is often harvested without their explicit consent. This situation creates a tension between the desire to innovate and the need to protect individual privacy rights. The Cambridge Analytica scandal exemplifies this issue, where data harvested from millions of Facebook users was used to influence political campaigns without their knowledge, highlighting the potential for ethical violations in the quest for innovation.

Practical Examples

Several organizations have successfully navigated the balance between innovation and ethics, serving as models for best practices in the field. One notable example is **IBM**, which has taken a proactive approach to ethical AI development. The company established the *IBM AI Ethics Board* to guide its AI initiatives, ensuring that ethical considerations are integrated into the design and deployment of AI systems. IBM's commitment to transparency is evident in its publication of AI ethics principles that prioritize fairness, accountability, and transparency.

Similarly, **Salesforce** has implemented a *Trust and Ethics* framework that emphasizes ethical considerations in its data-driven innovations. The company actively engages stakeholders, including customers and employees, in discussions about ethical data usage and the implications of its technologies. This collaborative approach fosters a culture of ethical awareness and responsibility within the organization.

In the realm of healthcare, the use of data analytics for personalized medicine presents both opportunities and ethical dilemmas. For instance, while leveraging patient data can lead to tailored treatment plans and improved outcomes, it also raises concerns about data privacy and informed consent. Organizations like **Mayo Clinic** have adopted stringent ethical guidelines for data usage, ensuring that patients are fully informed about how their data will be utilized and granting them control over their personal information.

Conclusion

Striking the balance between innovation and ethics is a complex yet essential endeavor in the field of data science. By employing robust ethical frameworks, addressing challenges head-on, and learning from practical examples, data scientists can foster a culture of responsible innovation. This balance not only enhances the credibility and trustworthiness of data-driven technologies but also ensures that the benefits of innovation are equitably distributed across society. As Fatima Wang continues to inspire future innovators, her legacy will undoubtedly emphasize the importance of ethical considerations in the pursuit of groundbreaking advancements in data science.

Inspiring the Next Generation

Encouraging Diversity in Data Science

The field of data science has seen exponential growth over the past decade, becoming a cornerstone of innovation across various industries. However, despite its rapid evolution, data science remains an arena that is predominantly homogenous, often reflecting the biases and limitations of a narrow demographic. Encouraging diversity in data science is not merely a matter of equity; it is essential for fostering creativity, improving decision-making, and driving innovation.

The Importance of Diversity

Research has consistently shown that diverse teams outperform their homogenous counterparts. According to a study by McKinsey [1], companies in the top quartile for gender diversity on executive teams were 21% more likely to experience above-average profitability. Furthermore, teams that are diverse in terms of race and ethnicity are 33% more likely to outperform their peers [2]. This correlation is attributed to the variety of perspectives and problem-solving approaches that diverse teams bring to the table.

In data science, diversity plays a crucial role in mitigating algorithmic bias. Algorithms trained on biased data can perpetuate and even amplify existing inequalities. For example, facial recognition technology has been shown to have significantly higher error rates for individuals with darker skin tones, primarily due to the lack of diverse representation in the datasets used for training [3]. By incorporating diverse voices and experiences in the data science process, practitioners can better identify potential biases and create more equitable algorithms.

Barriers to Diversity in Data Science

Despite the clear benefits, several barriers hinder diversity in data science. These include:

- **Educational Gaps:** Access to quality education in STEM fields is often inequitable, with marginalized communities facing systemic barriers that limit their opportunities to pursue careers in data science.

- **Workplace Culture:** Many tech companies have cultures that can be unwelcoming to underrepresented groups, leading to high turnover rates and low retention of diverse talent.

- **Bias in Recruitment:** Traditional hiring practices often favor candidates from specific backgrounds, perpetuating a cycle of homogeneity. For instance, a study by the National Bureau of Economic Research found that job applicants with traditionally African American names received 50% fewer callbacks than those with traditionally white names [4].

Strategies for Encouraging Diversity

To combat these barriers, organizations must implement targeted strategies to encourage diversity in data science:

1. **Outreach and Education** Engaging with underrepresented communities through outreach programs can help bridge the educational gap. Initiatives such as coding boot camps, scholarships, and mentorship programs can provide crucial support to aspiring data scientists from diverse backgrounds. For example, organizations like *Black Girls Code* and *Data Science Society* are working to empower underrepresented groups by providing training and resources.

2. **Inclusive Hiring Practices** Adopting inclusive hiring practices is vital for attracting diverse talent. This includes using blind recruitment techniques, where identifying information is removed from resumes to reduce bias, and implementing diverse interview panels to ensure a variety of perspectives in the selection process.

3. **Fostering an Inclusive Workplace Culture** Creating a supportive workplace culture is essential for retaining diverse talent. This can be achieved through diversity training, employee resource groups, and mentorship programs that foster connections among employees from different backgrounds. Companies like *Salesforce* have implemented diversity and inclusion training, resulting in a more cohesive and supportive environment.

4. Promoting Diversity in Leadership Leadership plays a crucial role in shaping organizational culture. By promoting diverse individuals to leadership positions, companies can ensure that diverse perspectives are represented in decision-making processes. Research shows that organizations with diverse leadership teams are more innovative and better equipped to address complex challenges [5].

Case Studies and Examples

Several organizations have successfully implemented diversity initiatives in data science:

1. Google Google has made significant strides in promoting diversity within its workforce. The company publishes annual diversity reports and has committed to increasing the representation of underrepresented groups in technical roles. Google's initiatives include partnerships with organizations that support minority groups in tech, such as *Code2040* and *Girls Who Code*.

2. IBM IBM has been at the forefront of promoting diversity in tech. The company has established a comprehensive diversity strategy that includes mentorship programs, employee resource groups, and partnerships with educational institutions to promote STEM education among underrepresented groups. IBM's commitment to diversity has resulted in a more inclusive workplace and improved innovation outcomes.

3. DataKind DataKind is a nonprofit organization that connects data scientists with social change organizations to address pressing social issues. By leveraging the skills of diverse data scientists, DataKind has tackled problems such as food insecurity, disaster response, and public health, demonstrating the power of diverse perspectives in data science.

Conclusion

Encouraging diversity in data science is not only a moral imperative but a strategic necessity. By fostering diverse teams, organizations can harness a wealth of perspectives that drive innovation and improve decision-making. Addressing the barriers to diversity requires concerted efforts in outreach, inclusive hiring, workplace culture, and leadership representation. As the field of data science continues to evolve, embracing diversity will be key to unlocking its full potential and creating solutions that are equitable and impactful for all.

Bibliography

[1] McKinsey & Company. (2015). *Why Diversity Matters*. Retrieved from https://www.mckinsey.com/business-functions/organization/our-insights/why-diversity-matters

[2] McKinsey & Company. (2018). *Delivering Through Diversity*. Retrieved from https://www.mckinsey.com/business-functions/organization/our-insights/delivering-through-diversity

[3] Buolamwini, J., & Gebru, T. (2018). *Gender Shades: Intersectional Accuracy Disparities in Commercial Gender Classification*. In *Proceedings of the 2018 Conference on Fairness, Accountability, and Transparency (FAT* 2018)*.

[4] Bertrand, M., & Mullainathan, S. (2004). *Are Emily and Greg More Employable Than Lakisha and Jamal? A Field Experiment on Labor Market Discrimination*. American Economic Review, 94(4), 991-1013.

[5] Herring, C. (2009). *Does Diversity Pay? Race, Gender, and the Business Case for Diversity*. American Sociological Review, 74(2), 208-224.

STEM Education and Data Literacy

In the modern world, the importance of STEM (Science, Technology, Engineering, and Mathematics) education cannot be overstated. As industries increasingly rely on data-driven decision-making, the ability to understand and manipulate data has become a fundamental skill. This subsection delves into the significance of STEM education, the challenges faced in promoting data literacy, and practical examples that illustrate the impact of these educational initiatives.

The Importance of STEM Education

STEM education equips students with critical thinking, problem-solving, and analytical skills necessary for success in a data-centric world. According to the National Math and Science Initiative, students engaged in STEM education are more likely to pursue careers in high-demand fields, fostering innovation and economic growth. Furthermore, a strong foundation in STEM subjects enhances students' abilities to engage with complex data, enabling them to interpret, analyze, and apply information effectively.

Challenges in Promoting Data Literacy

Despite the recognized importance of data literacy, several challenges persist in integrating data education into the STEM curriculum:

- **Curriculum Gaps:** Many educational institutions lack comprehensive curricula that effectively incorporate data literacy. Traditional education often emphasizes rote memorization over practical application, leaving students ill-prepared for real-world data challenges.

- **Resource Limitations:** Schools, particularly those in underfunded areas, may lack access to the necessary technology and resources to teach data literacy effectively. This digital divide exacerbates existing inequalities in education.

- **Teacher Training:** Educators often require training to teach data literacy effectively. Many teachers may not feel confident in their own data skills, which can hinder their ability to impart knowledge to students.

- **Rapidly Evolving Field:** The field of data science is continuously evolving, making it challenging for educational institutions to keep curricula up-to-date with the latest tools, technologies, and methodologies.

Theoretical Frameworks Supporting Data Literacy

Several educational theories support the integration of data literacy into STEM education:

- **Constructivist Learning Theory:** This theory posits that learners construct their own understanding and knowledge of the world through experiences and reflecting on those experiences. In the context of data literacy, students can engage in hands-on projects that allow them to analyze real datasets, fostering deeper understanding.

- **Project-Based Learning (PBL):** PBL encourages students to learn by engaging in projects that require critical thinking and problem-solving. For instance, students can work on projects involving data collection, analysis, and presentation, thereby enhancing their data literacy skills.

- **Inquiry-Based Learning:** This approach emphasizes the importance of questioning and investigation. By encouraging students to ask questions and seek answers through data analysis, educators can promote a culture of curiosity and engagement with data.

Practical Examples of Data Literacy Initiatives

Numerous initiatives have emerged to promote STEM education and data literacy:

- **Data Science for All:** This initiative aims to increase access to data science education for students from diverse backgrounds. It provides free online resources, including tutorials and courses, to help students develop data skills. The program emphasizes hands-on learning, allowing students to work with real datasets to solve problems.

- **Khan Academy:** Khan Academy offers a comprehensive platform for students to learn various subjects, including mathematics and computer science. Their interactive lessons on statistics and data analysis empower students to develop essential data skills at their own pace.

- **Girls Who Code:** This organization focuses on closing the gender gap in technology. By offering coding programs and data science workshops for girls, it encourages young women to pursue careers in STEM fields, fostering a more diverse future workforce.

Conclusion

In conclusion, STEM education and data literacy are crucial for preparing the next generation of innovators. By addressing the challenges in promoting data literacy and implementing effective educational strategies, we can empower students to thrive in a data-driven world. Initiatives that emphasize hands-on learning, collaboration, and real-world applications will play a vital role in fostering a culture of data literacy, ultimately leading to a more informed and capable society.

$$\text{Data Literacy} = \frac{\text{Understanding of Data}}{\text{Access to Data} + \text{Education and Training}} \tag{89}$$

This equation highlights that data literacy is dependent on both access to data and the education and training provided to individuals. As we strive to enhance data literacy, it is imperative to ensure that all students have equal access to quality education and resources.

By investing in STEM education and prioritizing data literacy, we can create a future where individuals are equipped to harness the power of data for innovation and societal advancement.

Mentorship and Support Networks

Mentorship and support networks play a critical role in the development of future innovators, particularly in fields as dynamic and complex as data science. These relationships not only provide guidance and knowledge but also foster a sense of community and belonging, which can be pivotal for individuals navigating the often intimidating landscape of technology and analytics.

The Importance of Mentorship

Mentorship can be defined as a professional relationship in which an experienced individual (the mentor) provides guidance, support, and advice to a less experienced individual (the mentee). According to Kram's (1985) theory of mentoring, there are two primary functions of mentorship: career development and psychosocial support.

$$\text{Mentorship} = \text{Career Development} + \text{Psychosocial Support} \quad (90)$$

Career development encompasses the mentor's role in providing opportunities for professional growth, such as networking, skill development, and career advancement. Psychosocial support, on the other hand, includes emotional encouragement, role modeling, and fostering a sense of identity and belonging within the field.

Challenges Faced by Mentees

Despite the clear benefits of mentorship, many aspiring data scientists encounter several challenges in finding suitable mentors. These challenges include:

- **Lack of Access:** Many individuals, particularly from underrepresented groups, may not have access to professional networks that facilitate mentorship opportunities. This can lead to feelings of isolation and hinder their career progression.

- **Imposter Syndrome:** Many mentees may struggle with feelings of inadequacy or self-doubt, commonly referred to as imposter syndrome. This can prevent them from seeking out mentorship or fully engaging in the relationship.
- **Mismatch of Expectations:** Sometimes, the expectations between mentors and mentees may not align, leading to dissatisfaction in the relationship. Clear communication about goals and objectives is essential to mitigate this issue.

Building Effective Support Networks

To address these challenges, it is essential to build effective support networks that extend beyond traditional mentorship. Support networks can include peer mentoring, professional organizations, and online communities. These networks can provide a range of benefits:

- **Diverse Perspectives:** Engaging with a variety of individuals can provide mentees with diverse perspectives and insights that can enhance their understanding of complex data science concepts.
- **Collaboration Opportunities:** Support networks can facilitate collaboration on projects, allowing mentees to gain practical experience and build their portfolios.
- **Emotional Support:** Sharing experiences and challenges with peers can help alleviate feelings of isolation and foster a sense of belonging in the data science community.

Examples of Successful Mentorship Programs

Several organizations and initiatives have successfully implemented mentorship programs aimed at fostering the next generation of data scientists:

- **Data Science Society:** This global community offers mentorship programs that connect aspiring data scientists with experienced professionals. Participants engage in workshops, hackathons, and networking events, fostering both technical skills and personal connections.
- **Women in Data Science (WiDS):** This initiative aims to inspire and educate women in data science and related fields. The WiDS conference features mentorship opportunities, panel discussions, and networking sessions, promoting female representation in the industry.

- **Black Girls Code:** This nonprofit organization focuses on providing young girls of color with the skills and resources needed to pursue careers in technology. Their mentorship program connects participants with industry professionals who provide guidance and support.

Conclusion

In conclusion, mentorship and support networks are vital for empowering future innovators in data science. By addressing the challenges faced by mentees and building effective support systems, we can create an environment that nurtures talent and fosters innovation. As Fatima Wang's legacy demonstrates, investing in mentorship not only benefits individuals but also strengthens the entire field of data science, paving the way for a more inclusive and innovative future.

Bibliography

[1] Kram, K. E. (1985). Mentoring at Work: Developmental Relationships in Organizational Life. Glenview, IL: Scott, Foresman.

Building a More Inclusive Tech Industry

The tech industry has long been criticized for its lack of diversity and inclusivity. As Fatima Wang recognized throughout her career, building a more inclusive tech industry is not only a moral imperative but also a strategic advantage that can lead to greater innovation and creativity. This section explores the theoretical frameworks, existing problems, and practical examples that illustrate the importance of inclusivity in technology.

Theoretical Frameworks

To understand the necessity of inclusivity in tech, we can draw on several theoretical frameworks, including:

- **Social Identity Theory:** This theory posits that individuals categorize themselves and others into various social groups. In a tech environment where homogeneous groups dominate, diverse perspectives are often overlooked, leading to a lack of innovation. By fostering an inclusive culture, companies can leverage the diverse backgrounds and experiences of their employees, leading to better problem-solving and creativity.

- **Intersectionality:** Coined by Kimberlé Crenshaw, intersectionality emphasizes that individuals have multiple identities that intersect, leading to unique experiences of privilege and oppression. Acknowledging intersectionality in the tech industry can help organizations understand the diverse needs of their employees and customers, leading to more inclusive products and services.

- **Systems Theory:** This theory posits that organizations are complex systems made up of interrelated parts. By viewing diversity and inclusion as a systemic issue, tech companies can implement comprehensive strategies that address the root causes of exclusion rather than merely treating the symptoms.

Existing Problems

Despite the growing awareness of the need for inclusivity, several persistent problems hinder progress in the tech industry:

- **Bias in Recruitment:** Many tech companies rely on traditional recruitment methods that often favor candidates from similar backgrounds. This bias can be exacerbated by algorithms that prioritize certain qualifications or experiences, further entrenching existing disparities.

- **Workplace Culture:** A lack of inclusivity can lead to toxic workplace cultures where underrepresented groups feel marginalized or unsupported. This environment can result in high turnover rates, decreased productivity, and a lack of employee engagement.

- **Representation in Leadership:** Women and minorities are significantly underrepresented in leadership positions within tech companies. According to a 2021 report by McKinsey & Company, women hold only 28% of senior vice president roles in the tech industry, while people of color make up only 15% of executive positions. This lack of representation perpetuates a cycle where the needs and perspectives of these groups are overlooked in decision-making processes.

Examples of Successful Initiatives

Several organizations and initiatives have successfully implemented strategies to promote inclusivity in the tech industry:

- **Girls Who Code:** This nonprofit organization aims to close the gender gap in technology by providing girls with the resources and support they need to pursue careers in computer science. Through coding camps and mentorship programs, Girls Who Code empowers young women to develop their skills and confidence in tech.

- **Black Girls Code:** Founded by Kimberly Bryant, this organization focuses on teaching girls of color aged 7-17 about computer programming and technology. By providing workshops and community events, Black Girls Code fosters a sense of belonging and encourages girls to pursue STEM careers.

- **Inclusive Hiring Practices:** Companies like Google and Microsoft have implemented blind recruitment processes to reduce bias in hiring. By anonymizing resumes and focusing on skills and qualifications rather than demographic information, these organizations have seen an increase in diversity among their new hires.

- **Employee Resource Groups (ERGs):** Many tech companies have established ERGs to create safe spaces for underrepresented employees. These groups provide support, networking opportunities, and a platform for employees to voice their concerns and ideas. ERGs have been shown to improve employee morale and retention, as well as contribute to a more inclusive workplace culture.

Challenges Ahead

While progress has been made, several challenges remain in the quest for a more inclusive tech industry:

- **Resistance to Change:** Changing organizational culture can be met with resistance, particularly from individuals who benefit from the status quo. It is crucial for leaders to advocate for inclusivity and demonstrate its value to the organization.

- **Sustainability of Initiatives:** Many diversity initiatives are implemented as short-term projects rather than long-term commitments. To create lasting change, organizations must integrate inclusivity into their core values and practices.

- **Measurement and Accountability:** Establishing metrics to measure inclusivity can be challenging. Organizations must develop clear benchmarks and hold themselves accountable for progress in diversity and inclusion efforts.

Conclusion

Building a more inclusive tech industry is essential for fostering innovation, creativity, and social equity. By understanding the theoretical frameworks that support inclusivity, addressing existing problems, and learning from successful initiatives, organizations can create a more equitable environment for all employees. As Fatima Wang's legacy demonstrates, inclusivity is not just a goal but a catalyst for transformative change in the tech landscape. Embracing diversity will ultimately lead to a more vibrant, innovative, and successful industry that reflects the rich tapestry of society.

Empowering Future Innovators

Empowering future innovators is essential for fostering creativity, critical thinking, and problem-solving skills in the next generation. This empowerment requires a multifaceted approach that includes education, mentorship, accessibility to resources, and the cultivation of a supportive community. In this section, we will explore the various strategies and initiatives that can be implemented to empower aspiring innovators in the field of data science and beyond.

Education and Curriculum Development

A robust educational framework is the foundation for empowering future innovators. Educational institutions must adapt their curricula to include data literacy, computational thinking, and interdisciplinary approaches that integrate science, technology, engineering, arts, and mathematics (STEAM). This integration allows students to see the connections between different fields and encourages innovative thinking.

$$\text{Innovation} = \text{Creativity} + \text{Knowledge} + \text{Collaboration} \qquad (91)$$

Here, innovation is seen as a product of creativity, knowledge acquisition, and collaborative efforts. Programs that emphasize hands-on learning, such as project-based learning and internships, can significantly enhance students' understanding and application of data analytics.

Mentorship Programs

Mentorship plays a crucial role in the development of future innovators. By connecting students with experienced professionals in the field, mentorship programs provide guidance, support, and valuable insights into the industry. Mentors can help mentees navigate challenges, explore career options, and develop essential skills.

A successful mentorship program should include:

- Regular one-on-one meetings to discuss goals and challenges.
- Opportunities for mentees to work on real-world projects.
- Networking events to connect mentees with industry professionals.

For example, initiatives like *Girls Who Code* and *Black Girls Who Code* focus on providing mentorship and resources to underrepresented groups in technology, empowering them to pursue careers in data science and related fields.

Accessibility to Resources

Access to resources is a critical factor in empowering future innovators. This includes access to technology, data sets, software tools, and educational materials. Educational institutions and organizations should strive to provide equitable access to these resources, particularly for underserved communities.

$$\text{Equity} = \frac{\text{Access to Resources}}{\text{Barriers to Entry}} \qquad (92)$$

In this equation, equity is achieved when access to resources outweighs the barriers to entry. Programs that offer free or low-cost workshops, online courses, and open-source tools can help bridge the gap for aspiring innovators.

Fostering a Supportive Community

Creating a supportive community is vital for empowering future innovators. This community can be built through networking events, hackathons, and collaborative projects that encourage interaction and knowledge sharing among peers. A strong community fosters a culture of innovation where individuals feel safe to share ideas and take risks.

- Organizing local meetups and workshops to discuss emerging trends in data science.
- Hosting hackathons that challenge participants to solve real-world problems using data analytics.
- Establishing online forums and social media groups for continuous engagement and support.

For instance, platforms like *Kaggle* provide a community for data enthusiasts to collaborate on projects, share insights, and compete in challenges, thereby enhancing their skills and confidence.

Promoting Diversity and Inclusion

To truly empower future innovators, it is essential to promote diversity and inclusion within the field of data science. Diverse teams bring a variety of perspectives and experiences, which can lead to more innovative solutions. Programs that actively recruit and support individuals from various backgrounds can help create a more inclusive environment.

Strategies to promote diversity and inclusion include:

- Implementing outreach programs in schools and communities to raise awareness of data science careers.

- Offering scholarships and financial support to underrepresented students pursuing degrees in data-related fields.

- Creating inclusive workplace cultures that value diverse perspectives and foster collaboration.

Case Studies and Success Stories

Several organizations and initiatives exemplify the empowerment of future innovators. For example, *Code.org* has successfully increased the number of students learning computer science in schools across the United States, particularly among underrepresented groups. Their efforts have led to increased enrollment in Advanced Placement (AP) Computer Science courses.

Another example is *DataKind*, which connects data scientists with nonprofit organizations to tackle social issues through data-driven solutions. By empowering data scientists to apply their skills for social good, DataKind inspires the next generation of innovators to leverage data for positive change.

Conclusion

Empowering future innovators requires a comprehensive approach that combines education, mentorship, accessibility, community support, and a commitment to diversity and inclusion. By implementing these strategies, we can cultivate a new generation of data scientists and innovators who are equipped to tackle the challenges of tomorrow. As we look to the future, it is imperative that we invest in the potential of young minds, ensuring that they have the tools, resources, and support they need to thrive in an increasingly data-driven world.

The Legacy of Fatima Wang

Impact on Future Innovations

Fatima Wang's contributions to the field of data analytics have paved the way for a new generation of innovations that are transforming industries and reshaping societal structures. Her work not only addressed existing challenges within data science but also opened new avenues for exploration and application. This subsection explores the profound impact of her innovations on future developments across various sectors.

Theoretical Foundations

At the core of Fatima's impact lies the integration of theoretical frameworks that govern data analytics. The application of statistical theories, such as Bayesian inference and regression analysis, has been crucial in developing robust algorithms that enhance predictive analytics. For instance, the use of Bayesian networks allows for the modeling of complex relationships between variables, enabling more accurate predictions in fields ranging from healthcare to finance.

The equation for a simple linear regression, which is foundational in predictive modeling, is given by:

$$y = \beta_0 + \beta_1 x + \epsilon \tag{93}$$

where:

- y is the dependent variable,
- x is the independent variable,
- β_0 is the y-intercept,
- β_1 is the slope of the line, and
- ϵ represents the error term.

Fatima's innovations in algorithm development have significantly enhanced the accuracy and efficiency of such models, allowing for real-time data processing and analysis.

Addressing Key Problems

One of the critical issues in data science is the challenge of handling vast amounts of unstructured data. Fatima's research focused on developing algorithms that could sift through this data efficiently, extracting meaningful insights. For example, her work in natural language processing (NLP) has enabled organizations to analyze customer feedback and sentiment on a massive scale, transforming how businesses approach customer service and product development.

Moreover, her emphasis on ethical data usage has addressed the growing concerns around data privacy and security. The implementation of differential privacy techniques, which allow for data analysis without compromising individual privacy, is a testament to her commitment to responsible innovation. The mathematical formulation of differential privacy can be expressed as:

$$\Pr[M(D) \in S] \leq e^{\epsilon} \cdot \Pr[M(D') \in S] \quad \forall S \subseteq \text{Range}(M) \qquad (94)$$

where:

- M is a randomized algorithm,
- D and D' are datasets differing by a single element,
- ϵ is the privacy parameter, and
- S is a subset of the output space.

This approach not only mitigates risks associated with data breaches but also fosters trust among users and stakeholders.

Examples of Innovations Influenced by Fatima's Work

Fatima's influence extends across various sectors, leading to notable innovations:

- **Healthcare:** Her advancements in predictive modeling have enabled healthcare providers to anticipate patient needs and optimize treatment plans. For instance, algorithms developed from her research have been instrumental in predicting outbreaks of diseases, allowing for timely interventions.

- **Finance:** In the financial sector, her work on algorithmic trading has revolutionized investment strategies. By utilizing machine learning techniques, investors can now analyze market trends and make informed decisions at unprecedented speeds.

- **Education:** Fatima's impact is also evident in educational technology, where her algorithms have facilitated personalized learning experiences. By analyzing student performance data, educational platforms can tailor content to meet individual learning needs, thereby improving educational outcomes.

Future Directions

The innovations sparked by Fatima Wang's research are only the beginning. As technology continues to evolve, the potential for data analytics to drive future innovations is immense. Emerging fields such as quantum computing and blockchain technology promise to further enhance the capabilities of data science. For example, quantum algorithms could exponentially increase the speed of data processing, enabling real-time analytics on previously unimaginable scales.

Moreover, the integration of artificial intelligence (AI) with data analytics is set to revolutionize decision-making processes across industries. The ability of AI to learn from data patterns and improve over time will lead to more sophisticated predictive models and automated insights.

Conclusion

In conclusion, Fatima Wang's impact on future innovations in data analytics is profound and far-reaching. By addressing critical challenges, developing robust theoretical frameworks, and inspiring new applications across various sectors, she has laid the groundwork for a future where data-driven decision-making is the norm. As we continue to navigate the complexities of the digital age, her legacy will undoubtedly guide the next generation of innovators in harnessing the power of data for societal good.

Recognition and Awards

Fatima Wang's contributions to the field of data science and analytics have not gone unnoticed. Her innovative research, groundbreaking methodologies, and tireless advocacy for ethical data practices have garnered her numerous accolades and recognitions, establishing her as a leading figure in the data revolution. This subsection explores the various awards and honors that Fatima has received throughout her career, highlighting the significance of these recognitions in both her professional journey and the broader context of the data science community.

Early Recognition

Fatima's journey in analytics began with her academic excellence during her undergraduate studies at a prestigious university. She was awarded the **Dean's List** honor for multiple semesters, showcasing her commitment to her studies and her exceptional performance in quantitative subjects. This early recognition laid the foundation for her future achievements and served as a motivator for her to pursue further research in data analytics.

Professional Accolades

As Fatima transitioned into her professional career, her work began to attract attention from industry leaders and academic institutions alike. One of her most notable early awards was the **Emerging Scholar Award** from the International Association for Data Science, which she received for her innovative research on machine learning algorithms. This award not only recognized her technical expertise but also her potential for future contributions to the field.

In addition, Fatima was honored with the **Data Innovation Award** by the Global Data Science Consortium for her pioneering work in predictive analytics. This award celebrated her ability to transform complex data sets into actionable insights, significantly impacting decision-making processes in various industries.

Industry Recognition

Fatima's influence extended beyond academia into the corporate world, where her analytics breakthroughs began to reshape industries. She was named one of **Forbes' 30 Under 30** in the category of Science and Technology, a prestigious recognition that highlights young innovators making significant contributions to their fields. This accolade not only elevated her profile but also positioned her as a role model for aspiring data scientists, particularly women and underrepresented minorities in tech.

Moreover, Fatima received the **Tech for Good Award** from the Tech Innovation Summit, acknowledging her commitment to using data science for social impact. Her projects focused on leveraging data to address global challenges such as healthcare disparities and environmental sustainability, demonstrating the power of analytics to drive positive change.

Academic Honors

Throughout her career, Fatima has also been recognized within the academic community. She has received multiple **Best Paper Awards** at international conferences, such as the Annual Conference on Data Science and Machine Learning. These awards highlight her contributions to advancing theoretical frameworks in data analytics and her ability to communicate complex ideas effectively.

In recognition of her teaching excellence, Fatima was awarded the **Excellence in Teaching Award** by her university. This honor reflects her dedication to mentoring the next generation of data scientists and her innovative approaches to teaching data literacy and analytics.

Lifetime Achievement and Impact Awards

As Fatima's career progressed, she began to receive more prestigious awards that acknowledged her lifetime contributions to the field of data science. The **Lifetime Achievement Award** from the Data Science Society was one such honor, recognizing her extensive body of work and her role in shaping the future of analytics. This award is reserved for individuals who have made significant contributions over the course of their careers, and Fatima's receipt of this award solidified her status as a pioneer in the field.

In addition to individual awards, Fatima has been instrumental in leading initiatives that have received collective recognition. For instance, her work on the **Open Data Initiative** earned her team the **Global Impact Award** for fostering transparency and collaboration in data sharing practices. This initiative not only advanced the field of data science but also promoted ethical standards in data usage.

Influence on Future Innovators

The recognition and awards that Fatima Wang has received serve not only to honor her individual achievements but also to inspire future innovators in data science. Her accolades highlight the importance of perseverance, creativity, and ethical considerations in analytics. As she often emphasizes in her talks and workshops, the journey to recognition is not merely about personal accolades but about making a meaningful impact on society through data.

Fatima's story exemplifies how recognition can empower individuals to pursue their passions and contribute to their fields. Her numerous awards have opened doors for her to mentor young data scientists, particularly those from underrepresented backgrounds, encouraging them to strive for excellence and innovate fearlessly.

In conclusion, Fatima Wang's recognition and awards reflect her significant contributions to the field of data science and analytics. From early academic honors to prestigious industry accolades, her journey underscores the transformative power of data and the importance of ethical practices in driving innovation. As the field continues to evolve, Fatima's legacy will undoubtedly inspire future generations of data scientists to push boundaries and create a more equitable and data-driven world.

Contributions to Data Science Education

Fatima Wang's impact on data science education is profound and multifaceted, reflecting her commitment to fostering a new generation of data-savvy individuals capable of navigating the complexities of the digital age. Her contributions can be categorized into several key areas: curriculum development, mentorship programs, advocacy for diversity in STEM, and the establishment of educational partnerships.

Curriculum Development

Recognizing the rapid evolution of data science as a discipline, Fatima played a pivotal role in the development of innovative curricula that integrate theoretical knowledge with practical applications. She advocated for a curriculum that encompasses a wide range of topics, including statistics, machine learning, data visualization, and ethical considerations in data usage.

An example of this is her collaboration with universities to create a modular data science program that allows students to build their skills progressively. The program includes core courses such as:

- **Introduction to Data Science:** Covers foundational concepts in data analysis, programming in Python, and the data science lifecycle.

- **Machine Learning Fundamentals:** Introduces key algorithms, including linear regression, decision trees, and clustering techniques, emphasizing hands-on projects.

- **Data Ethics and Privacy:** Discusses the ethical implications of data collection and analysis, including privacy laws and data governance.

Fatima's approach emphasizes not only technical skills but also the importance of ethical data practices, preparing students to make responsible decisions in their future careers.

Mentorship Programs

In addition to curriculum development, Fatima established mentorship programs aimed at providing guidance and support to aspiring data scientists. These programs connect students with industry professionals, offering them insights into real-world applications of data science.

For instance, through her initiative, the *Data Science Mentorship Network*, students are paired with mentors who provide:

- Career advice and networking opportunities.

- Guidance on technical skills and project development.

- Support in navigating challenges related to diversity and inclusion in tech fields.

Fatima's mentorship programs have been instrumental in helping students gain confidence and skills, particularly those from underrepresented backgrounds.

Advocacy for Diversity in STEM

Understanding the importance of diversity in driving innovation, Fatima has been a passionate advocate for increasing representation in data science and STEM fields. She has organized workshops and conferences aimed at inspiring young women and minorities to pursue careers in data science.

An example of her advocacy is the annual *Women in Data Science Conference*, which features keynote speakers, panel discussions, and hands-on workshops led by successful women in the field. The conference not only showcases role models but also provides a platform for participants to network and collaborate on projects.

Educational Partnerships

Fatima has also spearheaded partnerships between educational institutions and industry leaders to bridge the gap between academia and the workforce. These partnerships facilitate internships, co-op programs, and collaborative research projects that provide students with practical experience.

For example, she collaborated with a leading tech company to establish a summer internship program where students can work on real-world data projects. This initiative has proven beneficial for both students, who gain valuable experience, and companies, which benefit from fresh perspectives and innovative ideas.

Impact and Legacy

The impact of Fatima Wang's contributions to data science education is evident in the increasing number of graduates entering the field equipped with the skills and ethical understanding necessary to succeed. Her initiatives have not only elevated the standard of data science education but have also inspired a culture of continuous learning and innovation.

As a result of her efforts, educational institutions have reported higher enrollment rates in data science programs, particularly among underrepresented groups. Furthermore, many of her mentees have gone on to achieve significant milestones in their careers, a testament to the effectiveness of her mentorship and advocacy.

In summary, Fatima Wang's contributions to data science education have laid a strong foundation for the future of the field. By championing curriculum development, mentorship, diversity, and industry partnerships, she has created a legacy that will inspire and empower future generations of data scientists.

Philanthropy and Social Initiatives

Fatima Wang's journey in data science is not only characterized by her groundbreaking innovations but also by her commitment to philanthropy and social initiatives. Recognizing the potential of data to address pressing societal issues, Fatima has dedicated a significant portion of her career to leveraging analytics for the greater good. This section explores her philanthropic endeavors, the theoretical frameworks that underpin her initiatives, the challenges she faced, and the impact of her work on communities worldwide.

Theoretical Frameworks

At the core of Fatima's philanthropic efforts lies the theory of **data-driven social change**. This framework posits that data can be a powerful tool for identifying societal needs, measuring impact, and driving effective interventions. By applying advanced analytics, Fatima has been able to uncover patterns and insights that inform strategic decision-making in various social domains, including health, education, and poverty alleviation.

$$\text{Impact} = f(\text{Data Quality, Intervention Effectiveness, Community Engagement}) \tag{95}$$

In this equation, the overall impact of a social initiative is a function of the quality of the data collected, the effectiveness of the interventions designed, and the level of community engagement in the process. Fatima's initiatives often emphasize these three components, ensuring that her philanthropic efforts are both data-informed and community-centered.

Challenges in Philanthropy

Despite her successes, Fatima has encountered numerous challenges in her philanthropic journey. One significant issue is the **data divide**, which refers to the disparities in access to data and technology across different socio-economic groups. Many communities lack the resources to collect and analyze data effectively, which hampers their ability to advocate for their needs.

Furthermore, Fatima has faced the challenge of **data privacy and ethics**. In her efforts to use data for social good, she is acutely aware of the ethical implications of data collection and usage. Ensuring that data is collected transparently and used responsibly is paramount to maintaining trust within the communities she serves.

Examples of Initiatives

Fatima's philanthropic initiatives span various sectors, each showcasing her innovative approach to using data for social impact. One notable example is her collaboration with a non-profit organization focused on global health. By employing predictive analytics, Fatima helped the organization identify regions at high risk for disease outbreaks. This proactive approach allowed for targeted interventions, ultimately saving lives and resources.

Another initiative involved partnering with educational institutions to enhance data literacy among underserved communities. Fatima developed a curriculum that integrated data science education into local schools, empowering students with the skills necessary to navigate an increasingly data-driven world. This initiative not only improved educational outcomes but also fostered a sense of agency among students, enabling them to leverage data for their own community's benefit.

Impact on Communities

The impact of Fatima's philanthropic efforts is profound. By harnessing the power of data, she has enabled communities to advocate for their needs more effectively. For instance, in her work with a housing advocacy group, Fatima utilized data analytics to reveal patterns of housing inequality. The insights gained from this analysis empowered the organization to push for policy changes that addressed systemic injustices.

Moreover, Fatima's initiatives have inspired a new generation of data scientists committed to social good. Through mentorship programs and workshops, she has cultivated a community of aspiring data professionals who are eager to apply their skills to tackle social challenges. This ripple effect amplifies the impact of her work, as these individuals carry forward the ethos of using data for positive change.

Conclusion

In conclusion, Fatima Wang's philanthropy and social initiatives exemplify the transformative potential of data when applied with purpose and integrity. By addressing the challenges of the data divide and emphasizing ethical practices, she has set a standard for how data science can contribute to social good. Her legacy is not only in her innovations but also in the empowered communities and inspired individuals who continue to advocate for change through data. As we look to the future, Fatima's work serves as a beacon for those seeking to harness the power of data to create a more equitable and just society.

Remembering Fatima's Contributions

In the rapidly evolving landscape of data science, the contributions of visionaries like Fatima Wang are essential not only for their immediate impact but also for the enduring legacy they create for future generations. Fatima's innovative work has transformed not just the field of analytics but also the way we perceive and utilize data across various sectors. This section aims to explore the significance of her contributions, the challenges she faced, and the lasting influence she has had on both academia and industry.

The Impact on Future Innovations

Fatima's pioneering research in analytics has laid the groundwork for numerous advancements in the field. Her development of novel algorithms, such as the

Adaptive Learning Algorithm (ALA), has significantly enhanced the efficiency of data processing. The ALA is defined mathematically as:

$$ALA(x) = \alpha \cdot f(x) + (1 - \alpha) \cdot ALA(x - 1) \quad (96)$$

where α is a weighting factor that adjusts the influence of new data points relative to previous learning iterations. This algorithm has been instrumental in various applications, particularly in healthcare, where it has improved predictive models for patient outcomes.

Furthermore, Fatima's insights into machine learning frameworks have empowered organizations to leverage data more effectively. Her work on *ensemble methods* has shown that combining multiple models can lead to improved accuracy and robustness in predictions. This principle is mathematically represented as:

$$E(y) = \frac{1}{N} \sum_{i=1}^{N} f_i(x) \quad (97)$$

where $E(y)$ is the expected prediction, N is the number of models, and $f_i(x)$ represents the individual model predictions. This approach has been widely adopted in various industries, from finance to marketing, demonstrating the far-reaching implications of her contributions.

Recognition and Awards

Fatima's groundbreaking work has not gone unnoticed. Throughout her career, she has received numerous accolades that reflect her influence in the field of data science. Notable recognitions include:

- The **Data Science Innovator Award** for her contributions to predictive analytics in healthcare.

- The **Global Impact Award** from the World Data Forum, acknowledging her efforts in promoting data literacy and ethical data usage.

- The **IEEE Fellow** designation, recognizing her significant contributions to the advancement of technology and engineering in data science.

These awards not only honor her individual achievements but also highlight the importance of ethical and responsible data practices that she has championed throughout her career.

Contributions to Data Science Education

Recognizing the importance of nurturing the next generation of data scientists, Fatima has dedicated a significant portion of her career to education and mentorship. She has developed comprehensive curricula aimed at integrating data science into traditional educational frameworks. Her course on *Data Ethics and Responsibility* has been adopted by numerous universities, emphasizing the need for ethical considerations in data handling.

In her role as a mentor, Fatima has guided countless students and young professionals, providing them with the tools and knowledge necessary to navigate the complexities of data science. Her initiatives, such as the *Women in Data Science* program, have been pivotal in promoting diversity and inclusion within the field. This program has successfully increased female representation in data science by 30% over five years.

Philanthropy and Social Initiatives

Fatima's commitment to social good extends beyond academia and industry; she has actively engaged in philanthropic endeavors aimed at leveraging data for societal benefit. Through her foundation, *Data for Good*, she has funded projects focused on addressing global challenges such as poverty, health disparities, and climate change. One notable project involved using data analytics to improve access to clean water in underserved communities, showcasing her belief in the power of data to drive positive change.

Her work with *Data for Good* has not only provided resources to those in need but also served as a model for how data can be harnessed to create sustainable solutions. By collaborating with NGOs and government agencies, Fatima has demonstrated the potential of data-driven approaches to tackle some of the world's most pressing issues.

Remembering Fatima's Contributions

As we reflect on Fatima Wang's contributions, it is essential to recognize the principles that guided her work: curiosity, innovation, and a commitment to social responsibility. Her legacy is not merely in the algorithms and frameworks she developed, but in the minds she inspired and the communities she uplifted.

Fatima's journey serves as a reminder that data science is not just about numbers and algorithms; it is about people and the impact we can make on society. Her vision for a future where data is used ethically and responsibly continues to resonate, encouraging us all to strive for excellence in our endeavors.

In conclusion, remembering Fatima's contributions means embracing her vision and continuing the work she started. It involves fostering a culture of innovation, promoting diversity in the field, and ensuring that the power of data is harnessed for the greater good. As we move forward, let us honor her legacy by committing to the principles she championed and inspiring the next generation of innovators to carry the torch of progress in the data revolution.

Beyond the Data Revolution

The Continued Growth of Data Science

Emerging Technologies in Data Analytics

The landscape of data analytics is continuously evolving, driven by advancements in technology and the increasing volume of data generated across various sectors. Emerging technologies play a crucial role in shaping the future of data analytics, enabling organizations to derive deeper insights, make informed decisions, and enhance operational efficiencies. This section explores several key emerging technologies in data analytics, their theoretical foundations, associated challenges, and practical examples of their applications.

Artificial Intelligence and Machine Learning

Artificial Intelligence (AI) and Machine Learning (ML) are at the forefront of emerging technologies in data analytics. AI refers to the simulation of human intelligence in machines, while ML is a subset of AI that focuses on the development of algorithms that allow computers to learn from and make predictions based on data.

Theoretical Foundations The theoretical underpinnings of ML can be traced back to statistical learning theory, which provides a framework for understanding how algorithms generalize from training data to unseen data. The foundational equation governing many ML algorithms is the optimization problem, which can be expressed as:

$$\hat{f} = \arg\min_{f \in F} \sum_{i=1}^{n} L(y_i, f(x_i)), \tag{98}$$

where L is the loss function, y_i is the true output, $f(x_i)$ is the predicted output, and F is the hypothesis space of functions.

Challenges Despite the potential of AI and ML, several challenges persist, including data quality issues, algorithmic bias, and the need for interpretability in decision-making. For instance, biased training data can lead to biased predictions, which can have serious implications in sensitive applications such as hiring or law enforcement.

Examples A notable example of AI and ML in action is in the healthcare sector, where predictive analytics is utilized to forecast patient outcomes based on historical data. For instance, algorithms can analyze patterns in patient records to predict the likelihood of hospital readmissions, enabling healthcare providers to implement preventative measures.

Natural Language Processing

Natural Language Processing (NLP) is another emerging technology that enhances data analytics by enabling machines to understand and interpret human language. NLP combines linguistics, computer science, and AI to analyze textual data.

Theoretical Foundations The theoretical framework of NLP is grounded in statistical models and linguistic theories. A common approach is the use of vector space models, where words are represented as vectors in a high-dimensional space. The relationship between words can be quantified using cosine similarity, defined as:

$$\text{cosine\_similarity}(A, B) = \frac{A \cdot B}{\|A\| \|B\|}, \quad (99)$$

where A and B are vectors representing words.

Challenges NLP faces challenges such as ambiguity in language, context understanding, and the vast diversity of languages and dialects. Additionally, ethical concerns regarding data privacy and the potential misuse of NLP technologies must be addressed.

Examples Applications of NLP are widespread, from sentiment analysis in social media monitoring to chatbots in customer service. For example, companies like IBM utilize NLP in their Watson platform to analyze customer feedback and improve service delivery.

Big Data Technologies

The term "Big Data" refers to datasets that are so large or complex that traditional data processing applications are inadequate. Emerging technologies in this realm include distributed computing frameworks, such as Apache Hadoop and Apache Spark, which allow for the processing of large datasets across clusters of computers.

Theoretical Foundations The theoretical basis for Big Data technologies lies in distributed computing and parallel processing. The MapReduce programming model is a key concept, which can be expressed as:

$$\text{Map}(k, v) \to \text{list}(k', v'), \tag{100}$$

$$\text{Reduce}(k', \text{list}(v')) \to \text{list}(v''). \tag{101}$$

Here, the Map function processes input key-value pairs to generate a set of intermediate key-value pairs, while the Reduce function merges these intermediate values based on their keys.

Challenges Challenges in Big Data analytics include data integration from disparate sources, ensuring data quality, and managing the scalability of storage and processing resources. Additionally, organizations must navigate the complexities of data governance and compliance.

Examples A prominent example of Big Data technology in action is in the retail industry, where companies analyze vast amounts of transactional data to optimize inventory management and enhance customer experiences. For instance, Walmart employs Big Data analytics to predict customer purchasing patterns and adjust stock levels accordingly.

Data Visualization Technologies

Data visualization technologies are essential for transforming complex data into understandable visual formats, enabling stakeholders to make data-driven decisions. Emerging tools, such as Tableau and Power BI, allow users to create interactive dashboards and visualizations.

Theoretical Foundations The theoretical principles of data visualization encompass design theory, cognitive psychology, and statistical graphics. Effective visualizations adhere to principles such as simplicity, clarity, and the appropriate use of color. The effectiveness of a visualization can be quantified using metrics such as the information gain:

$$\text{Information Gain} = H(Y) - H(Y|X), \qquad (102)$$

where H denotes entropy, and Y is the outcome variable influenced by the predictor variable X.

Challenges Despite their advantages, data visualization technologies face challenges, including the potential for misrepresentation of data, overloading users with information, and ensuring accessibility for diverse audiences.

Examples An example of effective data visualization is seen in public health dashboards that track the spread of diseases. During the COVID-19 pandemic, various organizations utilized interactive maps and charts to convey critical information about infection rates and vaccination progress, aiding public understanding and response efforts.

Internet of Things (IoT)

The Internet of Things (IoT) refers to the interconnection of physical devices embedded with sensors and software that collect and exchange data. IoT technologies have transformed data analytics by enabling real-time data collection and analysis from various sources.

Theoretical Foundations The theoretical framework of IoT involves concepts from network theory, sensor technology, and data communication. The communication model can be represented as:

$$D = \sum_{i=1}^{n} S_i \cdot T_i, \qquad (103)$$

where D is the total data collected, S_i represents the sensor data from device i, and T_i is the transmission rate.

Challenges Challenges in IoT data analytics include managing the vast amounts of data generated, ensuring data security and privacy, and integrating data from heterogeneous devices. Additionally, issues related to network latency and connectivity must be addressed.

Examples IoT applications are prevalent in smart cities, where sensors monitor traffic patterns, air quality, and energy consumption. For instance, cities like Barcelona utilize IoT technology to optimize waste management through smart bins that signal when they need to be emptied, enhancing operational efficiency.

Conclusion

In conclusion, emerging technologies in data analytics are revolutionizing the way organizations approach data-driven decision-making. AI and ML provide powerful tools for predictive analytics, while NLP enables the extraction of insights from unstructured text. Big Data technologies facilitate the processing of vast datasets, and data visualization tools enhance the communication of complex information. Finally, IoT connects the physical and digital worlds, generating real-time data that can be analyzed for various applications. As these technologies continue to evolve, they will undoubtedly shape the future of data analytics, presenting both opportunities and challenges that organizations must navigate.

Predictions for the Future of Data

The future of data is poised for transformative changes driven by advancements in technology, evolving societal needs, and a growing emphasis on ethical considerations. As we look ahead, several key predictions can be made about the trajectory of data science and analytics.

Proliferation of Real-Time Data Analytics

One of the most significant trends is the increasing demand for real-time data analytics. With the rise of the Internet of Things (IoT), billions of devices will continuously generate data, necessitating systems capable of processing this information instantaneously. According to a report by *Gartner*, it is estimated that by 2025, over 75 billion IoT devices will be connected globally, producing a staggering amount of real-time data.

This influx of data will require advanced algorithms and machine learning models to analyze and derive insights quickly. For instance, in the healthcare sector, real-time analytics can facilitate immediate responses to patient needs, improving outcomes and operational efficiency. The mathematical representation of real-time data processing can be expressed as:

$$D(t) = \int_{t_0}^{t} d(t')\, dt'$$

where $D(t)$ represents the cumulative data processed up to time t, and $d(t')$ is the instantaneous data generated at time t'.

Increased Integration of Artificial Intelligence

The integration of Artificial Intelligence (AI) into data analytics will redefine how organizations interpret and utilize data. AI algorithms, particularly in machine learning and deep learning, will enhance predictive analytics capabilities, allowing for more accurate forecasting and decision-making processes.

For example, companies like *Netflix* utilize AI-driven algorithms to analyze viewer preferences, leading to personalized content recommendations. The effectiveness of these recommendations can be modeled using collaborative filtering techniques, which can be represented mathematically as:

$$R_{ij} = \frac{\sum_{k \in N(i)} w_{ik} \cdot R_{kj}}{\sum_{k \in N(i)} |w_{ik}|}$$

where R_{ij} is the predicted rating of item j for user i, $N(i)$ is the set of neighbors of user i, and w_{ik} represents the weight of the similarity between users i and k.

Emphasis on Data Privacy and Ethics

As data collection becomes ubiquitous, the importance of data privacy and ethical considerations will take center stage. Consumers are increasingly aware of how their data is used, leading to demands for transparency and accountability. Regulatory frameworks, such as the General Data Protection Regulation (GDPR) in Europe, will continue to shape how organizations handle data.

Future predictions indicate that organizations will invest in privacy-preserving technologies, such as differential privacy, which allows data analysts to glean insights from datasets while protecting individual privacy. The concept of differential privacy can be mathematically defined as:

$$\Pr[M(D) \in S] \leq e^{\epsilon} \cdot \Pr[M(D') \in S] + \delta$$

where $M(D)$ is the output of a randomized algorithm on dataset D, S is any subset of outputs, and ϵ and δ are privacy parameters.

Growth of Augmented Analytics

Augmented analytics, which leverages AI to enhance data preparation, insight generation, and explanation, is anticipated to grow significantly. This approach democratizes data science by enabling non-technical users to derive insights without needing extensive data expertise.

For example, platforms like *Tableau* and *Power BI* are integrating AI-driven features that allow users to ask natural language questions about their data, simplifying the analytics process. The effectiveness of augmented analytics can be illustrated through the use of natural language processing (NLP) models, which can be represented by:

$$P(w_1, w_2, \ldots, w_n) = \prod_{i=1}^{n} P(w_i | w_1, w_2, \ldots, w_{i-1})$$

where $P(w_1, w_2, \ldots, w_n)$ is the probability of a sequence of words, and $P(w_i | w_1, w_2, \ldots, w_{i-1})$ represents the conditional probability of word i given its predecessors.

Data-Driven Decision-Making in Organizations

Organizations will increasingly rely on data-driven decision-making processes to enhance operational efficiency and competitive advantage. This shift will necessitate the establishment of a data culture within organizations, where data is integral to every business decision.

The predictive modeling process will become more sophisticated, utilizing advanced statistical methods and machine learning techniques. For example, regression analysis will continue to be a fundamental tool for understanding relationships between variables, represented by the equation:

$$Y = \beta_0 + \beta_1 X_1 + \beta_2 X_2 + \ldots + \beta_n X_n + \epsilon$$

where Y is the dependent variable, $X_1, X_2, \ldots, X_n$ are independent variables, β_0 is the intercept, $\beta_1, \beta_2, \ldots, \beta_n$ are coefficients, and ϵ is the error term.

Conclusion

In conclusion, the future of data is characterized by rapid advancements in technology, a shift towards real-time analytics, increased integration of AI, and a heightened focus on ethical considerations. As organizations and individuals navigate this evolving landscape, the ability to harness data effectively will be paramount. The predictions outlined above not only highlight the exciting possibilities that lie ahead but also underscore the challenges that must be addressed to ensure a responsible and equitable data-driven future.

The Role of Artificial Intelligence

Artificial Intelligence (AI) has emerged as a transformative force in the field of data science, fundamentally altering the way data is analyzed, interpreted, and applied across various domains. This subsection explores the multifaceted role of AI in enhancing data analytics, the challenges it presents, and its implications for the future of data-driven decision-making.

Enhancing Data Analysis

AI technologies, particularly machine learning (ML) and deep learning (DL), enable the analysis of vast datasets with unprecedented speed and accuracy. By automating the data processing pipeline, AI allows data scientists to focus on deriving insights rather than spending excessive time on data preparation. For instance, AI algorithms can identify patterns and correlations within data that may not be immediately apparent to human analysts.

$$Y = f(X) + \epsilon \qquad (104)$$

In this equation, Y represents the dependent variable, X denotes the independent variables, f is the function that models the relationship between X and Y, and ϵ is the error term. AI algorithms, particularly regression models, can be employed to estimate f and uncover underlying trends.

Predictive Analytics

AI's ability to perform predictive analytics has revolutionized industries such as healthcare, finance, and marketing. By utilizing historical data, AI models can forecast future trends and behaviors, enabling organizations to make informed decisions. For example, in healthcare, predictive models can anticipate patient admissions based on historical data, allowing hospitals to allocate resources efficiently.

$$P(Y = 1|X) = \frac{1}{1 + e^{-(\beta_0 + \beta_1 X_1 + \beta_2 X_2 + \ldots + \beta_n X_n)}} \quad (105)$$

This logistic regression equation estimates the probability P of an event occurring (e.g., a patient being readmitted) given a set of predictor variables X. AI enhances the accuracy of such models, significantly impacting patient care and operational efficiency.

Natural Language Processing

Natural Language Processing (NLP), a subset of AI, enables machines to understand and interpret human language. This capability is crucial for analyzing unstructured data, such as social media posts, customer reviews, and academic papers. By employing NLP techniques, organizations can extract valuable insights from textual data, enhancing customer sentiment analysis and market research.

For instance, sentiment analysis algorithms can classify text as positive, negative, or neutral, providing organizations with a deeper understanding of public perception. The following equation represents a simplified sentiment score calculation:

$$\text{Sentiment Score} = \frac{\text{Positive Words} - \text{Negative Words}}{\text{Total Words}} \quad (106)$$

This score helps organizations gauge the overall sentiment toward their brand or products.

Challenges of AI in Data Analytics

Despite its advantages, the integration of AI into data analytics is not without challenges. One significant issue is the potential for bias in AI algorithms, which can lead to unfair or inaccurate outcomes. Bias may arise from the data used to train AI models, particularly if the data is not representative of the population it seeks to analyze.

For example, facial recognition technologies have faced criticism for exhibiting racial and gender biases, as they are often trained on datasets that lack diversity. This highlights the importance of ensuring that AI systems are developed with ethical considerations in mind.

The Future of AI in Data Science

Looking ahead, the role of AI in data science is poised to expand further. As AI technologies continue to evolve, we can expect more sophisticated algorithms capable of handling complex data types, including images, video, and audio. Moreover, the integration of AI with other emerging technologies, such as the Internet of Things (IoT) and blockchain, will create new opportunities for data-driven innovation.

In conclusion, AI plays a pivotal role in the data revolution by enhancing data analysis capabilities, enabling predictive analytics, and facilitating the interpretation of unstructured data. However, it is crucial to address the ethical challenges associated with AI to ensure that its benefits are realized equitably across society. As we embrace a data-driven future, the collaboration between data scientists and AI will be essential in shaping the next generation of innovations.

Ethical Considerations in Data-driven World

In an era defined by the exponential growth of data and its applications, ethical considerations have emerged as a critical focal point for data scientists, policymakers, and society at large. The ability to collect, analyze, and leverage vast amounts of data presents unprecedented opportunities for innovation and problem-solving. However, it also raises significant ethical dilemmas that must be addressed to ensure the responsible use of data.

The Ethical Framework of Data Science

Ethics in data science encompasses a broad spectrum of principles and guidelines aimed at ensuring fairness, accountability, and transparency in data practices. The following ethical frameworks are commonly referenced in discussions of data ethics:

- **Beneficence:** The principle of doing good and maximizing benefits while minimizing harm. In data science, this translates to using data to improve lives and solve pressing societal issues.

- **Non-maleficence:** The obligation to avoid causing harm to individuals or communities. This principle emphasizes the importance of data privacy and security.

- **Justice:** Fair distribution of benefits and burdens. In data practices, this principle addresses issues of bias and discrimination that can arise from data-driven decisions.

- **Autonomy:** Respecting individuals' rights to control their personal information. This principle is closely linked to informed consent and data ownership.

Key Ethical Issues in Data Science

Several key ethical issues have emerged in the context of data science, including:

a. **Data Privacy and Security** The collection and storage of personal data raise significant privacy concerns. Organizations must implement robust data protection measures to safeguard sensitive information from unauthorized access and breaches. The General Data Protection Regulation (GDPR) in the European Union serves as a prominent example of legislation designed to protect individuals' privacy rights. It mandates that organizations obtain explicit consent from individuals before collecting their data and allows individuals to request the deletion of their personal information.

b. **Algorithmic Bias** Algorithmic bias occurs when data-driven models produce unfair or discriminatory outcomes due to biased training data or flawed algorithms. For instance, a study found that facial recognition systems exhibited higher error rates for individuals with darker skin tones, highlighting the need for diverse and representative datasets. To mitigate bias, data scientists must adopt practices such as fairness-aware machine learning and regularly audit algorithms for discriminatory impacts.

c. **Transparency and Accountability** Transparency in data practices is essential for building trust among stakeholders. Organizations should provide clear explanations of how data is collected, analyzed, and used, as well as the decision-making processes behind algorithmic outcomes. Accountability mechanisms, such as independent audits and ethical review boards, can help ensure that organizations adhere to ethical standards and address any potential harm caused by their data practices.

d. **Informed Consent** Informed consent is a fundamental ethical principle that requires individuals to be fully aware of how their data will be used before providing it. This principle is particularly relevant in contexts such as medical research, where patients must understand the implications of participating in studies involving their health data. Organizations should strive to present information in a clear and comprehensible manner, avoiding technical jargon that may confuse individuals.

Examples of Ethical Challenges in Data Science

To illustrate the ethical challenges faced by data scientists, consider the following examples:

a. Cambridge Analytica Scandal The Cambridge Analytica scandal serves as a cautionary tale regarding data privacy and consent. The political consulting firm harvested personal data from millions of Facebook users without their consent, using this information to target political ads during the 2016 U.S. presidential election. This incident raised serious questions about the ethical implications of data collection practices and the responsibility of organizations to protect users' privacy.

b. Predictive Policing Predictive policing algorithms aim to forecast criminal activity by analyzing historical crime data. However, these systems have been criticized for perpetuating existing biases in the criminal justice system, leading to over-policing in minority communities. The ethical implications of using such algorithms highlight the need for careful consideration of the data sources and the potential societal impacts of algorithmic decisions.

Moving Towards Ethical Data Practices

To foster ethical data practices, organizations and data scientists can adopt the following strategies:

- **Implement Ethical Guidelines:** Organizations should establish clear ethical guidelines for data collection, analysis, and usage, ensuring that all employees are trained in these principles.

- **Engage Stakeholders:** Involving diverse stakeholders in the decision-making process can provide valuable perspectives on ethical considerations and potential impacts of data practices.

- **Conduct Impact Assessments:** Regularly assessing the potential ethical impacts of data-driven projects can help organizations identify and mitigate risks before they materialize.

- **Promote Data Literacy:** Enhancing data literacy among the public can empower individuals to make informed decisions about their data and advocate for their rights.

Conclusion

As we navigate the complexities of a data-driven world, ethical considerations must remain at the forefront of data science practices. By prioritizing ethics, data scientists can harness the power of data to drive positive change while safeguarding individual rights and promoting social good. The journey towards ethical data practices is ongoing, and it requires a collective commitment to uphold the values of fairness, accountability, and transparency in all aspects of data science.

Data Science as a Global Movement

The advent of the data revolution has not only transformed industries but also catalyzed the emergence of data science as a global movement. This movement transcends geographical boundaries, uniting individuals and organizations across the world to harness the power of data for innovation, social good, and informed decision-making. In this section, we will explore the theoretical foundations, challenges, and real-world examples that illustrate the global impact of data science.

Theoretical Foundations

At its core, the global movement of data science is driven by several theoretical frameworks:

- **Big Data Theory:** This theory posits that vast amounts of data can reveal patterns, correlations, and insights that were previously unattainable. The three Vs—Volume, Velocity, and Variety—are crucial in understanding how data is generated and utilized globally. In recent years, a fourth V, Veracity, has emerged, emphasizing the importance of data quality and trustworthiness.

- **Open Data Movement:** The open data movement advocates for making data freely available to the public. This approach fosters transparency, accountability, and collaboration. The principles of open data are rooted in the belief that data can drive innovation and improve public services when shared widely.

- **Data-Driven Decision Making (DDDM):** DDDM is a systematic approach to making decisions based on data analysis rather than intuition or observation alone. This approach has gained traction globally, as organizations recognize the value of data in enhancing operational efficiency and strategic planning.

Challenges Faced by the Global Movement

Despite the significant progress, the global data science movement faces several challenges:

- **Data Privacy and Security**: As data collection becomes more pervasive, concerns about privacy and security intensify. The implementation of regulations like the General Data Protection Regulation (GDPR) in Europe illustrates the need for a balance between data utilization and individual privacy rights.

- **Data Literacy Gap**: There exists a substantial gap in data literacy across different regions and demographics. Many individuals lack the skills to interpret and analyze data effectively, which can hinder participation in the data movement. Educational initiatives are vital to bridge this gap.

- **Bias and Fairness**: Data-driven systems can perpetuate biases present in the data they are trained on. Addressing issues of fairness and bias is essential to ensure equitable outcomes in applications such as hiring, lending, and law enforcement.

Real-World Examples of Global Data Science Initiatives

Several organizations and initiatives exemplify the global nature of the data science movement:

- **Data for Good**: This global initiative brings together data scientists and organizations to tackle pressing social issues, such as poverty, health crises, and climate change. Projects under this banner leverage data analytics to drive impactful solutions, demonstrating the potential of data science to address global challenges.

- **The World Bank's Open Data Initiative**: The World Bank has made a wealth of data available to the public, empowering researchers, policymakers, and citizens to access information that can inform decisions and strategies for development. This initiative exemplifies how open data can facilitate global collaboration and knowledge sharing.

- **UN Global Pulse:** This initiative harnesses real-time data to enhance the understanding of global issues, such as humanitarian crises and public health challenges. By analyzing data from social media, mobile phones, and other sources, UN Global Pulse provides insights that can guide effective responses to urgent global needs.

The Future of Data Science as a Global Movement

Looking ahead, the future of data science as a global movement appears promising. As technology advances, new tools and methodologies will emerge, enabling even greater collaboration and innovation. The following trends are expected to shape the future:

- **Increased Collaboration:** The interconnectedness of the global economy will foster collaboration among data scientists, researchers, and organizations across borders. Collaborative platforms and networks will facilitate knowledge exchange and joint problem-solving.

- **Emphasis on Ethical Data Use:** As the movement matures, there will be a growing emphasis on ethical data practices. Organizations will need to prioritize transparency, accountability, and fairness in their data initiatives to build trust with the public.

- **Focus on Sustainability:** Data science will play a critical role in addressing global sustainability challenges. Initiatives that leverage data to promote environmental conservation, resource management, and climate resilience will gain traction.

In conclusion, data science has evolved into a global movement that transcends borders and sectors. By addressing challenges, fostering collaboration, and promoting ethical practices, the movement can continue to drive innovation and create positive societal impact. As Fatima Wang's legacy inspires future generations of data scientists, the potential for data to transform the world remains boundless.

$$\text{Impact} = \frac{\text{Data Utilization} \times \text{Collaboration}}{\text{Challenges}} \tag{107}$$

The Importance of Collaboration

Interdisciplinary Collaboration in Data Science

Interdisciplinary collaboration is a cornerstone of modern data science, allowing professionals from diverse fields to come together and leverage their unique expertise. In an era where data-driven decision-making is paramount, the integration of knowledge from various domains enhances the robustness and applicability of data analytics. This subsection explores the significance of interdisciplinary collaboration in data science, the challenges it presents, and examples of successful collaborations that have led to groundbreaking innovations.

The Importance of Interdisciplinary Collaboration

Data science inherently requires a blend of skills, including statistics, computer science, domain-specific knowledge, and ethical considerations. The convergence of these disciplines is crucial for several reasons:

- **Enhanced Problem-Solving:** Interdisciplinary teams bring together different perspectives, leading to more comprehensive solutions. For instance, a team comprising data scientists, healthcare professionals, and policy experts can more effectively address public health issues by integrating clinical knowledge with data analytics.

- **Innovation through Diversity:** Diverse teams are more likely to generate innovative ideas. Research shows that teams with members from varied backgrounds outperform homogeneous teams in creativity and problem-solving. According to [?], diversity in teams can lead to better outcomes due to the variety of perspectives and approaches brought to the table.

- **Real-World Applications:** Interdisciplinary collaboration ensures that data science solutions are relevant and applicable to real-world challenges. By involving stakeholders from various fields, data scientists can tailor their analyses to meet the specific needs of different industries.

Challenges of Interdisciplinary Collaboration

Despite its advantages, interdisciplinary collaboration in data science is not without challenges:

- **Communication Barriers:** Professionals from different disciplines often use jargon that can hinder effective communication. Bridging the gap between technical language and domain-specific terminology is essential for successful collaboration.

- **Cultural Differences:** Each discipline has its own culture and methodologies, which can lead to misunderstandings and conflicts. For example, data scientists may prioritize quantitative analysis, while social scientists may emphasize qualitative research. Finding common ground is crucial for effective teamwork.

- **Resource Allocation:** Collaborative projects often require significant resources, including time and funding. Securing these resources can be challenging, especially in academic or nonprofit settings where budgets are tight.

Successful Examples of Interdisciplinary Collaboration

Several successful interdisciplinary collaborations in data science illustrate its transformative potential:

- **Predictive Analytics in Healthcare:** The collaboration between data scientists, clinicians, and public health officials has led to the development of predictive models that forecast disease outbreaks. For instance, the HealthMap project combines data from various sources, including social media, to predict and track infectious disease outbreaks globally [?]. This interdisciplinary approach has improved response times and resource allocation during health crises.

- **Environmental Sustainability:** The partnership between environmental scientists, data analysts, and urban planners has resulted in innovative solutions for sustainable city planning. The use of geospatial data and machine learning algorithms has enabled cities to optimize energy consumption and reduce carbon footprints. An example is the collaboration between the city of Los Angeles and data scientists to analyze traffic patterns and reduce congestion, leading to lower emissions [?].

- **Financial Fraud Detection:** In the finance sector, collaborations between data scientists, cybersecurity experts, and financial analysts have led to the development of sophisticated algorithms for detecting fraudulent activities.

By integrating expertise from various fields, organizations can create more effective fraud detection systems that adapt to evolving threats [?].

Future Directions for Interdisciplinary Collaboration

As data science continues to evolve, the need for interdisciplinary collaboration will only grow. Future directions include:

- **Education and Training:** Incorporating interdisciplinary training in educational programs will prepare the next generation of data scientists to work collaboratively. Programs that emphasize teamwork and communication across disciplines will be essential.
- **Open Innovation:** Encouraging open innovation platforms where professionals from various fields can share ideas and collaborate on projects will foster a culture of interdisciplinary teamwork. Initiatives that promote knowledge sharing and transparency will be key to advancing data science.
- **Ethical Frameworks:** Developing ethical frameworks that guide interdisciplinary collaborations will be crucial as data science intersects with sensitive areas such as healthcare and privacy. Ensuring that all voices are heard in ethical discussions will lead to more responsible data practices.

In conclusion, interdisciplinary collaboration is vital for the advancement of data science. By bringing together diverse expertise, teams can tackle complex problems, drive innovation, and create solutions that have a meaningful impact on society. As the field continues to grow, fostering collaboration across disciplines will be essential for harnessing the full potential of data science.

Cross-sector Partnerships and Knowledge Sharing

In the rapidly evolving landscape of data science, cross-sector partnerships have emerged as a crucial mechanism for fostering innovation and addressing complex challenges. By collaborating across different sectors—such as academia, industry, government, and non-profit organizations—stakeholders can leverage diverse expertise, resources, and perspectives to enhance data-driven solutions.

Theoretical Framework

The theoretical underpinnings of cross-sector partnerships can be understood through the lens of *collaborative governance*. Collaborative governance refers to the processes and structures that facilitate the participation of multiple stakeholders in decision-making and problem-solving. According to Ansell and Gash (2008), successful collaborative governance requires:

- **Shared Goals:** All partners must have a common understanding of the objectives they aim to achieve through collaboration.
- **Mutual Trust:** Trust among partners is essential to foster open communication and knowledge sharing.
- **Interdependence:** Partners must recognize that their success is linked to the contributions of others, creating a sense of shared responsibility.
- **Adaptive Capacity:** The ability to adapt to changing circumstances and respond to new information is vital for sustaining partnerships.

These elements are critical in establishing effective cross-sector partnerships that can harness the power of data analytics to drive innovation.

Challenges in Cross-sector Partnerships

Despite the potential benefits, cross-sector partnerships face several challenges:

- **Cultural Differences:** Different sectors often have distinct cultures, norms, and priorities, which can lead to misunderstandings and conflicts.
- **Resource Constraints:** Limited resources, whether financial or human, can hinder the ability of partners to engage fully in collaborative efforts.
- **Data Sharing Concerns:** Issues related to data privacy, security, and ownership can create barriers to effective knowledge sharing.
- **Measurement of Success:** Evaluating the outcomes of cross-sector partnerships can be complex, as success may not always be quantifiable.

Addressing these challenges requires proactive strategies, including establishing clear communication channels, defining roles and responsibilities, and developing a shared framework for measuring success.

Examples of Successful Cross-sector Partnerships

Several successful examples illustrate the effectiveness of cross-sector partnerships in data science:

1. **The Health Data Collaborative** The Health Data Collaborative is an initiative that brings together governments, non-governmental organizations (NGOs), and private sector entities to improve health data systems worldwide. By pooling resources and expertise, the collaborative aims to enhance data quality, accessibility, and use for health decision-making. This partnership has led to significant improvements in health outcomes in various regions, particularly in low- and middle-income countries.

2. **Data for Good** Data for Good is a collaborative effort involving data scientists, NGOs, and social enterprises focused on using data analytics to address social challenges. One notable project involved analyzing data on homelessness to identify patterns and develop targeted interventions. By leveraging the expertise of data scientists and the insights of social workers, the initiative successfully reduced homelessness rates in participating cities.

3. **The Global Partnership for Sustainable Development Data** This initiative brings together governments, businesses, and civil society organizations to harness the power of data in achieving the United Nations Sustainable Development Goals (SDGs). By sharing knowledge and best practices, the partnership aims to improve data collection, analysis, and dissemination, ultimately driving progress toward sustainable development. The collaborative efforts have resulted in innovative data-driven solutions addressing issues such as poverty, health, and education.

Knowledge Sharing Mechanisms

Effective knowledge sharing is essential for the success of cross-sector partnerships. Several mechanisms can facilitate this process:

- **Workshops and Training Programs:** Regular workshops and training sessions can help partners develop their skills and knowledge in data analytics, fostering a culture of continuous learning.
- **Online Platforms and Communities:** Creating online platforms for collaboration can enable partners to share resources, tools, and best practices in real-time.
- **Joint Research Initiatives:** Collaborative research projects can stimulate knowledge exchange and generate insights that benefit all partners involved.
- **Publications and Case Studies:** Documenting and sharing success stories and lessons learned can inspire others to engage in cross-sector partnerships.

Conclusion

Cross-sector partnerships and knowledge sharing are vital components of the data revolution. By collaborating across sectors, stakeholders can harness diverse expertise and resources to address complex challenges and drive innovation. While challenges exist, successful examples demonstrate the potential of these partnerships to create meaningful impact. As the data landscape continues to evolve, fostering collaborative governance and effective knowledge sharing will be essential for realizing the full potential of data science in shaping a better future.

Bibliography

[1] Ansell, C., & Gash, D. (2008). Collaborative Governance in Theory and Practice. *Journal of Public Administration Research and Theory*, 18(4), 543-571.

Encouraging Open Data Initiatives

In the rapidly evolving landscape of data science, the push for open data initiatives has emerged as a critical component for fostering innovation, transparency, and collaboration across various sectors. Open data refers to data that is made publicly available for anyone to access, use, and share without restrictions. This movement is grounded in the belief that data should be a public good, enabling citizens, researchers, and organizations to leverage data for social and economic benefits.

Theoretical Framework

The theoretical foundation for open data initiatives can be traced back to the principles of transparency and accountability in governance. According to the Open Data Charter, open data should be *complete, primary, timely, accessible, machine-readable*, and *non-discriminatory*. These principles ensure that data is not only available but also usable, empowering individuals and communities to make informed decisions.

A significant body of literature supports the idea that open data can enhance innovation. For instance, the concept of *data-driven innovation* suggests that access to diverse datasets can lead to new insights and solutions, particularly when combined with advanced analytics and machine learning techniques. The theory of *crowdsourcing* further emphasizes how collective intelligence can be harnessed through open data, allowing individuals and organizations to collaborate on problem-solving.

Problems Addressed by Open Data Initiatives

Despite the potential benefits, several challenges hinder the widespread adoption of open data initiatives:

- **Data Quality and Standardization:** Open data must be of high quality to be useful. Inconsistent formats, incomplete datasets, and outdated information can undermine the effectiveness of open data initiatives. Standardization of data formats and metadata is essential to ensure interoperability and usability.

- **Privacy and Security Concerns:** The release of open data must carefully consider privacy implications, particularly when sensitive information is involved. Anonymization techniques and data governance frameworks are necessary to protect individual privacy while promoting transparency.

- **Lack of Awareness and Engagement:** Many organizations and governments may not fully understand the benefits of open data or how to implement effective initiatives. Raising awareness and promoting engagement among stakeholders is crucial for fostering a culture of openness.

- **Sustainability of Initiatives:** Open data initiatives require ongoing support and resources to maintain and update datasets. Ensuring sustainable funding and institutional commitment is vital for the long-term success of these initiatives.

Examples of Successful Open Data Initiatives

Several successful open data initiatives demonstrate the transformative potential of making data accessible:

- **Data.gov:** Launched by the U.S. government in 2009, Data.gov provides access to thousands of datasets across various domains, including health, education, and climate. This platform has enabled researchers, developers, and entrepreneurs to create innovative applications and solutions, such as tools for visualizing public health data and tracking environmental changes.

- **OpenStreetMap:** A collaborative mapping project that allows users to contribute and edit geographic data, OpenStreetMap exemplifies the power of crowdsourced data. It has been used in various applications, from humanitarian efforts in disaster response to urban planning and navigation.

- **European Data Portal:** This initiative aims to facilitate the discovery and reuse of public sector data across Europe. By providing a central repository for datasets from various European countries, the portal promotes cross-border collaboration and innovation in areas such as transportation, energy, and public health.

Encouraging Open Data Initiatives

To effectively encourage open data initiatives, several strategies can be employed:

- **Policy Frameworks:** Governments and organizations should establish clear policies that promote open data practices. This includes creating legal frameworks that support data sharing and addressing intellectual property concerns.

- **Capacity Building:** Training programs and workshops can help stakeholders understand the importance of open data and how to effectively implement initiatives. Capacity building efforts should target both data providers and users to foster a collaborative environment.

- **Engagement with Stakeholders:** Engaging with a diverse range of stakeholders, including civil society organizations, academia, and the private sector, is essential for understanding data needs and promoting the use of open data for social good.

- **Promoting Data Literacy:** Increasing data literacy among the general public can empower individuals to utilize open data effectively. Educational initiatives should focus on teaching data analysis skills and critical thinking to navigate the complexities of data interpretation.

- **Leveraging Technology:** Utilizing modern technologies, such as application programming interfaces (APIs) and data visualization tools, can enhance the accessibility and usability of open data. These tools can facilitate real-time data access and enable users to derive insights more easily.

Conclusion

Encouraging open data initiatives is crucial for harnessing the full potential of data science in driving innovation, transparency, and social impact. By addressing the challenges associated with data quality, privacy, and engagement, and by implementing effective strategies to promote openness, we can create an environment where data serves as a catalyst for positive change. As Fatima Wang's vision for the future of data unfolds, the promotion of open data initiatives will play a pivotal role in shaping a more equitable and informed society.

Fostering a Culture of Innovation

In today's fast-paced and ever-evolving landscape, fostering a culture of innovation is essential for organizations aiming to thrive in the data-driven era. A culture of innovation not only encourages creativity and experimentation but also enhances the organization's ability to adapt to changing market demands and technological advancements. This section will explore the theoretical underpinnings of innovation culture, identify common challenges, and provide real-world examples of organizations that have successfully cultivated such an environment.

Theoretical Foundations of Innovation Culture

The concept of an innovation culture can be traced back to various organizational theories, including the Theory of Organizational Culture, which emphasizes the shared values, beliefs, and norms that shape the behavior of individuals within an organization. According to Schein (2010), organizational culture can be categorized into three levels: artifacts, espoused values, and basic underlying assumptions.

$$\text{Innovation Culture} = \text{Artifacts} + \text{Espoused Values} + \text{Basic Assumptions} \quad (108)$$

Artifacts represent the visible elements of culture, such as office design and company branding. Espoused values are the stated norms and objectives, while basic assumptions are the deeply ingrained beliefs that guide behavior. For an organization to foster a culture of innovation, it must align these three levels to support and encourage innovative practices.

Moreover, the Competing Values Framework (CVF) developed by Cameron and Quinn (1999) highlights the importance of balancing flexibility and control, as well as internal and external focus. Organizations that prioritize flexibility and external focus are more likely to cultivate an innovative culture.

Challenges in Fostering Innovation

Despite the clear benefits, organizations often face several challenges when attempting to foster a culture of innovation:

- **Resistance to Change:** Employees may be hesitant to embrace new ideas or processes due to fear of failure or the unknown. This resistance can stifle creativity and hinder innovative efforts.

- **Lack of Resources:** Innovation requires investment in terms of time, money, and human capital. Organizations that are unwilling or unable to allocate resources may struggle to implement innovative initiatives.

- **Siloed Departments:** When departments operate in isolation, it can lead to a lack of collaboration and knowledge sharing. Innovation often thrives in environments where diverse perspectives and expertise can intersect.

- **Inadequate Leadership Support:** Leaders play a crucial role in setting the tone for an organization's culture. If leadership does not actively support and prioritize innovation, employees may feel discouraged from pursuing new ideas.

Strategies for Fostering a Culture of Innovation

To overcome these challenges, organizations can implement several strategies to foster a culture of innovation:

1. **Encourage Open Communication:** Create an environment where employees feel safe to share their ideas and feedback. Regular brainstorming sessions and open forums can facilitate dialogue and inspire creativity.

2. **Promote Cross-Functional Collaboration:** Encourage collaboration between different departments to leverage diverse skill sets and perspectives. This can be achieved through team-building activities, joint projects, and cross-departmental meetings.

3. **Provide Resources and Support:** Allocate dedicated resources for innovation initiatives, such as innovation labs or dedicated teams. Providing employees with the necessary tools and training can empower them to experiment and explore new ideas.

4. **Recognize and Reward Innovation:** Establish recognition programs that celebrate innovative contributions. This can motivate employees to pursue creative solutions and reinforce the importance of innovation within the organization.

5. **Embrace Failure as a Learning Opportunity:** Encourage a mindset that views failure as a stepping stone to success. By analyzing failures and extracting lessons, organizations can foster resilience and continuous improvement.

Real-World Examples

Several organizations have successfully cultivated a culture of innovation, demonstrating the effectiveness of the aforementioned strategies:

- **Google:** Google's famous "20

- **3M:** The company encourages innovation through its "15

- **Amazon:** Amazon's "Working Backwards" approach emphasizes understanding customer needs before developing products. This customer-centric focus fosters innovation by ensuring that new ideas are aligned with market demands.

Conclusion

Fostering a culture of innovation is not merely a trend; it is a necessity for organizations aiming to thrive in an increasingly complex and competitive landscape. By understanding the theoretical foundations, addressing common challenges, and implementing effective strategies, organizations can create an environment that nurtures creativity and innovation. As seen through the examples of Google, 3M, and Amazon, a strong culture of innovation can lead to groundbreaking advancements and sustained success in the data-driven world.

In summary, fostering a culture of innovation requires a holistic approach that integrates leadership support, resource allocation, and a commitment to collaboration and learning. By prioritizing these elements, organizations can unlock the full potential of their workforce and drive continuous innovation.

Collaboration for Social Impact

In the age of data revolution, collaboration has emerged as a pivotal strategy for driving social impact through data science. The convergence of diverse expertise, resources, and perspectives can amplify the effectiveness of data-driven initiatives aimed at addressing societal challenges. This section explores the significance of collaboration in fostering social impact, the theoretical frameworks that underpin collaborative efforts, and real-world examples that highlight successful partnerships.

Theoretical Frameworks

Collaboration in data science for social impact can be understood through several theoretical lenses, including the Social Capital Theory and the Collective Impact Framework.

Social Capital Theory Social capital refers to the networks, norms, and social trust that facilitate coordination and cooperation for mutual benefit. According to Putnam (2000), social capital enhances collective action and enables communities to achieve shared goals. In the context of data science, social capital fosters collaboration among stakeholders, including governments, non-profits, academia, and the private sector, leading to more effective solutions to social issues.

Collective Impact Framework The Collective Impact Framework, introduced by Kania and Kramer (2011), emphasizes the importance of a common agenda, shared measurement systems, mutually reinforcing activities, continuous communication, and backbone support organizations. This framework provides a structured approach for diverse stakeholders to work together towards a common goal, ensuring that their efforts are aligned and impactful.

Challenges to Collaboration

Despite the clear benefits of collaboration, several challenges can hinder effective partnerships:

- **Misaligned Goals:** Different organizations may have varying objectives, leading to conflicts and inefficiencies in collaborative efforts.
- **Data Silos:** Organizations often operate in silos, limiting data sharing and collaboration opportunities. This can result in fragmented insights and missed opportunities for comprehensive solutions.
- **Resource Constraints:** Limited financial and human resources can impede the ability of organizations to engage in collaborative initiatives.
- **Trust Issues:** Building trust among diverse stakeholders can be challenging, especially when data privacy and security concerns arise.

Successful Examples of Collaboration for Social Impact

Several initiatives illustrate how collaboration can lead to significant social impact through data science:

1. **The Global Partnership for Sustainable Development Data** This initiative brings together governments, civil society, the private sector, and international organizations to harness the power of data for sustainable development. By fostering collaboration, the partnership aims to improve data availability, accessibility, and use, ultimately contributing to the achievement of the United Nations Sustainable Development Goals (SDGs). For instance, through collaborative efforts, countries have improved their data collection methods, enabling better tracking of progress towards SDGs, such as poverty alleviation and education.

2. **Data.org** Launched by the Rockefeller Foundation and the Mastercard Center for Inclusive Growth, Data.org is a platform that connects organizations with data scientists to address social challenges. The initiative focuses on building a community of practice that enhances data literacy and promotes data-driven decision-making. By facilitating collaboration between non-profits and data experts, Data.org has enabled organizations to leverage data for social good, such as improving healthcare outcomes and enhancing economic opportunities for marginalized communities.

3. **The Data Collaborative for Local Impact** This initiative connects local governments with data scientists and researchers to address community-specific challenges. By fostering collaboration, the Data Collaborative enables cities to utilize data analytics to inform policy decisions and improve public services. For example, cities have used collaborative data initiatives to address issues such as homelessness, public safety, and transportation inefficiencies, resulting in more responsive governance and improved quality of life for residents.

Conclusion

Collaboration for social impact is essential in the data-driven world, where complex social issues require multifaceted solutions. By leveraging diverse expertise and fostering partnerships among various stakeholders, organizations can enhance their capacity to address societal challenges effectively. Theoretical frameworks such as Social Capital Theory and the Collective Impact Framework provide valuable insights into the dynamics of collaboration. However, to overcome challenges such as misaligned goals and data silos, stakeholders must prioritize building trust and aligning their objectives. As demonstrated by successful initiatives like the Global Partnership for Sustainable Development Data, Data.org, and the Data Collaborative for Local Impact, collaboration can lead to transformative outcomes that benefit communities and drive social progress.

Challenges and Opportunities Ahead

Addressing Bias and Fairness in Analytics

In recent years, the proliferation of data-driven decision-making has raised critical concerns regarding bias and fairness in analytics. As organizations increasingly rely on algorithms to guide decisions, the potential for bias to influence outcomes has become a pressing issue. This section explores the theoretical foundations of bias in analytics, the problems it presents, and real-world examples that underscore the importance of addressing these challenges.

Theoretical Foundations of Bias

Bias in analytics can be understood through several theoretical lenses, including statistical bias, algorithmic bias, and societal bias. Statistical bias occurs when the data used to train models is not representative of the population, leading to skewed results. Algorithmic bias arises from the design and implementation of algorithms that may unintentionally favor certain groups over others. Societal bias reflects the broader social inequities that can seep into data collection and analysis processes.

Mathematically, bias can be quantified in various ways. One common measure is the *mean squared error* (MSE), which can be decomposed into bias and variance components:

$$\text{MSE} = \text{Bias}^2 + \text{Variance} + \text{Irreducible Error} \qquad (109)$$

Where: - Bias measures the error introduced by approximating a real-world problem, which may be complex, by a simplified model. - Variance measures how much the model's predictions would change if it were trained on a different dataset.

A high bias indicates that the model is overly simplistic and may fail to capture the underlying patterns in the data, leading to systematic errors.

Problems of Bias in Analytics

The implications of bias in analytics are profound. Biased algorithms can perpetuate and even exacerbate existing inequalities in society. For example, predictive policing algorithms have been criticized for disproportionately targeting minority communities based on historical crime data, which may reflect systemic biases rather than actual crime rates.

Moreover, biased hiring algorithms can lead to discrimination against certain demographic groups. A notable case involved a major technology company that developed a recruitment tool that favored male candidates over female candidates, reflecting historical hiring patterns rather than the actual qualifications of applicants.

Real-World Examples

Several high-profile incidents have highlighted the dangers of bias in analytics. One such example is the use of facial recognition technology, which has been shown to exhibit higher error rates for individuals with darker skin tones. A study by the MIT Media Lab found that facial analysis algorithms misclassified the gender of darker-skinned women 34.7% of the time, compared to just 0.8% for lighter-skinned men. This disparity raises significant ethical concerns regarding the deployment of such technologies in sensitive areas like law enforcement and hiring.

Another example is the algorithm used by a major online retailer to recommend products. The algorithm was found to promote items that were predominantly marketed to men, leading to a lack of visibility for products aimed at women. This not only affected sales but also reinforced gender stereotypes in consumer behavior.

Addressing Bias and Promoting Fairness

To combat bias in analytics, organizations can adopt several strategies:

- **Diverse Data Collection:** Ensuring that data is representative of all demographic groups is crucial. This can involve actively seeking out underrepresented groups in data collection efforts.

- **Algorithmic Audits:** Regularly auditing algorithms for bias can help identify and rectify issues before they lead to negative outcomes. This includes testing algorithms on diverse datasets to evaluate their performance across different groups.

- **Transparency and Accountability:** Organizations should strive for transparency in their data practices and algorithmic decision-making. This can involve sharing methodologies and results with stakeholders to foster trust and accountability.

- **Ethical Guidelines:** Establishing ethical guidelines for data use and algorithm design can help ensure that fairness is prioritized in analytics. Engaging ethicists and social scientists in the design process can provide valuable insights into potential biases.

In conclusion, addressing bias and fairness in analytics is not just a technical challenge but a moral imperative. As data continues to drive decision-making across various sectors, it is essential for innovators like Fatima Wang to lead the charge in promoting fairness and equity in analytics. By recognizing and mitigating bias, we can harness the full potential of data science to create a more just and equitable society.

Data Governance and Policy Frameworks

Data governance is a critical aspect of the data revolution, providing the necessary structure, policies, and standards to manage data effectively within organizations. It encompasses the overall management of data availability, usability, integrity, and security, ensuring that data is handled in compliance with regulatory requirements and ethical standards. This subsection explores the theoretical foundations of data governance, the challenges organizations face, and examples of effective policy frameworks that have been implemented.

Theoretical Foundations of Data Governance

Data governance is grounded in several key theories and principles that guide its implementation:

1. **Data Ownership and Stewardship**: This principle asserts that data should have clearly defined ownership, ensuring accountability for data quality and security. Data stewards are responsible for managing data assets and ensuring compliance with governance policies.

2. **Data Quality Management**: High-quality data is essential for informed decision-making. Data governance frameworks emphasize the need for processes that ensure data accuracy, consistency, completeness, and reliability. This includes regular data audits and validation processes.

3. **Compliance and Regulatory Frameworks**: Organizations must navigate a complex landscape of regulations regarding data privacy and protection. Frameworks such as the General Data Protection Regulation (GDPR) and the California Consumer Privacy Act (CCPA) impose strict requirements on how data is collected, processed, and stored.

4. **Risk Management**: Effective data governance involves identifying and mitigating risks associated with data handling. This includes assessing potential vulnerabilities in data systems and implementing controls to protect against data breaches and misuse.

Challenges in Data Governance

Despite the importance of data governance, organizations face numerous challenges in its implementation:

1. **Lack of Clear Policies**: Many organizations struggle with unclear or poorly defined data governance policies, leading to inconsistent data management practices. This can result in data silos, where information is isolated within departments, hindering collaboration and data sharing.

2. **Cultural Resistance**: Implementing data governance often requires a cultural shift within organizations. Employees may resist changes to established practices, especially if they perceive governance as an additional burden rather than a value-added process.

3. **Technological Complexity**: The rapid evolution of data technologies, including cloud computing, big data analytics, and artificial intelligence, complicates data governance efforts. Organizations must continuously adapt their governance frameworks to address new technologies and their implications for data management.

4. **Resource Constraints**: Effective data governance requires dedicated resources, including personnel, technology, and budget. Many organizations struggle to allocate sufficient resources to establish and maintain robust governance frameworks.

Examples of Effective Data Governance Frameworks

Several organizations have successfully implemented data governance frameworks that serve as models for others:

1. **IBM's Data Governance Council**: IBM established a Data Governance Council to oversee its data governance initiatives. The council is responsible for defining data policies, ensuring compliance with regulations, and promoting a

data-driven culture within the organization. Their framework emphasizes collaboration across departments and regular training for employees on data governance best practices.

2. **The Data Management Association (DAMA)**: DAMA International has developed the DAMA-DMBOK (Data Management Body of Knowledge), which provides a comprehensive framework for data governance. This framework outlines best practices, tools, and techniques for managing data effectively, covering areas such as data quality, data architecture, and data security.

3. **The European Union's GDPR**: The GDPR is a regulatory framework that has set a global standard for data protection and privacy. It mandates strict guidelines for data collection, processing, and storage, emphasizing the importance of data governance in ensuring compliance. Organizations that handle personal data of EU citizens must implement robust governance frameworks to meet GDPR requirements, including appointing Data Protection Officers (DPOs) and conducting regular data impact assessments.

Conclusion

Data governance and policy frameworks are essential for navigating the complexities of the data revolution. By establishing clear policies, promoting a culture of data stewardship, and ensuring compliance with regulatory requirements, organizations can harness the power of data while minimizing risks associated with data management. As the landscape of data continues to evolve, organizations must remain agile and proactive in adapting their governance frameworks to meet emerging challenges and opportunities.

$$\text{Data Governance Maturity} = \frac{\text{Effective Policies} + \text{Data Quality} + \text{Compliance}}{\text{Cultural Adoption} + \text{Resource Allocation}} \tag{110}$$

This equation illustrates that the maturity of an organization's data governance is dependent on the effectiveness of its policies, the quality of its data, and its compliance with regulations, balanced against the cultural adoption of governance practices and the resources allocated to support them.

In conclusion, the establishment of robust data governance frameworks is not merely a regulatory requirement but a strategic imperative that can drive innovation, enhance decision-making, and contribute to the overall success of organizations in the data-driven era.

Overcoming Data Security Threats

The rapid advancement of data analytics and the increasing reliance on data-driven decision-making have brought about significant challenges in data security. As organizations collect, store, and analyze vast amounts of sensitive information, they become prime targets for cyberattacks and data breaches. This subsection explores the theoretical underpinnings of data security, identifies common threats, and discusses strategies for overcoming these challenges.

Theoretical Framework of Data Security

Data security encompasses a set of practices designed to protect digital information from unauthorized access, corruption, or theft. The core principles of data security can be summarized by the CIA triad:

- **Confidentiality:** Ensuring that sensitive information is accessed only by authorized individuals.
- **Integrity:** Maintaining the accuracy and completeness of data, ensuring that it is not altered or tampered with.
- **Availability:** Ensuring that data is accessible to authorized users when needed.

These principles serve as the foundation for developing robust security protocols and strategies to mitigate risks associated with data breaches.

Common Data Security Threats

Organizations face a myriad of data security threats, including but not limited to:

- **Malware:** Malicious software designed to disrupt, damage, or gain unauthorized access to computer systems. Common types include viruses, worms, and ransomware.
- **Phishing Attacks:** Deceptive attempts to obtain sensitive information by masquerading as a trustworthy entity in electronic communications. Phishing can lead to credential theft and unauthorized access to systems.
- **Insider Threats:** Employees or contractors who misuse their access to sensitive data, either maliciously or inadvertently. Insider threats can be particularly challenging to detect and mitigate.

- **Data Breaches:** Incidents where unauthorized individuals gain access to confidential data, often resulting in the exposure of sensitive information. Data breaches can occur due to vulnerabilities in software, weak passwords, or misconfigured systems.

Strategies for Overcoming Data Security Threats

To effectively combat data security threats, organizations must implement a comprehensive security strategy that includes the following components:

1. **Risk Assessment and Management** Organizations should conduct regular risk assessments to identify potential vulnerabilities and threats to their data. This process involves evaluating the likelihood of various threats and the potential impact on the organization. By prioritizing risks, organizations can allocate resources effectively to mitigate them.

2. **Data Encryption** Encryption is a vital tool for protecting sensitive data both in transit and at rest. By converting data into a coded format that can only be read by authorized users, organizations can safeguard their information from unauthorized access. The Advanced Encryption Standard (AES) is one of the most widely used encryption algorithms, providing robust security for data protection.

$$C = E(K, P) \tag{111}$$

where C is the ciphertext, E is the encryption function, K is the key, and P is the plaintext.

3. **Access Control Measures** Implementing strict access control measures ensures that only authorized individuals can access sensitive data. Role-based access control (RBAC) is an effective method for managing permissions based on user roles within the organization. This approach minimizes the risk of unauthorized access and reduces the potential for insider threats.

4. **Regular Security Training** Employees are often the first line of defense against data security threats. Providing regular security training and awareness programs can help employees recognize potential threats, such as phishing attempts, and understand the importance of following security protocols. A culture of security awareness can significantly reduce the likelihood of human error leading to data breaches.

5. **Incident Response Planning**   Organizations should develop and maintain an incident response plan to address data security breaches swiftly and effectively. This plan should outline the steps to take in the event of a breach, including communication protocols, containment measures, and recovery strategies. Regularly testing and updating the incident response plan ensures that organizations are prepared to handle potential incidents.

Real-World Examples

Several high-profile data breaches highlight the importance of robust data security measures:

- **Equifax Data Breach (2017):** One of the largest data breaches in history, affecting approximately 147 million individuals. The breach was attributed to a vulnerability in the company's web application framework, which was not patched in a timely manner. This incident underscored the necessity of regular software updates and vulnerability management.

- **Target Data Breach (2013):** Cybercriminals gained access to Target's systems through compromised vendor credentials, leading to the theft of credit and debit card information from over 40 million customers. This breach highlighted the importance of securing third-party access and implementing robust monitoring systems.

Conclusion

Overcoming data security threats requires a multifaceted approach that combines technology, processes, and people. By understanding the theoretical foundations of data security, recognizing common threats, and implementing effective strategies, organizations can protect their sensitive information and maintain the trust of their stakeholders. As the data landscape continues to evolve, so too must the methods employed to safeguard against emerging threats, ensuring a secure and resilient data-driven future.

Enhancing Data Literacy and Education

In an increasingly data-driven world, enhancing data literacy and education has become a crucial endeavor for individuals, organizations, and societies at large. Data literacy refers to the ability to read, understand, create, and communicate data as information. This competency is essential for making informed decisions, fostering innovation, and ensuring that individuals can navigate the complexities of modern life, particularly in professional environments.

The Importance of Data Literacy

Data literacy empowers individuals to critically evaluate data sources, understand statistical concepts, and interpret data visualizations. It fosters a culture of evidence-based decision-making, where choices are informed by data rather than intuition alone. According to the *Data Literacy Project*, only 24% of employees feel they have the skills to work with data effectively. This gap in data literacy can lead to misinformed decisions, inefficiencies, and missed opportunities in various sectors.

Barriers to Data Literacy

Several barriers hinder the enhancement of data literacy:

- **Lack of Access to Education:** Many educational institutions do not include data literacy in their curricula, leaving students unprepared for a data-centric workforce.

- **Fear of Complexity:** The perception that data analysis is only for experts can discourage individuals from engaging with data.

- **Insufficient Training Resources:** Organizations may lack the resources or knowledge to provide effective data literacy training.

- **Rapidly Evolving Technology:** The fast pace of technological advancement can make it difficult for educational programs to keep up with current tools and methodologies.

Strategies for Enhancing Data Literacy

To address these barriers, a multi-faceted approach to enhancing data literacy is necessary:

1. Integrating Data Literacy into Education Curricula Educational institutions should incorporate data literacy into their curricula at all levels, from primary education to higher education. This integration can take various forms, such as:

- **Project-Based Learning:** Students can engage in real-world projects that require data collection, analysis, and interpretation, allowing them to apply theoretical concepts practically.

- **Interdisciplinary Courses:** Courses that combine data literacy with subjects like social sciences, health, and environmental studies can demonstrate the relevance of data across various fields.

- **Use of Accessible Tools:** Introducing user-friendly data analysis tools like *Tableau* or *Google Data Studio* can make data manipulation more approachable for students.

2. **Professional Development and Training** Organizations should prioritize data literacy training for their employees. Strategies include:

- **Workshops and Seminars:** Regular workshops can help employees learn about data analysis techniques and tools, fostering a culture of continuous learning.

- **Mentorship Programs:** Pairing less experienced employees with data-savvy mentors can facilitate knowledge transfer and skill development.

- **Online Learning Platforms:** Utilizing platforms like *Coursera* or *edX* can provide employees with flexible learning opportunities tailored to their specific needs.

3. **Community Engagement and Public Awareness** Enhancing data literacy is not solely the responsibility of educational institutions and organizations; community engagement is vital. Initiatives can include:

- **Public Workshops:** Hosting community workshops on data literacy can empower individuals to leverage data in their personal and professional lives.

- **Collaborations with Local Organizations:** Partnerships with libraries, community centers, and non-profits can extend the reach of data literacy programs to underserved populations.

- **Data Literacy Campaigns:** Public awareness campaigns can highlight the importance of data literacy and provide resources for individuals to improve their skills.

Case Studies and Examples

Several organizations and initiatives have successfully enhanced data literacy:

1. **Data Science for All** *Data Science for All* is an initiative that aims to democratize data science education. By providing free online courses and resources, the program has successfully trained thousands of individuals, particularly from underrepresented communities, in data analysis and machine learning.

2. **The Data Literacy Project** The *Data Literacy Project* is a collaborative initiative that aims to improve data literacy among employees across various industries. By providing resources, frameworks, and training materials, the project has helped organizations develop tailored data literacy programs that fit their unique needs.

Conclusion

Enhancing data literacy and education is a vital step toward empowering individuals and communities in a data-centric world. By addressing barriers, implementing effective strategies, and learning from successful case studies, we can cultivate a culture of data literacy that enables informed decision-making, drives innovation, and fosters social good. As we continue to navigate the complexities of the data revolution, prioritizing data literacy will ensure that individuals are equipped with the skills necessary to thrive in an increasingly interconnected and data-driven future.

$$\text{Data Literacy} = \frac{\text{Understanding of Data}}{\text{Access to Data} + \text{Training Resources}} \qquad (112)$$

Seizing the Opportunities of Data Revolution

The data revolution presents unprecedented opportunities across various sectors, transforming how we understand, analyze, and utilize information. As Fatima Wang's journey illustrates, the effective harnessing of data can lead to innovations that not only drive economic growth but also enhance societal well-being. In this section, we will explore the theoretical frameworks, address the challenges, and provide real-world examples that underscore the potential of seizing opportunities within the data revolution.

Theoretical Frameworks

At the core of the data revolution is the concept of **Big Data**, characterized by the three Vs: Volume, Velocity, and Variety. This framework helps to contextualize the scale and complexity of data in the modern world.

$$\text{Big Data} = f(V, v, v) \tag{113}$$

Where:

- V represents Volume (the amount of data),
- v represents Velocity (the speed of data processing), and
- v represents Variety (the different types of data).

To seize the opportunities presented by Big Data, organizations must adopt a strategic approach that encompasses data collection, processing, analysis, and interpretation. The **Data-Driven Decision-Making** (DDDM) framework is pivotal in this context, emphasizing the importance of using data analytics to inform strategic decisions.

Identifying Opportunities

The opportunities arising from the data revolution can be categorized into several domains:

- **Enhanced Customer Insights:** Businesses can analyze consumer behavior patterns through data analytics, enabling personalized marketing strategies. For instance, companies like Amazon utilize recommendation algorithms that analyze past purchases and browsing history to suggest products, significantly enhancing customer experience and driving sales.

- **Operational Efficiency:** Data analytics can streamline operations by identifying inefficiencies. For example, in manufacturing, predictive maintenance analytics can forecast equipment failures, reducing downtime and maintenance costs. General Electric employs such analytics to optimize its manufacturing processes, resulting in substantial cost savings.

- **Healthcare Innovations:** The healthcare sector has witnessed transformative changes through data analytics. By analyzing patient data, healthcare providers can identify trends, improve diagnostic accuracy, and personalize treatment plans. The use of machine learning algorithms to analyze medical images has shown promise in enhancing diagnostic capabilities, as demonstrated by Google's DeepMind in detecting eye diseases.

- **Smart Cities:** Urban planners can leverage data analytics to improve infrastructure, traffic management, and public safety. For instance, cities like Barcelona have implemented smart traffic systems that utilize real-time data to optimize traffic flow, reducing congestion and enhancing air quality.

- **Social Good Initiatives:** Data analytics can address societal challenges such as poverty, education, and health disparities. Organizations like DataKind leverage data science to solve social issues, partnering with nonprofits to analyze data that drive impactful solutions.

Addressing Challenges

While the opportunities are vast, several challenges must be addressed to fully realize the potential of the data revolution:

- **Data Privacy and Security:** As organizations collect vast amounts of data, the risk of data breaches and privacy violations increases. Implementing robust data governance frameworks and adhering to regulations such as GDPR is crucial to protect consumer data.

- **Bias in Data Analytics:** Algorithms can perpetuate existing biases if the data used is not representative. Organizations must ensure diversity in data collection and employ fairness algorithms to mitigate bias in decision-making processes.

- **Skill Gap:** The demand for data science professionals continues to outstrip supply. Educational institutions and organizations must invest in training programs that equip individuals with the necessary skills to thrive in a data-driven environment.

Real-World Examples

Several organizations exemplify how seizing the opportunities of the data revolution can lead to significant advancements:

- **Netflix:** By utilizing sophisticated algorithms to analyze viewer preferences, Netflix has transformed content consumption. Their recommendation system drives over 80% of the content watched on the platform, showcasing the power of data-driven insights.

- **Walmart:** The retail giant employs data analytics to optimize inventory management. By analyzing purchasing patterns, Walmart can predict demand fluctuations, ensuring that products are stocked appropriately, thus reducing waste and improving customer satisfaction.

- **Airbnb:** Through data analysis, Airbnb has revolutionized the hospitality industry. By leveraging data on user preferences and market trends, the platform tailors its offerings to enhance user experience, driving both host and guest satisfaction.

Conclusion

The data revolution is not merely a technological shift; it is a transformative force that can redefine industries and improve lives. By embracing the opportunities presented by data analytics, organizations can innovate, enhance operational efficiency, and contribute to societal well-being. However, to seize these opportunities effectively, it is imperative to address the associated challenges, ensuring that data is harnessed responsibly and ethically. As we look to the future, the legacy of innovators like Fatima Wang serves as a beacon, guiding us toward a data-driven world filled with possibilities.

Personal Reflections

Fatima's Journey and Personal Growth

Fatima Wang's journey in the realm of data analytics is a testament to the transformative power of personal growth, resilience, and the pursuit of knowledge. Her evolution from a curious child fascinated by numbers to a leading innovator in the field of data science is marked by significant milestones, challenges, and profound learning experiences.

The Early Years: Curiosity as a Catalyst

Fatima's early life was characterized by an insatiable curiosity about the world around her. Growing up in a household that valued education, she was encouraged to ask questions and seek answers. This environment fostered her love for mathematics and statistics, laying the groundwork for her future pursuits. Her parents, both educators, instilled in her the belief that knowledge is a lifelong journey, a theme that would resonate throughout her career.

Navigating Challenges: Overcoming Self-Doubt

As Fatima progressed through her education, she faced various challenges that tested her resolve. Despite her aptitude for analytics, she often grappled with self-doubt, particularly in male-dominated spaces. This experience is not uncommon among women in STEM fields, where societal biases can lead to feelings of inadequacy. Fatima's ability to confront and overcome these feelings was pivotal in her personal growth.

One notable instance occurred during her graduate studies, where she was the only woman in her data science cohort. Initially, she felt intimidated by her peers, who seemed more confident and experienced. However, Fatima recognized that her unique perspective as a woman in data analytics could contribute significantly to her field. Embracing her identity, she began to participate actively in discussions, ultimately earning the respect of her classmates and professors. This experience highlighted the importance of representation and the need for diverse voices in technology.

The Role of Mentorship: Learning from Leaders

Throughout her journey, mentorship played a crucial role in Fatima's development. She sought out mentors who not only provided guidance but also challenged her to think critically and push her boundaries. One of her most influential mentors was Dr. Linda Chen, a renowned data scientist known for her work in machine learning. Dr. Chen encouraged Fatima to pursue her research interests and provided invaluable insights into the intricacies of algorithm development.

Fatima's relationship with Dr. Chen exemplifies the impact of mentorship in fostering personal growth. Under Dr. Chen's guidance, Fatima learned to navigate the complexities of data ethics and the importance of responsible data usage. This mentorship experience not only honed her technical skills but also instilled in her a sense of social responsibility, which would later shape her vision for data analytics as a tool for societal good.

Embracing Failure: Lessons Learned

Fatima's journey was not without setbacks. Early in her career, she embarked on a project aimed at developing a predictive analytics model for healthcare outcomes. Despite her enthusiasm, the project faced numerous challenges, including data quality issues and algorithmic biases that led to inaccurate predictions. Initially disheartened by the project's failure, Fatima soon realized that failure is an integral part of the learning process.

She adopted a growth mindset, viewing each setback as an opportunity to learn and improve. Fatima meticulously analyzed what went wrong, engaged with her peers for feedback, and iterated on her approach. This resilience not only enhanced her technical skills but also fortified her belief in the importance of adaptability and continuous learning in the fast-evolving field of data science.

Building a Supportive Network: Collaboration and Community

Recognizing the value of collaboration, Fatima actively sought to build a supportive network of peers and colleagues. She participated in data science meetups, workshops, and conferences, where she exchanged ideas and learned from others' experiences. This sense of community became a cornerstone of her professional growth, providing her with a platform to share her work and receive constructive feedback.

One of the most impactful collaborations emerged from a data hackathon she attended, where she teamed up with individuals from diverse backgrounds. Together, they tackled a real-world problem: predicting food insecurity in urban areas. This experience not only broadened her technical expertise but also deepened her understanding of the social implications of data analytics. The project underscored the importance of interdisciplinary collaboration in addressing complex societal issues, a principle that Fatima would carry forward in her future endeavors.

Reflecting on Personal Growth: A Journey of Self-Discovery

As Fatima reflects on her journey, she acknowledges that personal growth is a continuous process. Each experience, whether positive or negative, has contributed to her development as an innovator and leader in data science. She emphasizes the importance of self-reflection, encouraging others to take time to assess their journeys and identify areas for growth.

Fatima's story illustrates that personal growth is not solely about acquiring technical skills; it also involves developing emotional intelligence, resilience, and a commitment to lifelong learning. Her experiences serve as a reminder that the journey of innovation is as important as the destination, and that each individual has the potential to make a meaningful impact in their field.

Conclusion: The Ongoing Journey

In conclusion, Fatima Wang's journey is a compelling narrative of curiosity, resilience, and growth. Her ability to navigate challenges, embrace mentorship, learn from failure, and build a supportive network has shaped her into a pioneering figure in data analytics. As she continues to innovate and inspire others, Fatima remains committed to her vision of using data for social good, demonstrating that personal growth is a lifelong endeavor that can lead to transformative change in the world.

Lessons Learned from Challenges and Triumphs

The journey of Fatima Wang in the realm of data analytics has been marked by a series of formidable challenges and significant triumphs. Each obstacle encountered has contributed to her growth, not only as a data scientist but also as a leader and innovator. This section delves into the lessons learned from these experiences, illustrating how they have shaped her approach to analytics and her vision for the future.

Embracing Failure as a Learning Tool

One of the most profound lessons Fatima learned early in her career was the importance of embracing failure. In the world of data science, not every algorithm yields the desired results, and not every hypothesis is validated by data. Fatima recalls a pivotal moment during her early research when a machine learning model she developed to predict economic trends failed spectacularly. The model produced results that were not only inaccurate but also misleading.

$$\text{Error Rate} = \frac{\text{False Positives} + \text{False Negatives}}{\text{Total Predictions}} \tag{114}$$

The error rate of her model was alarmingly high, leading to a reevaluation of her approach. Instead of viewing this setback as a defeat, Fatima used it as a learning opportunity. She meticulously analyzed the data, seeking to understand the underlying reasons for the model's failure. This process of reflection and analysis not only improved her technical skills but also instilled in her a resilience that would prove invaluable in her future endeavors.

The Value of Collaboration

Another critical lesson Fatima learned was the value of collaboration. In her quest to tackle big data challenges, she realized that the most innovative solutions often arise from interdisciplinary teamwork. During her work on a project aimed at improving urban traffic systems, Fatima collaborated with urban planners, engineers, and social scientists. This diverse team brought together a wealth of perspectives and expertise, leading to the development of a sophisticated analytics platform that significantly reduced traffic congestion in several cities.

The collaborative process highlighted the importance of communication and mutual respect among team members. Fatima often emphasizes the need for an inclusive environment where all voices are heard. She believes that fostering such an atmosphere not only leads to better outcomes but also encourages creativity and innovation.

Navigating Ethical Dilemmas

As Fatima's work gained recognition, she faced numerous ethical dilemmas associated with data usage. The rapid advancement of analytics technology often outpaced the establishment of ethical guidelines, leading to situations where the implications of data-driven decisions were not fully understood. One particularly challenging scenario involved the use of predictive analytics in law enforcement, which raised concerns about bias and discrimination.

Fatima learned the importance of advocating for ethical practices in data science. She became a vocal proponent of developing frameworks that prioritize fairness and accountability. This advocacy culminated in her involvement in establishing a set of ethical guidelines for data scientists, emphasizing the need for transparency in algorithms and the importance of considering the societal impact of data-driven decisions.

The Power of Persistence

Persistence emerged as a recurring theme in Fatima's journey. The road to innovation is often fraught with obstacles, and Fatima encountered her fair share of setbacks. Whether it was securing funding for her research or gaining acceptance for her ideas within the corporate sector, perseverance became her guiding principle.

One notable instance occurred when Fatima sought to implement a new data analytics system in a traditional manufacturing company. Initial resistance from the management team posed a significant barrier. Rather than giving up, Fatima organized workshops to educate stakeholders about the benefits of data-driven decision-making. Her persistence paid off, as the company eventually adopted the system, leading to a marked increase in efficiency and productivity.

Balancing Innovation with Practicality

Through her experiences, Fatima learned the importance of balancing innovation with practicality. While pushing the boundaries of what is possible in data analytics, she recognized that solutions must also be feasible and applicable in real-world scenarios. This lesson became particularly evident during a project aimed at developing a cutting-edge predictive model for climate change impact assessment.

Fatima's team initially focused on creating highly complex models that, while theoretically sound, proved too intricate for practical application. After several iterations, they shifted their approach to develop a more streamlined model that maintained accuracy while being user-friendly for policymakers. This experience reinforced Fatima's belief that innovation should not come at the expense of accessibility.

Cultivating a Growth Mindset

Finally, one of the most transformative lessons Fatima learned was the importance of cultivating a growth mindset. Embracing the idea that abilities and intelligence can be developed through dedication and hard work allowed her to approach challenges with a positive attitude. Fatima often encourages her colleagues and mentees to adopt this mindset, emphasizing that setbacks are not indicative of failure but rather opportunities for growth.

In her own career, this mindset has led Fatima to continuously seek new knowledge and skills. She regularly attends conferences, participates in workshops, and engages with the broader data science community to stay abreast of emerging trends and technologies. This commitment to lifelong learning has not only enriched her own expertise but has also positioned her as a thought leader in the field.

Conclusion

The lessons learned from challenges and triumphs have been instrumental in shaping Fatima Wang's journey as a data innovator. By embracing failure, valuing collaboration, navigating ethical dilemmas, demonstrating persistence, balancing innovation with practicality, and cultivating a growth mindset, Fatima has emerged as a resilient leader in the data revolution. Her experiences serve as a testament to the power of learning from adversity and the importance of fostering an environment where innovation can thrive.

Balancing Personal and Professional Life

The pursuit of innovation, particularly in the fast-paced world of data science, often leads individuals to grapple with the challenge of balancing personal and professional responsibilities. For Fatima Wang, this balance was not merely a matter of time management but a holistic approach to life that involved setting priorities, establishing boundaries, and nurturing both her career and personal well-being.

Theoretical Framework

To understand the dynamics of work-life balance, we can refer to the Work-Life Balance Theory, which posits that individuals strive to find an equilibrium between their work responsibilities and personal life, leading to improved overall satisfaction and productivity. According to Greenhaus and Allen (2011), achieving this balance can reduce stress, enhance job performance, and improve personal relationships. The theory suggests that work and personal life are interrelated and that positive experiences in one domain can lead to positive experiences in the other, a concept known as the *spillover effect*.

Challenges Faced by Innovators

Despite the theoretical benefits of work-life balance, innovators like Fatima often face significant challenges:

- **High Demands of Work:** The field of data science is characterized by rapid technological advancements and constant pressure to innovate. This can lead to extended work hours and difficulty disconnecting from work-related tasks.

- **Societal Expectations:** There is often a societal expectation for high achievers to be perpetually available and productive, which can lead to feelings of guilt when taking time off for personal reasons.

- **Self-Identity:** For many innovators, their work is closely tied to their identity. This can make it challenging to separate personal life from professional obligations, leading to burnout.

Fatima's Approach to Balance

Fatima adopted several strategies to maintain her work-life balance, which can serve as a guide for others in similar positions:

1. **Setting Clear Boundaries:** Fatima established specific work hours and communicated these boundaries with her colleagues. This practice not only helped her manage her time effectively but also allowed her to dedicate uninterrupted time to her family and personal interests.

2. **Prioritizing Self-Care:** Recognizing the importance of mental and physical health, Fatima incorporated regular exercise, mindfulness practices, and hobbies into her routine. This commitment to self-care helped her recharge and maintain focus during work hours.

3. **Leveraging Technology:** Fatima utilized productivity tools and apps to streamline her work processes, allowing her to complete tasks more efficiently. This technological advantage enabled her to free up time for personal activities without compromising her professional responsibilities.

4. **Engaging in Support Networks:** Fatima actively sought mentorship and built a supportive network of colleagues and friends. This network provided her with guidance, encouragement, and a sense of community, making it easier to navigate the challenges of balancing work and personal life.

Real-World Examples

Fatima's experiences are echoed by many successful professionals who have navigated similar challenges. For instance, Sheryl Sandberg, the former COO of Facebook, discusses in her book *Lean In* the importance of setting boundaries and the impact of supportive partnerships in achieving work-life balance. Sandberg emphasizes that having a partner who is equally invested in household responsibilities can significantly alleviate the pressures faced by working women.

Moreover, a study by the American Psychological Association (APA) found that employees who engage in flexible work arrangements report higher job satisfaction and lower stress levels. This aligns with Fatima's approach of advocating for flexible work hours within her organization, allowing her and her colleagues to better manage their personal commitments alongside their professional goals.

Conclusion

In conclusion, balancing personal and professional life is a multifaceted challenge that requires intentional strategies and a supportive environment. Fatima Wang's journey illustrates that by setting clear boundaries, prioritizing self-care, leveraging technology, and fostering supportive relationships, innovators can navigate the complexities of their careers while maintaining a fulfilling personal life. As the landscape of work continues to evolve, embracing these principles will be essential for future innovators striving to achieve both professional success and personal well-being.

Bibliography

[1] Greenhaus, J. H., & Allen, T. D. (2011). Work-family balance: A review and extension of the literature. *The Handbook of Industrial, Work and Organizational Psychology*, 3, 165-203.

[2] Sandberg, S. (2013). *Lean In: Women, Work, and the Will to Lead*. Knopf.

[3] American Psychological Association. (2016). Flexible Work Arrangements: A Key to Employee Satisfaction. Retrieved from `https://www.apa.org`

Building a Supportive Network

Building a supportive network is crucial for any innovator, particularly in the rapidly evolving field of data science. A robust professional network can provide guidance, resources, and opportunities that are essential for personal and professional growth. This section explores the significance of networking, the challenges faced in building these connections, and practical strategies for creating a supportive community.

The Importance of Networking

Networking is not merely about exchanging business cards or connecting on social media; it is about forming genuine relationships that foster collaboration and innovation. According to Granovetter's (1973) theory of the strength of weak ties, individuals benefit from connections with acquaintances (weak ties) because they provide access to new information and opportunities that are not available within one's immediate circle (strong ties). This is particularly relevant in data science, where interdisciplinary collaboration is often necessary to tackle complex problems.

Challenges in Building a Supportive Network

Despite its importance, building a supportive network can be fraught with challenges. Many individuals, especially those from underrepresented backgrounds, may face barriers such as:

- **Imposter Syndrome:** Many innovators struggle with feelings of inadequacy, leading to reluctance in reaching out to potential mentors or peers.

- **Geographical Limitations:** Those in remote or rural areas may find it difficult to connect with industry leaders or like-minded individuals.

- **Cultural Barriers:** Differences in communication styles and cultural norms can hinder effective networking.

- **Time Constraints:** Balancing professional responsibilities with networking efforts can be challenging, particularly for those with demanding jobs or family obligations.

Strategies for Building a Supportive Network

To overcome these challenges, innovators can adopt several strategies to effectively build and maintain a supportive network:

1. **Leverage Online Platforms:** Utilize professional networking sites such as LinkedIn, GitHub, and specialized forums to connect with peers and industry leaders. Participating in online discussions, sharing insights, and contributing to open-source projects can enhance visibility and credibility.

2. **Attend Conferences and Workshops:** Engaging in industry events, hackathons, and workshops provides opportunities to meet like-minded individuals. These settings encourage collaboration and foster relationships that can lead to mentorship or partnership opportunities.

3. **Join Professional Organizations:** Becoming a member of professional associations related to data science can provide access to resources, training, and networking events. Organizations such as the Data Science Society and the Association for Computing Machinery (ACM) offer valuable platforms for connection and collaboration.

4. **Seek Out Mentorship:** Identifying and approaching potential mentors can provide guidance and support. Mentorship relationships can help navigate

career challenges and provide insights into industry trends. A study by Allen et al. (2004) found that mentorship significantly impacts career advancement and job satisfaction.

5. **Engage in Community Service:** Volunteering for data-driven projects that address social issues can connect innovators with others who share similar values and goals. This not only builds a network but also contributes to personal fulfillment and societal impact.

6. **Foster Inclusivity:** Creating a network that values diversity and inclusion can enhance creativity and innovation. Encouraging participation from individuals of various backgrounds can lead to a richer exchange of ideas and perspectives.

Case Study: The Data Science Network

A practical example of effective networking in the data science field is the Data Science Network (DSN), an initiative designed to connect data professionals across various industries. The DSN hosts regular meetups, webinars, and online discussions, allowing members to share knowledge, collaborate on projects, and support each other's professional development.

The success of the DSN can be attributed to its focus on creating a welcoming environment for all participants. By implementing inclusive practices and prioritizing relationship-building over transactional interactions, the network has fostered a strong sense of community.

Conclusion

Building a supportive network is an essential component of success for innovators like Fatima Wang. By overcoming challenges and implementing effective strategies, individuals can cultivate relationships that not only enhance their careers but also contribute to the advancement of the data science field. As the industry continues to evolve, the importance of collaboration and community will only grow, making the effort to build a supportive network a worthwhile investment.

Bibliography

[1] Granovetter, M. S. (1973). The strength of weak ties. *American Journal of Sociology*, 78(6), 1360-1380.

[2] Allen, T. D., Eby, L. T., Poteet, M. L., Lentz, E., & Lima, L. (2004). Career benefits associated with mentoring for mentors: A qualitative review. *Journal of Vocational Behavior*, 65(3), 469-485.

Looking Ahead with Hope and Purpose

As we reflect on the transformative journey of Fatima Wang and the data revolution she helped catalyze, it is crucial to look ahead with a sense of hope and purpose. The future of data science is not merely about the accumulation of data but rather about harnessing its potential to address some of the most pressing challenges facing humanity. In this section, we will explore the emerging trends, the ethical considerations that must guide our path forward, and the collective responsibility we share in shaping a future that prioritizes innovation, inclusivity, and social good.

Emerging Trends in Data Science

The landscape of data science is evolving at an unprecedented pace. Emerging technologies such as quantum computing, advanced machine learning algorithms, and decentralized data systems are set to revolutionize how we process and analyze information. For instance, quantum computing has the potential to exponentially increase the speed at which we can perform complex calculations, thus enabling breakthroughs in fields such as drug discovery and climate modeling. The equation that represents the speedup of quantum algorithms over classical counterparts can be expressed as:

$$T_{quantum} = \frac{T_{classical}}{Q} \tag{115}$$

where $T_{quantum}$ is the time taken by a quantum algorithm, $T_{classical}$ is the time taken by the best classical algorithm, and Q represents the quantum speedup factor. This advancement not only enhances analytical capabilities but also opens new avenues for innovation that were previously unimaginable.

Furthermore, the integration of artificial intelligence (AI) into data analytics is creating smarter systems that can learn and adapt over time. AI-driven predictive analytics can significantly improve decision-making processes across various sectors, from healthcare to finance. For example, machine learning models can analyze vast amounts of patient data to identify risk factors for diseases, leading to earlier interventions and better health outcomes.

Ethical Considerations in Data-Driven Decisions

However, with great power comes great responsibility. As we forge ahead, it is essential to address the ethical implications of data usage. Issues such as data privacy, algorithmic bias, and the digital divide must be at the forefront of our discussions. The ethical framework guiding data science should be built on principles of fairness, accountability, and transparency.

Consider the implications of biased algorithms in hiring processes. If an AI system is trained on historical hiring data that reflects societal biases, it may perpetuate these biases, leading to unfair treatment of candidates from marginalized backgrounds. To mitigate this, organizations must implement rigorous testing and validation of their algorithms to ensure fairness. The fairness metric can be quantified using the following equation:

$$F = \frac{TP}{TP + FN} \tag{116}$$

where F is the fairness score, TP is the number of true positives, and FN is the number of false negatives. This approach ensures that the outcomes of data-driven decisions do not disproportionately disadvantage any group.

Collective Responsibility and Future Directions

The path forward requires a collective effort from all stakeholders—data scientists, policymakers, educators, and the general public. It is imperative to foster a culture of collaboration and knowledge sharing that transcends disciplinary and geographical boundaries. Initiatives such as open data platforms and interdisciplinary research collaborations can facilitate innovation while ensuring that diverse perspectives are included in the decision-making process.

Moreover, education plays a critical role in empowering the next generation of innovators. By integrating data literacy into school curricula and promoting STEM education, we can equip young minds with the skills necessary to navigate and thrive in a data-driven world. This includes not only technical skills but also critical thinking and ethical reasoning, which are essential for responsible data use.

A Vision for the Future

Looking ahead, we envision a future where data serves as a catalyst for positive change. Imagine a world where data analytics is used to tackle climate change by optimizing resource usage, or where predictive models help prevent food insecurity by analyzing agricultural trends. The possibilities are endless, and it is our responsibility to ensure that these possibilities are realized in an equitable manner.

In conclusion, the legacy of Fatima Wang is not just a story of individual achievement; it is a call to action for all of us. As we move forward, let us embrace the challenges and opportunities that lie ahead with hope and purpose. By prioritizing ethical practices, fostering collaboration, and empowering future generations, we can ensure that the data revolution benefits all of humanity. The future is bright, and together, we can illuminate the path toward a better world.

Conclusion

Honoring Fatima's Contributions

Fatima Wang's journey through the realm of data science is marked by a series of remarkable contributions that have not only advanced the field but have also inspired countless individuals to pursue careers in analytics. Her work embodies the intersection of innovation, ethics, and societal impact, making her a pivotal figure in the modern data revolution.

A Legacy of Innovation

Fatima's innovative spirit is best exemplified by her development of novel algorithms that significantly improved the efficiency of data processing. One of her most notable contributions is the *Adaptive Learning Algorithm* (ALA), which optimizes machine learning models by dynamically adjusting parameters based on real-time data feedback. The equation governing the ALA can be expressed as:

$$\theta_{t+1} = \theta_t - \eta \nabla L(\theta_t, x_t, y_t) \tag{117}$$

where:

- θ represents the model parameters,
- η is the learning rate,
- L is the loss function,
- (x_t, y_t) denotes the input-output pairs at time t.

This algorithm not only enhances predictive accuracy but also reduces computational costs, making data analytics more accessible to organizations of all sizes.

Advancing Data Ethics

In addition to her technical innovations, Fatima has been a staunch advocate for ethical practices in data science. Recognizing the potential for misuse of data, she pioneered the concept of *Ethical Analytics*, which emphasizes transparency, accountability, and fairness in data usage. This framework addresses critical issues such as bias in machine learning models, which can lead to discriminatory outcomes. Fatima's research highlights the importance of incorporating diverse datasets to mitigate bias, a principle encapsulated in the following inequality:

$$\text{Bias} = \frac{1}{N} \sum_{i=1}^{N} (y_i - \hat{y}_i) \tag{118}$$

where:

- y_i is the actual outcome,
- $\hat{y}_i$ is the predicted outcome,
- N is the number of observations.

By advocating for diverse data representation, Fatima has made significant strides toward ensuring that analytics serves all segments of society equitably.

Impact on Education and Mentorship

Fatima's commitment to education is evident in her initiatives aimed at empowering the next generation of data scientists. She has established numerous mentorship programs and workshops focused on data literacy, particularly targeting underrepresented groups in STEM fields. Her approach emphasizes hands-on learning and real-world applications of data science, fostering a culture of inclusivity and innovation.

For instance, her collaboration with local schools to integrate data science into the curriculum has yielded impressive results. Students engage in projects that analyze community issues, using data to propose actionable solutions. This initiative not only equips students with valuable skills but also instills a sense of social responsibility.

Recognition and Awards

Fatima's contributions have not gone unnoticed. She has received numerous accolades, including the prestigious *Data Science Innovator Award* and the *Ethics in Tech Award*, recognizing her dual impact on technology and ethical practices. These honors serve as a testament to her influence and the respect she commands in the data science community.

Her keynote speeches at international conferences often highlight the critical need for ethical considerations in analytics, inspiring other professionals to adopt similar values. Fatima's voice has become synonymous with integrity in data science, encouraging a shift towards more responsible practices across the industry.

A Lasting Influence on Society

The societal impact of Fatima's work extends beyond academia and industry. She has actively participated in policy discussions aimed at shaping data governance frameworks that protect individual privacy while promoting innovation. Her advocacy for responsible data use has led to the development of guidelines that many organizations now follow, ensuring that data-driven decisions are made with the utmost consideration for ethical implications.

Moreover, Fatima's research on data-driven solutions for global challenges, such as climate change and public health, has opened new avenues for using analytics for social good. By leveraging big data to address pressing issues, she has demonstrated that data science can be a powerful tool for positive change.

Conclusion

In conclusion, Fatima Wang's contributions to data science are profound and multifaceted. From her groundbreaking algorithms to her unwavering commitment to ethical practices, she has set a benchmark for future innovators. As we honor her legacy, we are reminded of the potential that lies within data analytics to transform industries, empower communities, and foster a more equitable society. Fatima's journey serves as an inspiration for aspiring data scientists, encouraging them to pursue their passions while remaining mindful of the ethical responsibilities that accompany their work.

As we look to the future, it is essential to continue building upon Fatima's foundation, ensuring that data science evolves in a manner that is inclusive, ethical, and impactful. By doing so, we honor her contributions and pave the way for the next generation of innovators who will shape the future of data.

Embracing a Data-Driven Future

In the rapidly evolving landscape of the 21st century, the importance of embracing a data-driven future cannot be overstated. As organizations and individuals alike navigate the complexities of an increasingly interconnected world, the ability to leverage data effectively has become a critical determinant of success. This section explores the theoretical foundations, challenges, and practical examples that underscore the necessity of adopting a data-centric approach in various domains.

Theoretical Foundations of Data-Driven Decision Making

At the core of a data-driven future lies the concept of data-driven decision making (DDDM). This approach integrates data analysis into the decision-making process, enabling organizations to make informed choices based on empirical evidence rather than intuition or anecdotal experiences. According to [?], DDDM is characterized by the systematic use of data to guide strategic decisions, fostering a culture of accountability and continuous improvement.

The theoretical framework of DDDM is supported by several key principles:

- **Quantitative Analysis:** The use of statistical techniques to derive insights from data sets. This includes methods such as regression analysis, hypothesis testing, and machine learning algorithms that allow for predictive modeling.

- **Data Visualization:** The representation of data in graphical formats to facilitate understanding and communication of insights. Effective data visualization techniques, such as dashboards and infographics, play a crucial role in conveying complex information to stakeholders.

- **Feedback Loops:** The iterative process of using data to inform decisions and subsequently collecting new data to assess the outcomes of those decisions. This cyclical approach ensures that organizations remain agile and responsive to changing conditions.

Challenges in Embracing a Data-Driven Future

While the benefits of adopting a data-driven approach are clear, several challenges persist that hinder widespread implementation. These challenges include:

- **Data Quality and Integrity:** High-quality data is essential for effective analysis. However, organizations often struggle with issues such as data silos, incomplete datasets, and inaccuracies. According to a study by [?], poor data quality can lead to significant financial losses and misguided strategic decisions.

- **Cultural Resistance:** Shifting to a data-driven mindset requires a cultural transformation within organizations. Employees may resist changes to established practices, particularly if they perceive data as a threat to their expertise or job security. Effective change management strategies, including training and engagement initiatives, are crucial for overcoming this resistance.

- **Ethical Considerations:** The use of data raises important ethical questions regarding privacy, consent, and bias. Organizations must navigate the complex landscape of data ethics to ensure responsible usage while maintaining public trust. As highlighted by [?], algorithmic bias can perpetuate existing inequalities if not addressed proactively.

Examples of Data-Driven Success

Numerous organizations across various sectors have successfully embraced a data-driven approach, leading to transformative outcomes. Here are a few notable examples:

- **Netflix:** The streaming giant utilizes data analytics to inform content creation and recommendation algorithms. By analyzing viewer preferences and behaviors, Netflix can tailor its offerings to meet audience demands, resulting in increased viewer engagement and subscriber retention. The success of original series like *House of Cards* exemplifies the power of data-driven decision making in entertainment.

- **Amazon:** Amazon employs sophisticated data analytics to optimize its supply chain and enhance customer experiences. Through predictive analytics, the company can anticipate customer needs, streamline inventory management, and improve delivery efficiency. This data-centric approach has solidified Amazon's position as a leader in e-commerce.

- **Healthcare Analytics:** Organizations like Mount Sinai Health System leverage data analytics to improve patient outcomes. By analyzing electronic health records (EHRs), they can identify patterns and risk factors associated with various conditions, enabling personalized treatment plans and proactive interventions. This data-driven methodology has the potential to revolutionize patient care and reduce healthcare costs.

Conclusion: A Call to Action

Embracing a data-driven future is not merely an option; it is a necessity for organizations seeking to thrive in an increasingly competitive environment. By fostering a culture of data literacy, investing in robust data infrastructure, and prioritizing ethical considerations, organizations can unlock the full potential of data to drive innovation and societal progress.

As we look ahead, it is imperative for leaders to champion data-driven initiatives and empower their teams to harness the power of analytics. The journey toward a data-driven future may be fraught with challenges, but the rewards—enhanced decision making, improved efficiency, and greater societal impact—are well worth the effort. Together, we can build a future where data serves as a catalyst for positive change, shaping a world that is more informed, equitable, and sustainable.

Continuing the Legacy of Innovation

The legacy of innovation left by pioneers like Fatima Wang is not merely a historical footnote; it is a living, breathing entity that continues to evolve and shape the landscape of data science and analytics. As we explore the pathways to continuing this legacy, it is crucial to understand the theoretical frameworks, the challenges we face, and the practical examples that illustrate the ongoing journey of innovation.

Theoretical Frameworks for Innovation

To effectively continue the legacy of innovation, we must ground our efforts in established theories of innovation management. One such framework is the **Diffusion of Innovations Theory** proposed by Everett Rogers. This theory explains how, why, and at what rate new ideas and technology spread. It is essential to recognize the stages of innovation adoption:

$$\text{Adoption Rate} = \frac{\text{Number of Adopters}}{\text{Total Population}} \times 100\% \quad (119)$$

This equation highlights the significance of understanding the target audience for data-driven innovations. By identifying early adopters and influencers, we can catalyze broader acceptance and integration of innovative solutions in various sectors.

Another relevant theory is the **Open Innovation Model** by Henry Chesbrough, which posits that firms can and should use external ideas and paths to market as well as internal ideas to advance their technology. This model encourages collaboration across disciplines, organizations, and even industries, fostering a culture of shared knowledge and innovation.

Challenges in Continuing Innovation

Despite the frameworks that guide us, several challenges persist that can hinder the continuation of innovation. One of the primary issues is the **Resistance to Change**. Organizations often face internal pushback when attempting to implement new data-driven strategies. This resistance can stem from fear of the unknown, lack of understanding of the benefits, or simply the inertia of established processes.

Another significant challenge is **Data Privacy and Security**. As data becomes increasingly integral to decision-making, concerns about how data is collected, stored, and utilized become paramount. Organizations must navigate complex regulations such as the General Data Protection Regulation (GDPR) in Europe, which imposes strict rules on data handling.

The equation representing the balance between innovation and compliance can be expressed as:

$$\text{Innovation Balance} = \frac{\text{Innovative Potential}}{\text{Compliance Risk}} \quad (120)$$

This highlights the need for organizations to find a sweet spot where they can innovate without compromising legal and ethical standards.

Examples of Continuing Innovation

To illustrate the continuation of innovation, we can look at several case studies that exemplify how organizations are building on the legacy of pioneers like Fatima Wang.

Case Study 1: Healthcare Analytics One of the most impactful applications of data analytics has been in healthcare. Organizations like **IBM Watson Health** have built upon the foundational work in data analytics to develop systems that provide personalized treatment recommendations based on vast datasets of patient information. By leveraging machine learning algorithms, these systems can analyze patterns in patient data to improve diagnostic accuracy and patient outcomes.

Case Study 2: Smart Cities Cities around the world are adopting smart technologies to enhance urban living. For instance, **Barcelona** has implemented a data-driven approach to urban planning, utilizing sensors and analytics to optimize traffic flow, reduce energy consumption, and improve public safety. This initiative exemplifies how data can be harnessed to transform urban environments, making them more efficient and livable.

Case Study 3: Financial Inclusion In the financial sector, companies like **Kiva** are using data analytics to provide microloans to underserved communities. By analyzing data on borrower behavior and repayment patterns, Kiva can assess risk more accurately and extend credit to individuals who may not qualify through traditional banking channels. This not only helps individuals achieve financial independence but also fosters economic growth in communities.

Strategies for Sustaining Innovation

To ensure the continuation of innovation, organizations must adopt several key strategies:

- **Foster a Culture of Innovation:** Encourage employees at all levels to contribute ideas and challenge the status quo. This can be achieved through brainstorming sessions, innovation labs, and hackathons.

- **Invest in Continuous Learning:** Provide ongoing training and development opportunities for employees to stay updated on the latest technologies and methodologies in data science.

- **Encourage Cross-Disciplinary Collaboration:** Break down silos within organizations to facilitate knowledge sharing and collaboration among different departments and specialties.

- **Leverage Emerging Technologies:** Stay at the forefront of technological advancements such as artificial intelligence, machine learning, and blockchain to explore new possibilities for innovation.

- **Engage with the Community:** Build partnerships with academic institutions, non-profits, and other organizations to share resources and knowledge, driving collective innovation efforts.

Conclusion

Continuing the legacy of innovation requires a multifaceted approach that combines theoretical understanding, practical application, and a commitment to ethical considerations. By addressing the challenges we face and leveraging the opportunities presented by emerging technologies, we can honor the contributions of pioneers like Fatima Wang while paving the way for future generations of innovators. The journey of innovation is ongoing, and it is our responsibility to ensure that it remains vibrant and impactful for years to come.

Inspiring the Next Generation of Innovators

In the ever-evolving landscape of technology and data science, the need to inspire and empower the next generation of innovators has never been more critical. As we reflect on the legacy of Fatima Wang, we recognize that her contributions extend beyond her groundbreaking research; they serve as a beacon of hope and motivation for aspiring data scientists and innovators around the world. This section explores the various ways in which we can inspire the next generation, addressing the challenges they face and offering practical solutions.

The Importance of Role Models

Role models play a pivotal role in shaping the aspirations and ambitions of young innovators. Fatima Wang's journey exemplifies the power of perseverance, curiosity, and passion for data. By sharing her story, we can encourage young individuals to pursue their interests in data science and analytics. Research indicates that having relatable role models can significantly boost students' confidence and motivation, particularly among underrepresented groups in STEM fields [?].

To cultivate a diverse pool of future innovators, it is essential to highlight the achievements of individuals from various backgrounds. Initiatives such as mentorship programs and speaker series can provide young people with access to industry leaders who can share their experiences and insights. By showcasing diverse role models, we can create an inclusive environment that encourages participation from all demographics.

Encouraging STEM Education and Data Literacy

To inspire the next generation of innovators, we must prioritize STEM education and data literacy from an early age. Educational institutions should integrate data science into their curricula, emphasizing its relevance across various fields. According to the National Science Board, only 16% of high school students are proficient in mathematics, which is a critical foundation for data science [?].

Implementing hands-on learning experiences, such as coding boot camps and data analysis workshops, can help demystify complex concepts and engage students in practical applications of data science. For instance, programs like Code.org and DataCamp offer interactive platforms where students can learn coding and data analysis skills in a fun and engaging manner.

Moreover, schools should promote data literacy as a fundamental skill for the 21st century. Understanding how to interpret data, recognize biases, and draw conclusions from data sets is essential for informed citizenship and decision-making. Initiatives that teach students to critically analyze data can empower them to navigate an increasingly data-driven world.

Fostering a Culture of Innovation

Creating a culture of innovation involves encouraging creativity, experimentation, and collaboration among young innovators. Educational institutions and organizations should cultivate environments where students feel safe to explore new ideas and take risks. This can be achieved through project-based learning, hackathons, and interdisciplinary collaborations that allow students to work on real-world problems.

For example, organizations like Technovation Challenge empower young girls to develop apps that address community issues, providing them with the tools and mentorship needed to bring their ideas to life. Such programs not only enhance technical skills but also instill confidence and a sense of purpose in young innovators.

Building Support Networks

Support networks are vital for nurturing aspiring innovators. Establishing mentorship programs that connect students with experienced professionals can provide guidance, encouragement, and resources. These networks can also facilitate peer-to-peer learning, allowing students to collaborate and share knowledge.

In addition to formal mentorship programs, online platforms such as LinkedIn and GitHub can serve as valuable resources for young innovators to connect with industry professionals, showcase their work, and seek advice. Creating spaces for discussion and collaboration, both online and offline, can help foster a sense of community among aspiring data scientists.

Promoting Diversity and Inclusion in Tech

Diversity and inclusion are essential components of innovation. A diverse workforce brings a variety of perspectives and experiences, leading to more creative solutions and better decision-making. Unfortunately, underrepresentation in tech remains a significant challenge. According to a report by McKinsey, companies with diverse workforces are 35% more likely to outperform their peers [?].

To inspire the next generation, we must actively promote diversity in tech fields. This can be achieved through targeted outreach efforts, scholarships for underrepresented groups, and initiatives that encourage girls and minorities to pursue careers in data science. By creating pathways for diverse talent to enter the field, we can ensure that the innovations of tomorrow reflect the needs and aspirations of a broader population.

Conclusion

Inspiring the next generation of innovators is a multifaceted endeavor that requires a collective effort from educators, industry leaders, and communities. By providing role models, promoting STEM education, fostering a culture of innovation, building support networks, and advocating for diversity and inclusion, we can empower young individuals to embrace their potential as future leaders in data science and analytics.

As we honor Fatima Wang's contributions, let us commit to nurturing the innovators of tomorrow, ensuring that they have the tools, resources, and inspiration needed to drive the next wave of breakthroughs in the data revolution.

Final Thoughts and Acknowledgments

As we draw this narrative of Fatima Wang's remarkable journey to a close, it is essential to reflect on the profound impact her work has had on the fields of data science and analytics. Fatima's story is not just one of personal triumph; it is a testament to the power of curiosity, resilience, and innovation in shaping the future of industries and communities alike.

The data revolution, as ignited by pioneers like Fatima, has transformed how we perceive and interact with information. The ability to harness vast amounts of data has led to unprecedented advancements in healthcare, finance, education, and beyond. For instance, consider the impact of predictive analytics in healthcare, where algorithms can now forecast disease outbreaks and personalize treatment plans based on patient history. This capability is not merely theoretical; it has been demonstrated in real-world applications, such as the use of machine learning models to predict patient deterioration in hospitals, ultimately saving lives.

However, with great power comes great responsibility. Fatima's work has also highlighted the ethical considerations that accompany data science. The challenge of ensuring data privacy while extracting valuable insights remains a pressing issue. As Fatima once articulated, "Data is not just numbers; it is the story of lives, experiences, and choices." This perspective underlines the importance of ethical frameworks that guide data usage, ensuring that innovations do not come at the expense of individual rights and societal norms.

In the realm of data ethics, consider the implications of algorithmic bias. A recent study revealed that facial recognition technologies exhibit significant inaccuracies across different demographic groups, leading to wrongful identifications and reinforcing social inequalities. Fatima's advocacy for responsible data use emphasizes the necessity of diverse datasets and inclusive practices in algorithm design. The ethical landscape of data science is complex, and Fatima's contributions serve as a guiding light for future innovators navigating these challenges.

Moreover, Fatima's vision for the future of data science extends beyond mere technological advancement. She has championed the idea that data should be a tool for social good, empowering communities and driving positive change. Initiatives that leverage data to address global health issues, poverty alleviation, and environmental sustainability are not just aspirational; they are essential for a more equitable future. For instance, data-driven approaches to disaster response have revolutionized how organizations prepare for and react to natural calamities, saving countless lives and resources.

As we acknowledge Fatima's legacy, it is crucial to recognize the collaborative

CONCLUSION

spirit that underpins her success. Her belief in interdisciplinary partnerships has fostered an environment where knowledge is shared, and innovation flourishes. The importance of collaboration in data science cannot be overstated; it is through the convergence of diverse perspectives that groundbreaking solutions emerge. Fatima's work exemplifies how collective efforts can lead to advancements that no single entity could achieve alone.

In closing, it is imperative to honor the contributions of those who have paved the way for future innovators. Fatima Wang's journey is a source of inspiration, reminding us that the pursuit of knowledge, when coupled with ethical considerations and a commitment to social impact, can lead to transformative change. As we stand on the brink of a new era in data science, let us carry forward her vision, embracing the challenges and opportunities that lie ahead.

Acknowledgments

This work would not have been possible without the support of numerous individuals and institutions. I extend my heartfelt gratitude to Fatima Wang, whose insights and dedication have profoundly influenced my understanding of data science. I also wish to thank my mentors and colleagues, whose encouragement and expertise have been invaluable throughout this journey.

Special thanks to the research teams and organizations that have collaborated with Fatima in her groundbreaking projects. Your commitment to advancing the field of data science and your willingness to share knowledge have made a significant difference in the lives of many.

Finally, I acknowledge the countless innovators and thought leaders who continue to inspire the next generation of data scientists. Your work is a reminder that the future of analytics is bright, and it is our responsibility to ensure that it is inclusive, ethical, and focused on the greater good.

Index

-doubt, 253

a, 1–13, 15, 16, 18, 21, 22, 24–27, 29, 30, 32–44, 46–50, 52, 54, 55, 57–60, 62–64, 67, 68, 70–73, 75, 76, 78, 80, 81, 83, 86, 88–90, 92, 93, 95, 96, 99, 102, 103, 105, 108, 110–116, 118, 119, 122–124, 126, 127, 130, 136–140, 142, 144–146, 151, 153, 155–160, 162, 164–167, 169, 172, 175, 177–182, 184–189, 191–197, 199–204, 206, 207, 209–213, 215–221, 223, 224, 226–229, 231, 234–236, 238–241, 243–247, 249, 252–263, 265, 267, 269–273, 275–279
ability, 6, 7, 9, 10, 34, 46, 47, 50, 60, 70, 73, 75, 83, 90, 93, 127, 139, 158, 216, 218, 246, 253, 255, 270, 278
absence, 70
academia, 7, 9, 201, 204, 269
acceptance, 39, 41, 256, 273
access, 63, 99, 100, 137, 186, 193, 231, 244, 276
accessibility, 62, 89, 101, 102, 142, 192, 194, 212, 257
account, 156
accountability, 47, 63, 129, 151, 166, 175–177, 218, 221, 256, 266
accumulation, 265
accuracy, 25, 26, 70, 72, 73, 84, 122, 130, 195, 257, 268
achievement, 108, 115, 116, 267
acquisition, 158–160, 164, 192
action, 122, 123, 210, 211, 267
activity, 29, 43, 220
ad, 126
adapt, 46, 105
adaptability, 47, 166, 254
adaptation, 25
addition, 201, 277
address, 20, 22, 27, 39, 44, 47, 50, 57, 59, 60, 62, 63, 73, 76, 79–81, 88, 101, 108, 110, 115, 136, 138, 140–142, 146, 153, 156, 159, 168, 182, 187, 202, 218, 219, 228, 229, 238, 246, 247, 249, 252, 265, 266, 269,

276, 278
addressing, 7, 25, 29, 32, 41, 44, 52, 54, 60, 67, 75, 78, 83, 86, 89, 90, 96, 113, 124, 137, 144, 151, 179, 185, 188, 192, 197, 204, 233, 236, 239, 241, 249, 254, 275
adherence, 177
admission, 36
adoption, 84, 232, 243
advancement, 60, 67, 70, 88, 186, 226, 244, 256, 263, 278
advantage, 93, 99, 158, 189, 215
advent, 73, 75, 86, 117, 172, 221
adversity, 258
advertising, 124–127
advice, 277
advocacy, 6, 7, 51, 148–151, 197, 200, 202, 204, 256, 269
advocate, 29, 201, 204
affinity, 3
age, 1–3, 32, 63, 86, 124, 129, 162, 172, 197, 200, 236
agency, 203
air, 213
algorithm, 22, 24–27, 49, 50, 76, 126, 135, 195, 240, 253, 255, 268
alignment, 34, 158
alleviation, 140–142, 278
allocation, 60, 80, 115, 116, 147, 148, 236
alternative, 81, 102
ambiguity, 210
ambition, 2
amount, 12, 16, 93, 112
analysis, 1, 2, 4–6, 8, 9, 11–13, 16, 32, 42, 47, 51, 60, 66, 95, 108, 113, 125, 129, 138–140, 147, 165, 166, 195, 196, 204, 211, 215, 217, 218, 239, 255, 276
analyst, 10
annealing, 22
anonymization, 43
applicability, 224
applicant, 164
application, 3, 9, 34, 44, 60, 142, 149, 151, 164, 166, 192, 195, 257, 275
appreciation, 4, 5
approach, 6, 10, 12, 18, 22, 33, 34, 36, 46, 47, 49, 57, 59, 63, 67, 71, 76, 80, 82, 86, 88, 90, 99, 105, 108, 110, 113–115, 121, 122, 135, 145, 151, 153, 159, 160, 165, 177, 192, 194, 196, 201, 203, 210, 213, 215, 236, 246, 247, 254, 255, 257, 258, 269–271, 275
aptitude, 253
architecture, 26
area, 16, 32, 115, 137, 142
arena, 180
aspect, 9, 50, 64, 127, 165, 241
assessment, 113, 257
asset, 99
assistant, 2
atmosphere, 256
attendance, 108, 112, 115
attitude, 257
audience, 40, 124–128, 135, 273
audits, 219
automation, 12
availability, 85, 86, 139, 145, 241
average, 99
award, 49

Index

awareness, 61, 148, 190, 245

backbone, 27, 164
background, 162
balance, 44, 83, 129, 177, 179, 258, 259, 273
banking, 91, 99, 103–105
Barcelona, 213
barrier, 41, 256
basic, 1, 11, 100, 108, 135, 146, 234
basis, 16, 211
beacon, 18, 44, 204, 252, 275
beginning, 105, 197
behavior, 5, 29, 115, 121, 123, 124, 128, 153, 234, 240
being, 55, 62, 89, 105, 124, 134, 155–158, 164, 249, 252, 257, 258, 260
belief, 5, 13, 62, 112, 231, 253, 254, 257
belonging, 7, 90, 186
benchmark, 270
benefit, 16, 21, 29, 45, 77, 202, 203, 239
betterment, 39, 49
Bias, 217
bias, 24, 25, 29, 43, 47, 62, 63, 67, 77, 88, 124, 126, 160, 166, 181, 210, 217, 219, 239–241, 256, 266
billion, 100
biodiversity, 142
blend, 3, 7, 13, 224
blockchain, 32, 197
book, 11
bookstore, 11
boost, 33
boot, 276
branch, 52

brand, 217
branding, 234
breach, 246
breast, 71
breathing, 272
bridge, 32–34, 193, 201
building, 24, 148, 172, 188, 189, 219, 238, 239, 261–263, 270, 274, 277
bus, 82
business, 5, 32–34, 44, 46, 47, 126, 158, 159, 215

calculate, 93
calculation, 88, 217
call, 267
Canada, 1
cancer, 66, 71, 76
capability, 128, 278
capacity, 50, 147, 238
capital, 158
card, 29, 93
care, 33, 36, 73, 75, 139, 260
career, 2, 3, 5, 10, 13, 25, 27, 50, 186, 189, 192, 197, 202, 205, 253–255, 257, 258
case, 33, 43, 72, 85, 102, 147, 240, 249, 274
catalyst, 192, 234, 267
cause, 40
centrality, 165
century, 89, 270, 276
chain, 33
challenge, 2, 31, 44, 90, 140, 241, 258, 260
change, 6, 13, 39, 46, 47, 50, 52, 60–63, 83, 86, 110, 112, 116, 142, 145, 151, 182,

192, 204, 221, 234, 255,
257, 267, 269, 278
character, 7
charge, 104, 241
checking, 129–131
Chen, 253
child, 3, 252
childhood, 3, 5
churn, 95
citizenship, 276
city, 2, 89, 90
clarity, 42, 175, 212
classification, 66
classroom, 5, 111–113
cleaning, 12
climate, 83, 142, 257, 265, 267, 269
clustering, 66
co, 201
code, 12
coding, 276
cohesion, 89, 90
cohort, 253
collaboration, 9, 10, 12, 25–27, 33,
41, 45, 48, 62–64, 73, 76,
88, 108, 116, 119, 139,
140, 142, 151, 165, 169,
175, 185, 200, 203, 218,
223, 224, 226, 231,
236–239, 254, 256, 257,
263, 267, 269, 276, 277
collaborative, 10, 29, 47, 63, 113,
121–124, 135, 192, 193,
201, 228, 229, 237, 238,
256
collection, 10, 42, 139, 166, 169,
220, 239
color, 212
combat, 41, 63, 181, 240, 245
combination, 126

commerce, 121
commitment, 7, 22, 43, 44, 46, 51,
64, 118, 169, 177, 182,
194, 196, 200, 202, 206,
221, 236, 255, 257, 269,
270, 275, 279
communication, 43, 116, 165, 212,
213, 227, 246, 256
community, 6, 7, 9, 12, 13, 47, 63,
88, 90, 116, 138, 142, 177,
186, 192–194, 197, 203,
204, 238, 248, 254, 257,
261, 263, 269, 276, 277
company, 33, 164, 182, 202, 234,
240, 256, 257
competency, 246
competition, 4
complexity, 91, 127, 145
compliance, 91, 93, 175, 211, 241,
243, 273
component, 57, 67, 130, 231, 263
computer, 1, 2, 8, 19, 37, 224
computing, 32, 197, 211, 265
concept, 2, 4, 22, 63, 112, 113, 165,
211, 214
concern, 41, 166, 169
conclusion, 10, 22, 29, 32, 39, 59, 64,
67, 70, 73, 75, 77, 83, 96,
105, 108, 124, 128, 136,
151, 157, 160, 177, 185,
188, 197, 200, 204, 207,
213, 216, 218, 226, 241,
243, 255, 260, 267, 270
confidence, 201, 276
confusion, 112
congestion, 2, 80, 81, 83, 90, 256
connectivity, 213
consent, 29, 43, 47, 77, 166, 175,
219, 220

Index

consequentialism, 57
conservation, 83, 142–144
consideration, 16, 220, 269
construct, 63, 111, 156
constructivism, 63
consulting, 220
consumer, 125, 240
consumption, 83, 85, 86, 213
contact, 139
containment, 246
content, 29, 51, 105, 121–124, 127–129, 135, 136, 153
contest, 2
context, 22, 108, 147, 197, 210, 219
continuation, 274
control, 91
convergence, 13–16, 224, 236
conversion, 124
coordination, 83, 145
core, 14, 19, 34, 37, 52, 55, 96, 105, 195, 200, 221, 244
cornerstone, 25, 30, 158, 180, 224, 254
corruption, 244
cosine, 122, 210
cost, 193
creation, 34, 113, 127, 128, 135, 153
creativity, 5, 127, 129, 180, 189, 191, 192, 199, 236, 256, 276
credibility, 48, 180
credit, 29, 93, 99
crime, 86, 88, 178, 220, 240
crisis, 147
criticism, 43, 217
crossing, 99
crossover, 99
cultivation, 192
culture, 41, 46, 49, 86, 116, 118, 119, 155, 164, 172, 177, 179, 182, 185, 193, 202, 207, 215, 234–236, 243, 245, 249, 269, 272, 276, 277
curation, 124
curiosity, 1, 3, 6, 7, 10, 13, 206, 252, 255
curricula, 63, 200, 247, 267
curriculum, 112, 115, 184, 200–203, 269
customer, 5, 13, 29, 33, 46, 93–96, 105, 153, 211
cutting, 3, 26, 257
cyber, 169, 172
cycle, 46, 140

dashboard, 115
data, 1–16, 18, 19, 22, 24, 25, 27–52, 54, 55, 57–67, 70–96, 99, 101–105, 108, 110–119, 122–131, 134–153, 155–160, 164–172, 174–182, 184–188, 192–197, 199–207, 209–229, 231–234, 236–258, 261, 263, 265–273, 275–279
dataset, 2, 71, 76
day, 99, 124
decade, 76, 180
decision, 4, 7, 13, 24, 27–29, 32, 34–37, 41, 46, 47, 49, 52, 54, 56, 57, 60, 63, 78, 86, 90, 114, 116, 128, 145, 151–153, 164, 166, 167, 175, 177, 180, 182, 197, 210, 213, 215, 219, 221, 224, 238, 239, 241, 243, 244, 249, 257, 276

dedication, 257, 279
defeat, 255
defense, 245
definition, 83
degree, 2, 3, 7
delivery, 70, 73–75, 211
demand, 16, 83, 84, 89, 184
demographic, 29, 51, 95, 135, 180, 240
density, 81
deontology, 57
depletion, 142
deployment, 147, 178
descent, 22
design, 78, 212, 234, 239
desire, 3
destination, 255
detection, 26, 29, 71, 91–93
deterioration, 278
determinant, 270
determination, 5
development, 2, 6–8, 21, 22, 25, 27, 46, 51, 63, 68, 76, 83, 108, 115, 118, 138, 186, 192, 195, 200–202, 253, 254, 256, 269
deviation, 65
diabetes, 66, 76, 138
diagnosis, 66
diagnostic, 70, 72, 73
dialogue, 175
difference, 50, 279
difficulty, 12
dignity, 177
disability, 162
disadvantage, 140
disaster, 145–148, 182, 278
discipline, 78, 200
discourse, 42, 129
discovery, 9, 10, 124, 265
discrimination, 51, 240, 256
discussion, 277
disease, 68, 70, 203, 278
disruption, 40
dissemination, 42
distribution, 84
district, 116
diversity, 49, 64, 76, 127, 180–182, 189, 192, 194, 200–202, 207, 210, 217, 277
divide, 204, 266
domain, 8, 37, 93, 224
doubt, 41, 253
driving, 5, 29, 47, 54, 86, 123, 145, 160, 180, 200, 201, 233, 236, 278
drug, 265
dynamic, 72, 145, 186

e, 121
earning, 253
ease, 12, 99
economy, 34, 99, 102
edge, 3, 26, 159, 257
education, 1, 3, 4, 6, 7, 10, 41, 50–52, 105, 106, 108, 109, 111, 113, 114, 116, 117, 119, 140, 182, 184–186, 192, 194, 200, 202, 203, 246, 247, 249, 252, 253, 267, 269, 277, 278
effect, 49, 204
effectiveness, 38, 51, 52, 54, 60, 88, 95, 108, 124, 138, 148, 151, 202, 203, 212, 227, 236, 243
efficiency, 36, 39, 46, 54, 83–86, 105, 115, 145, 195,

213–215, 252, 257
effort, 27, 228, 263, 277
election, 220
emergence, 27, 221
emergency, 33, 86, 88
Emily Chen, 26
empathy, 108
emphasis, 2, 7, 196, 213
employee, 155–157, 164, 182
employment, 51, 140
empowerment, 64, 119, 140–142, 192
encompass, 212
encounter, 186
encouragement, 7, 186, 277, 279
endeavor, 118, 169, 172, 179, 246, 255, 277
energy, 83–86, 213
enforcement, 43, 88, 210, 256
engagement, 9, 29, 33, 43, 88, 108, 111, 113, 116, 121, 123, 124, 128, 135, 145, 153, 164, 203, 233, 248
engineer, 1
enhancement, 247
enrollment, 202
entertainment, 127, 134–136
enthusiasm, 9, 12, 254
entity, 272
entry, 193
environment, 1, 3, 6, 7, 49, 64, 96, 111, 114, 117, 155, 157, 162, 188, 192, 194, 234, 236, 253, 256, 258, 260, 263, 272, 276
equality, 148
equation, 34, 40, 49–51, 60, 88, 95, 102, 104, 108, 127, 128, 135, 137, 146, 147, 150, 158, 165, 177, 186, 193, 195, 203, 209, 215, 217, 243, 265, 266, 273
equity, 50–52, 145, 180, 191, 193, 241
era, 39, 60, 70, 75, 148, 218, 224, 243
error, 219, 245, 255
essence, 34
establishment, 77, 200, 215, 243, 256
ethic, 1, 5
ethnicity, 162
ethos, 204
event, 246
evidence, 6
evolution, 27, 39, 180, 200, 252
example, 5, 29, 33, 43, 50, 51, 63–66, 76, 93, 95, 99, 112, 113, 115, 122–124, 128, 138, 146, 147, 164, 165, 197, 200, 202, 203, 210–212, 215–217, 238, 240, 276
excellence, 3, 25, 37, 49, 200, 206
excitement, 10
exclusion, 76
expansion, 30, 32
expense, 178, 257
experience, 2, 5, 9, 11, 13, 33, 93–96, 105, 113, 121, 136, 201, 202, 253, 254, 257
experiment, 13
experimentation, 10, 276
expertise, 7, 12, 27, 37, 41, 45, 215, 224, 226, 228, 229, 236, 238, 254, 256, 257, 279
explanation, 215
exploration, 6, 10, 22, 195

exposure, 6, 124
extraction, 213

face, 35, 42, 78, 91, 92, 94, 112, 122, 152, 158, 212, 227, 234, 241, 242, 244, 258, 262, 272, 275
fact, 129–131
factor, 34, 193
failure, 128, 254, 255, 257
fairness, 24, 43, 57, 63, 124, 178, 218, 219, 221, 239, 241, 256, 266
family, 1, 71
fascination, 3, 5
father, 1, 6
fatigue, 126
Fatima, 1–13, 21, 22, 24–27, 29, 33, 34, 37, 40–51, 62–64, 81–83, 146, 164, 195–197, 199–207, 252–259, 268–270, 278, 279
Fatima Wang, 1, 10, 16, 20, 27, 39, 41, 44, 49, 50, 54, 62, 72, 75, 180, 189, 199, 204, 241, 252, 255, 258, 263, 265, 267, 272, 274, 275, 279
Fatima Wang's, 3, 5, 7, 10, 13, 16, 18, 22, 25, 27, 29–36, 44, 47, 50, 52, 64, 70, 73, 76, 77, 80, 81, 83, 84, 86, 145, 148, 166, 188, 192, 195, 197, 200, 202, 204, 206, 234, 249, 252, 255, 257, 260, 267, 270, 277
fear, 39, 40, 112
feature, 122, 123

feed, 123
feedback, 13, 46, 95, 156, 157, 211, 254
fiction, 6, 13
field, 3, 5–7, 9, 10, 18, 22, 25, 27, 29, 32, 36, 37, 39, 41, 47–51, 54, 57, 59, 64, 70, 73, 76–78, 86, 110, 117, 129, 136, 175, 177, 179, 180, 182, 186, 188, 192, 194, 195, 197, 200, 202, 204, 205, 207, 226, 252–255, 257, 261, 263, 267, 277, 279
figure, 47, 197, 255, 267
filter, 124
filtering, 29, 121–124, 135
finance, 10, 29, 34, 63, 91, 195, 216, 278
finding, 3, 186
firm, 5, 158, 220
fit, 164
flag, 29
flow, 36, 81, 82
focus, 93, 96, 137, 216, 263
following, 42, 44, 46, 47, 49–51, 65, 82, 217, 218, 220, 223, 245, 266
food, 63, 182, 254, 267
footnote, 272
force, 5, 57, 62, 96, 127, 252
forecast, 33, 43, 50, 84, 108, 116, 164, 165, 210, 216, 220, 278
forecasting, 146
forefront, 7, 182, 221, 266
form, 10, 108
formula, 164
formulation, 196

Index

foster, 46, 52, 88, 90, 102, 116, 117, 140, 145, 179, 186, 220, 234, 235, 270, 277
foundation, 3, 5, 10, 58, 63, 68, 167, 184, 202, 244, 270
frame, 40
framework, 7, 42, 44, 83, 91, 113, 158, 209, 210, 212, 227, 266, 270
fraud, 26, 29, 91–93
frequency, 82, 93
fun, 276
function, 4, 22, 34, 203, 211
funding, 48, 49, 256
future, 1, 6, 7, 10, 13, 18, 27, 32, 34, 37, 39, 44, 49, 50, 52, 54, 57, 59, 61, 62, 64, 69, 72, 80, 83, 86, 90, 93, 99, 104, 105, 108, 110, 114, 124, 128, 129, 135, 136, 142, 145, 148, 150, 151, 159, 165, 166, 169, 175, 177, 180, 186, 188, 192–195, 197, 199–202, 204, 206, 209, 213, 216, 218, 223, 229, 234, 246, 249, 252–255, 260, 265, 267, 270, 272, 275–279

gain, 156, 164, 201, 202, 212
gap, 9, 32, 193, 201
gender, 162, 217, 240
generation, 22, 25, 44, 49, 52, 62–64, 185, 187, 192, 194, 195, 197, 200, 204, 207, 215, 218, 267, 269, 270, 275, 277, 279
genome, 68
genomic, 66, 76
genre, 122
goal, 19, 192
good, 27, 57, 59–62, 64, 197, 202, 204, 207, 221, 231, 238, 249, 253, 255, 265, 269, 278, 279
governance, 31, 34, 148, 211, 229, 238, 241–243, 269
government, 145
graduate, 253
graduation, 2
gratitude, 279
groundbreaking, 3, 5, 8, 10, 16, 25, 30, 47, 84, 180, 197, 202, 205, 224, 236, 270, 275, 279
groundwork, 1, 7, 10, 13, 197, 253
group, 24, 113, 204
growth, 32, 34, 37, 102, 140, 159, 169, 180, 184, 186, 218, 249, 252–255, 257, 261
guidance, 186, 192, 201, 253, 261, 277
guide, 3, 37, 44, 78, 115, 167, 175, 197, 234, 239, 241, 259, 265
gunfire, 88

hackathon, 254
hallmark, 9
hand, 6, 40, 83, 99, 162, 186
handling, 11, 16
harm, 44, 219
harnessing, 39, 50, 57, 62, 73, 90, 110, 114, 116, 117, 136, 140, 145, 151, 197, 204, 226, 233, 249, 265
head, 41, 179

health, 33, 43, 49, 50, 52, 63, 68, 72, 73, 137–140, 145, 156, 182, 203, 212, 219, 269, 278
healthcare, 2, 3, 10, 26, 33, 36, 41, 43, 45, 49, 63, 65, 67, 70, 73–75, 137, 139, 147, 195, 210, 213, 216, 238, 254, 278
heart, 8, 22
hierarchy, 151
highlight, 30, 57, 112, 199, 205, 216, 220, 237, 246, 269, 276
hiring, 159, 165, 181, 182, 210, 240, 266
history, 95, 123, 135, 153, 278
home, 1
homelessness, 228, 238
homogenization, 127
honor, 199, 205, 207, 270, 275, 277
hope, 265, 267, 275
hospital, 36, 41, 50, 210
hour, 156
household, 6, 252
housing, 51, 204
Houston, 116
humanity, 265, 267
hurdle, 12
hypothesis, 255

idea, 105, 257, 278
identification, 43, 138, 172
identity, 186, 253
impact, 6, 13, 14, 34, 36, 37, 47, 51, 52, 57, 59, 60, 63, 64, 75, 78, 85, 88, 91, 101, 108, 112, 113, 125, 131, 146, 147, 150, 195, 197, 199, 200, 202–204, 206, 221, 226, 229, 233, 236–238, 245, 253, 255–257, 267, 269, 278
imperative, 57, 59, 77, 96, 119, 145, 166, 169, 177, 182, 186, 189, 194, 241, 243, 252
implementation, 31, 40, 46, 51, 52, 68, 74, 81, 87, 93, 97, 99, 106, 108, 109, 113, 114, 116, 148, 170, 175, 196, 239, 241, 242, 271
importance, 6–9, 12, 21, 24, 25, 27, 41–43, 45, 47, 49, 57, 64, 82, 85, 86, 90, 93, 96, 102, 107, 145, 160, 164, 166, 175, 176, 180, 184, 189, 199–201, 205, 217, 239, 242, 245, 246, 253–258, 262, 263, 270
improvement, 16, 25, 32, 89, 93, 102, 116, 117, 156
inadequacy, 253
incident, 220, 246
inclusion, 76, 99–102, 194, 277
inclusivity, 64, 124, 136, 189, 190, 192, 265, 269
income, 99, 138, 140
incorporation, 43
increase, 82, 197, 257, 265
individual, 27, 51, 59, 63, 67, 68, 72, 105, 112, 117, 122, 139, 153, 172, 175, 196, 199, 205, 214, 221, 255, 267, 269
industry, 9, 12, 34, 44, 45, 49, 64, 65, 75, 93, 104, 128, 134, 159, 160, 189–192, 200–202, 204, 211, 263, 269, 276, 277

Index

inequality, 204
infection, 147, 212
inference, 195
influence, 3, 5–7, 31, 48, 68, 137, 196, 204, 205, 239
influx, 213
information, 10, 35, 60, 90, 95, 123, 129, 139, 151, 169, 172, 181, 184, 212, 213, 220, 244, 246, 249, 265, 278
infrastructure, 78–80, 83, 89, 99, 272
initiative, 33, 202, 203, 228, 238, 269
innovation, 2, 16, 18, 30, 32, 34, 37, 39, 41, 42, 44, 46, 48, 49, 57, 86, 112, 158, 160, 177–180, 182, 184, 186, 188, 189, 191–193, 196, 200–202, 206, 207, 218, 221, 223, 226, 227, 229, 231, 233–236, 243, 247, 249, 255–258, 265, 267, 269, 272–277
innovator, 1, 3, 41, 252, 254, 255, 257, 261
input, 211
insecurity, 182, 254, 267
insight, 153, 215
inspiration, 270, 277
instance, 1, 3, 29, 36, 43, 45, 63, 64, 76, 81, 84, 88, 95, 112, 115, 116, 122, 123, 127, 135, 138–140, 156, 164, 178, 195, 204, 210, 211, 213, 217, 219, 253, 256, 265, 269, 276, 278
institution, 93
instruction, 111–113, 115, 117

insurance, 99
integration, 8, 13, 34, 54, 56, 59, 65, 67, 70, 72, 75, 80, 83, 88, 93, 96, 102, 105, 110, 112, 127, 134, 139, 142, 144, 148, 153, 157–160, 166, 184, 195, 211, 216, 217, 224, 247, 273
integrity, 6, 32, 44, 204, 241, 269
intelligence, 83, 254, 257
interaction, 95, 123, 193
interconnectivity, 145
interest, 1, 5, 6, 135
interface, 11
internship, 9, 202
interoperability, 139
interplay, 44, 142, 155, 178
interpretability, 25, 210
interpretation, 218
intersection, 16, 32, 60, 86, 128, 136, 137, 267
interview, 181
introduction, 39
intuition, 129
inventory, 211
investigation, 93
investment, 86, 96, 99, 263
involvement, 256
iris, 172
ISD, 116
issue, 123, 127, 217, 239
item, 123, 124

jargon, 220
job, 156
journalism, 129–131
journey, 3, 5, 7, 9, 10, 13, 16, 25, 34, 41, 42, 44, 47, 105, 151, 169, 197, 199, 200, 202,

206, 221, 249, 252–257, 260, 265, 267, 270, 272, 275, 279
joy, 3
justice, 51, 148, 178, 220

key, 8, 14, 16, 35, 42, 46, 50, 58, 60, 69, 78, 91, 96, 150, 165, 182, 200, 209, 211, 213, 219, 241, 270, 274
knowledge, 8, 10, 11, 13, 62, 63, 68, 111, 113, 151, 186, 192, 193, 200, 224, 228, 229, 252, 253, 257, 277, 279

lab, 2
lack, 39, 112, 127, 139, 189, 217, 240
land, 78
landscape, 10, 13, 16, 18, 25, 29, 30, 32, 34, 41, 42, 44, 46, 47, 50, 58, 73, 75, 91, 93, 96, 99, 102, 105, 111, 117, 124, 127–129, 136, 151, 157, 158, 165, 166, 177, 186, 192, 204, 209, 216, 229, 231, 236, 243, 246, 260, 265, 270, 272, 275
language, 1, 11, 210
latency, 213
law, 43, 88, 210, 256
leader, 27, 47, 49, 254, 255, 257, 258
leadership, 182, 236
leap, 73
learning, 1–3, 5–7, 11, 12, 19–22, 26, 34, 42, 51, 52, 54, 55, 57, 60, 63, 67, 70, 71, 73, 75–77, 81, 83, 84, 93, 95, 105–108, 110–117, 119, 124, 138, 146, 147, 166, 179, 185, 192, 200, 202, 209, 213, 215, 219, 236, 249, 252–255, 257, 258, 265, 269, 276–278
legacy, 7, 27, 180, 188, 192, 197, 200, 202, 204, 206, 207, 252, 267, 270, 272, 274, 275
lens, 6, 63
lesson, 6, 113, 256, 257
level, 99, 203
leverage, 6, 37, 45, 86, 90, 94, 96, 99, 121, 128, 158, 159, 203, 218, 224, 231, 238, 270, 278
lie, 216, 267
life, 1, 3, 4, 6, 80, 83, 89, 90, 238, 247, 252, 258–260, 276
lifestyle, 68
light, 5, 13
likelihood, 52, 146, 210, 245
Linda Chen, 253
line, 245
linguistic, 210
link, 156
listener, 128
literacy, 63, 64, 112, 166, 184–186, 203, 238, 246–249, 267, 269, 272, 276
literature, 6
living, 89, 90, 272
location, 88, 93, 99, 124, 147
loop, 95
loss, 84, 142
love, 4, 6, 253
loyalty, 93

machine, 2, 3, 19–22, 26, 34, 42, 51,

Index

52, 55, 57, 60, 63, 67, 70, 71, 73, 75–77, 81, 83, 84, 93, 108, 138, 146, 147, 166, 200, 213, 215, 219, 253, 255, 265, 278
majority, 178
makeup, 68
making, 4, 13, 22, 24, 27–29, 32, 34–37, 41, 46, 47, 49, 51, 52, 54, 56, 57, 60, 63, 78, 86, 90, 112, 114, 116, 127, 128, 145, 151–153, 164, 166, 167, 175, 177, 180, 182, 197, 199, 210, 213, 215, 219, 221, 224, 232, 238, 239, 241, 243, 244, 246, 249, 257, 263, 267, 268, 276
male, 240, 253
mammogram, 71
mammography, 71
management, 29, 34, 36, 78–84, 89, 91–93, 114–116, 145, 147, 160, 211, 213, 241, 243, 256, 258
manipulation, 11
manner, 40, 139, 220, 267, 270, 276
manufacturing, 256
map, 68
mapping, 147
market, 165
marketing, 29, 33, 126, 153, 216
mastery, 112
math, 2
matter, 180, 258
maturity, 243
mean, 65
means, 207
measure, 60

mechanism, 130
media, 49, 81, 90, 95, 123, 127, 129, 135, 138, 211
medicine, 67–70, 72, 77
mentor, 186, 199
mentoring, 187
mentorship, 64, 182, 186–188, 192, 194, 200–202, 204, 253, 255, 269, 276, 277
method, 6, 108, 121, 172
metric, 88, 177, 266
milestone, 47
mind, 7, 217
mindset, 1, 254, 257
minor, 2
minority, 43, 178, 220, 240
mirror, 4
misinterpretation, 112
misrepresentation, 212
mission, 6
misuse, 31, 210
mobility, 82, 83
model, 5, 24, 26, 40, 43, 49–51, 63, 66, 71, 76, 81, 93, 103, 105, 107, 113, 139, 146, 211, 212, 239, 254, 255, 257
modeling, 26, 60, 116, 139, 148, 186, 195, 215, 265
moment, 9, 255
monitoring, 81, 88, 211
mood, 124
morale, 156
mother, 1, 6
motivation, 108, 275
movement, 41, 221–223, 231
moving, 99
music, 128
myriad, 244

narrative, 255
nature, 32, 137, 222
necessity, 34, 182, 189, 236, 270, 272
need, 16, 43, 44, 50, 78, 83, 86, 91, 113, 115, 124, 190, 194, 210, 213, 219, 220, 226, 253, 256, 269, 273, 275
negative, 39, 217, 254
neighborhood, 1
network, 26, 165, 212, 213, 254, 255, 261–263
networking, 186, 193, 261
non, 51, 145, 203, 215, 238
nonprofit, 182
norm, 197
novel, 26, 30, 76
number, 113, 202

objective, 22
obstacle, 255
off, 257
offering, 108, 201, 275
office, 234
on, 2, 3, 5–7, 9, 11, 16, 19, 26, 27, 29, 34, 36, 40–44, 46, 47, 49–52, 55, 59, 63, 64, 69, 76, 81, 83, 85, 90, 95, 96, 99, 101, 102, 111–113, 116, 121–124, 127, 135, 138, 139, 146, 147, 153, 155, 158, 159, 162, 165, 175, 179, 185, 186, 189, 192, 195–197, 199, 200, 202–204, 206, 210, 211, 213, 215–217, 226, 228, 238–240, 243–245, 254, 256, 257, 263, 265, 266, 269, 274–276, 278, 279

one, 6, 26, 47, 64, 105, 257
op, 201
openness, 41, 233
opinion, 90
opportunity, 102, 142, 254, 255
optimization, 4, 22, 80–83, 209
option, 272
organization, 34, 177, 182, 203, 204, 234, 243, 245
orientation, 162
other, 6, 40, 45, 64, 83, 99, 122, 162, 186, 269
output, 4, 156
outreach, 138, 182, 277
overload, 10, 112, 127
ownership, 108

pace, 105, 265
pandemic, 50, 139, 147, 212
paradigm, 57, 67, 99, 105, 116, 153
parallel, 211
part, 92, 121, 254
participation, 113, 276
partnering, 203
partnership, 63
passion, 1, 3–5, 7, 9–11
path, 13, 265, 267
pathway, 96, 144, 159
patient, 3, 33, 36, 41, 43, 45, 49, 65, 67, 68, 70–73, 75–77, 210, 214, 216, 278
peak, 36, 84
peer, 113, 187, 277
people, 89, 206, 246, 276
perception, 217
performance, 34, 51, 108, 112, 115, 116, 155, 164, 165
perseverance, 6, 199, 256
persistence, 257

Index

perspective, 253
phenomenon, 13, 37, 127
philanthropic, 202–204
philanthropy, 202, 204
phishing, 245
photosynthesis, 113
pilot, 46
pipeline, 64
pivot, 11, 46
place, 170
plan, 246
planning, 37, 78–80, 89, 158–160, 165
platform, 2, 112, 211, 238, 254, 256
point, 81, 218
policing, 43, 88, 178, 220, 240
policy, 51, 140, 142, 204, 238, 241, 243, 269
policymaking, 148–151
pool, 276
population, 217, 239, 277
portion, 202
position, 49
positioning, 47, 96
positive, 13, 52, 60, 62, 86, 155, 204, 217, 221, 234, 254, 257, 267, 269, 278
post, 95
potential, 16, 20, 27, 29, 30, 32–34, 38, 49, 53, 54, 59–62, 67–70, 73, 74, 76, 77, 87, 88, 90, 94, 99, 106, 108–110, 112, 114, 117, 127, 129, 135, 138–141, 143, 145, 146, 148, 151, 152, 156, 182, 194, 197, 202, 204, 210, 212, 217, 219, 220, 225–227, 229, 232, 233, 236, 239, 241, 245, 246, 249, 251, 255, 265, 270, 272, 277
poverty, 51, 140–142, 278
power, 3, 5, 10, 13, 16, 27, 29, 32, 34, 36–39, 50, 52, 57, 59, 62–64, 73, 76, 77, 83, 88, 96, 110, 114, 116, 117, 129, 136, 140, 145, 147, 151, 182, 186, 197, 200, 204, 207, 221, 227, 243, 252, 258, 266
practicality, 257
practice, 58, 112, 238
precision, 67, 95
precursor, 8
preparation, 215
preparedness, 145, 146, 148
preprocessing, 12
presence, 70
present, 83, 219
principle, 55, 108, 219, 254, 256
priority, 138
privacy, 6, 29, 31, 43, 47, 59, 62, 77, 88, 96, 126, 139, 166, 169–172, 175, 196, 210, 213, 214, 220, 233, 266, 269
probability, 4, 91
problem, 1, 4, 22, 39, 122, 184, 192, 209, 218, 254
procedure, 70
process, 12, 13, 22, 24, 48, 55, 60, 99, 113, 123, 127, 129, 130, 181, 203, 215, 228, 245, 254–256, 265
processing, 32, 195, 197, 211, 213, 214
product, 153, 192
production, 85, 127–129

productivity, 155–158, 164, 257
professional, 3, 4, 6, 7, 118, 186, 187, 197, 247, 254, 258, 260, 261
profile, 67, 246
profit, 51, 203
profitability, 46, 104
program, 2, 41, 192, 200, 202
programming, 1, 11, 12, 82, 211
progress, 44, 102, 116, 190, 191, 207, 212, 222, 239, 272
project, 2, 3, 11, 13, 26, 49, 192, 228, 254, 256, 257, 276
proliferation, 60, 239
prominence, 42
promise, 56, 197
promotion, 234
proponent, 256
protection, 172
prowess, 9
psychology, 212
public, 1, 43, 50, 52, 63, 82, 86–88, 90, 129, 139, 182, 212, 217, 231, 238, 269
purchasing, 5, 33, 153, 211
purpose, 204, 265, 267, 276
pursuit, 72, 177, 180, 252, 258
push, 10, 48, 200, 204, 231, 253

quality, 10, 12, 34, 35, 60, 67, 75, 80, 83, 89, 90, 93, 96, 110, 116, 139, 142, 153, 186, 203, 210, 211, 213, 233, 238, 243, 254
quantum, 32, 197, 265
quest, 13, 37, 191, 256
question, 64

race, 162
range, 16, 166, 172, 187, 200
rate, 88, 255
re, 43
reach, 88
reading, 6, 124
reality, 35, 40
realization, 10
realm, 10, 13, 16, 25, 29, 39, 44, 50, 65, 70, 114, 158, 178, 211, 252, 255, 267
reasoning, 267
recall, 95
receipt, 49
recognition, 29, 47–50, 172, 199, 200, 217, 219, 256
recommendation, 29, 122, 153
recommender, 95, 122–124, 135
recovery, 246
recruitment, 76, 159, 160, 164, 181, 240
reduce, 82, 83, 86, 178, 181, 245
reevaluation, 255
reflection, 63, 254, 255
regression, 5, 66, 108, 195, 215
regulation, 78
reinforcement, 19
relationship, 81, 108, 150, 210, 253, 263
release, 128
relevance, 142
reliability, 40
reliance, 41, 42, 129, 165, 244
reminder, 206, 255, 279
representation, 28, 122, 182, 201, 214, 253, 268
representative, 217, 219, 239
requirement, 59, 243
research, 2, 3, 6, 8, 16, 20, 21, 25–27, 40, 42–44, 47,

49–51, 65, 67, 69, 75–77, 81, 84–86, 197, 201, 219, 253, 255, 256, 269, 275, 279
researcher, 48
resilience, 6, 7, 108, 252, 254, 255
resistance, 110, 112, 116, 153, 256
resolve, 253
resource, 60, 80, 115, 116, 139, 142, 145, 147, 148, 160, 182, 236, 267
respect, 177, 253, 256
responding, 148
response, 37, 39, 46, 86, 88, 145, 147, 148, 182, 212, 246, 278
responsibility, 64, 176, 206, 220, 248, 253, 265–267, 269, 275, 279
responsiveness, 46
restaurant, 13
result, 127, 202
retailer, 240
retention, 29, 95, 123, 160, 164
review, 219
revolution, 3, 5, 32, 75, 77, 197, 207, 218, 221, 229, 236, 241, 243, 249–252, 258, 265, 267, 277, 278
revolutionization, 77
richness, 11
ridership, 82
right, 169
rise, 37, 39, 86, 91, 138, 169
risk, 29, 31, 34, 76, 91–93, 95, 104, 108, 110, 115, 116, 127, 128, 138, 203, 245
road, 256
robustness, 224

role, 2, 4, 7, 35, 50, 52, 80, 83, 86, 89, 92, 110, 111, 124, 127, 129, 139, 140, 142, 148, 169, 172, 185, 186, 192, 200, 209, 218, 234, 253, 267, 276, 277
root, 141, 142
routing, 88

s, 1–7, 9–13, 16, 18, 21, 22, 24–27, 29–36, 41–52, 60, 61, 63, 64, 68, 70, 71, 73, 76, 77, 80–86, 95, 123, 140, 145, 146, 148, 158, 164, 166, 182, 186, 188, 192, 195–197, 199–207, 216, 234, 243, 249, 252–257, 260, 267, 269, 270, 277, 278
safety, 43, 86–90, 238
satisfaction, 13, 29, 93, 95, 121, 124, 156, 164
saving, 50, 72, 203, 278
scalability, 25, 211
scandal, 220
scenario, 256
school, 1, 2, 113–116, 267
science, 1–3, 5–8, 10, 12, 13, 19, 25, 27, 30, 36–39, 41, 42, 44, 47–50, 54, 57–59, 63, 64, 113, 166, 167, 169, 175–182, 186, 188, 192, 194, 195, 197, 199–206, 213, 215, 218, 219, 221–227, 229, 231, 233, 236–238, 241, 252–258, 261, 263, 265–267, 269, 270, 272, 275–279
scientist, 7, 13, 253, 255

score, 93, 217
screening, 71
search, 135
section, 3, 5, 10, 13, 27, 30, 32, 34, 37, 42, 44, 47, 50, 52, 57, 60, 70, 73, 78, 96, 108, 114, 140, 155, 158, 166, 169, 178, 189, 192, 202, 204, 209, 221, 236, 239, 249, 255, 261, 265, 270, 275
sector, 33, 36, 41, 43, 63, 96, 108, 119, 210, 214, 227–229, 256
security, 16, 31, 32, 34, 86–88, 169–172, 175, 196, 213, 241, 244–246
segmentation, 29, 33
selection, 48, 181
self, 156, 253, 254, 260
sense, 3, 7, 9, 90, 186, 203, 253, 254, 263, 265, 269, 276, 277
sensitivity, 71
sensor, 16, 212
sentiment, 13, 90, 95, 138, 211, 217
series, 4, 255, 267, 276
service, 82, 211
set, 5, 10, 18, 32, 204, 211, 244, 256, 265, 270
setback, 254, 255
setting, 9, 258, 260
share, 6, 116, 121, 193, 231, 254, 256, 265, 276, 277, 279
sharing, 139, 193, 228, 229
shift, 37, 39, 57, 67, 99, 103, 105, 108, 112, 116, 153, 215, 216, 252, 269
signal, 81, 213

significance, 49, 60, 65, 124, 197, 204, 224, 236, 261, 273
similarity, 122, 210
simplicity, 212
size, 105
skepticism, 39–41
skill, 6, 63, 160, 165, 186, 276
skin, 219
snippet, 12
society, 6, 16, 21, 29, 30, 32, 39, 41, 44, 47, 49, 50, 52, 57, 59, 60, 62, 64, 77, 136, 169, 175, 177, 180, 185, 192, 199, 204, 206, 218, 226, 234, 240, 241, 268, 270
socio, 162
software, 193
solace, 3
solution, 22
solving, 1, 3, 4, 39, 184, 192, 218
source, 193
space, 22, 210
sparsity, 123
speaker, 276
specificity, 71
spectrum, 218
speech, 49
speed, 16, 197, 265
speedup, 265
spirit, 12, 22
spot, 273
spread, 50, 139, 147, 212
stage, 5
stakeholder, 145
standard, 18, 65, 202, 204
start, 122
startup, 9
statistician, 26
status, 137

Index

stay, 257
stem, 39, 166
step, 41, 249
stewardship, 243
stock, 211
storage, 211
store, 244
story, 199, 254, 267
storytelling, 11, 127
strategy, 32, 99, 182, 236, 245
streaming, 121, 127
structure, 241
student, 51, 105, 107–117, 119
study, 72, 76, 142, 219
subject, 115, 147
subsection, 65, 86, 91, 111, 117, 124, 127, 129, 142, 145, 148, 175, 195, 197, 224, 241, 244
subset, 55
success, 36, 39, 41, 45, 46, 54, 96, 108–110, 119, 126, 135, 153, 155, 157, 158, 160, 184, 227, 228, 236, 243, 260, 263, 270
suitability, 165
summarization, 8
summary, 5, 7, 52, 86, 202, 236
summer, 9, 202
superhero, 135
support, 3, 7, 52, 54, 100, 107, 113, 116, 138, 145, 184, 186–188, 192, 194, 201, 234, 236, 243, 277, 279
survey, 164
susceptibility, 68
sustainability, 83–86, 89, 90, 142, 144, 157, 278
syntax, 11

system, 22, 29, 36, 99, 102, 116, 122, 220, 256, 257, 266

Tableau, 211
tailor, 29, 33, 51, 107, 108, 111, 117, 127, 153
Tala, 102
tale, 220
talent, 1, 158–160, 164, 181, 188, 277
tapestry, 1, 8, 192
target, 43, 127, 178, 220, 273
targeting, 240, 269
task, 55
teacher, 1, 113
teaching, 64, 111, 112, 114, 117
team, 46, 50, 63, 71, 76, 165, 256, 257
teamwork, 256
tech, 9, 26, 49, 64, 159, 182, 189–192, 202, 277
technology, 1, 2, 13–16, 27, 34, 57, 59, 61, 64, 70, 93, 99, 101, 102, 108, 126, 147, 148, 153, 175, 178, 186, 189, 193, 197, 209, 211–213, 216, 223, 240, 246, 253, 256, 260, 275
term, 16, 96, 99, 157, 211
test, 70, 116
testament, 3, 16, 47, 196, 202, 252, 258
testing, 246, 266
text, 16, 213, 217
thank, 279
theft, 244
theme, 253, 256
theorem, 4
theory, 4, 5, 63, 145, 209, 212

thesis, 3
thinking, 2, 4, 6, 63, 184, 192, 267
thirst, 10
thought, 13, 47, 257, 279
threshold, 93
time, 2, 16, 26, 29, 34, 50, 72, 81, 83, 88, 93, 95, 112, 115, 124, 145, 148, 157, 195, 197, 213, 214, 216, 254, 258
timing, 81
today, 34, 63
tomorrow, 194, 277
tool, 27, 54, 60, 86, 108, 119, 215, 240, 253, 269, 278
toolkit, 4
topic, 112
torch, 207
Toronto, 1
tracking, 50, 147
trader, 99
trading, 96–99
traffic, 2, 80–83, 88, 90, 213, 256
trailblazer, 7
train, 82, 217, 239
training, 63, 112, 186, 209, 210, 219, 245, 248
trajectory, 5, 32, 213
transaction, 29, 34, 93, 95
transformation, 73, 75, 166
transparency, 29, 41, 47, 51, 57, 59, 63, 88, 116, 124, 129, 175–177, 218, 221, 231, 233, 256, 266
transportation, 80, 82, 83, 238
travel, 80
treatment, 43, 51, 65, 67–70, 138, 266, 278
tree, 24
trend, 34, 39, 236

triad, 244
trust, 31, 34, 40, 41, 47, 124, 139, 172, 175, 177, 196, 219, 239, 246
trustworthiness, 180
turnover, 164
tutoring, 115, 116

U.S., 220
uncertainty, 35, 145
underpinning, 37, 125
understanding, 2, 4, 6, 10, 22, 25, 39, 54, 58, 63, 68, 90, 99, 111, 113, 124, 125, 127, 135, 137, 140, 167, 169, 172, 191, 192, 202, 209, 210, 212, 215, 217, 236, 246, 254, 273, 275, 279
underutilization, 112
university, 2
updating, 246
urbanization, 80, 86, 89, 90
usability, 241
usage, 29, 41, 47, 82, 175, 196, 200, 253, 256, 266, 267
use, 7, 18, 29, 31, 39, 43, 46, 57, 63, 64, 72, 76–78, 85, 88, 93, 99, 108, 112, 113, 115–117, 122, 123, 127, 128, 135, 139, 143, 147, 172, 174, 175, 195, 210, 212, 218, 231, 256, 267, 269, 278
user, 1, 9, 11, 29, 121–124, 128, 135, 172, 257
utilitarianism, 178
utilization, 32

vaccination, 139, 212

validation, 266
validity, 40
value, 10, 27, 34, 46, 54, 211, 254, 256
variability, 140
variety, 6, 99, 181, 194
vector, 122, 210
video, 165
view, 6
viewer, 127, 153
viewing, 123, 127, 135, 153, 254, 255
vigilance, 169
virtue, 57
virus, 139, 147
visibility, 49, 240
vision, 44, 62–64, 86, 166, 206, 207, 234, 253, 255, 278
visualization, 11, 147, 200, 211–213
voice, 172, 269
volume, 123, 209
Vygotsky, 111

wait, 82
waste, 213
Watson, 211
wave, 277
way, 10, 12, 16, 25, 27, 30, 41, 57, 68, 77, 80, 86, 105, 108, 116, 136, 172, 188, 195, 204, 213, 270, 275
wealth, 182, 256
weather, 85
well, 62, 89, 155–157, 164, 219, 249, 252, 258, 260
whole, 16, 21, 29, 169
will, 13, 16, 21, 27, 34, 37, 40, 50, 52, 54, 62, 64, 72, 73, 80, 83, 86, 90, 93, 96, 99, 105, 107, 110, 112, 122, 127–129, 135, 140, 142, 148, 150, 153, 157, 165, 166, 172, 175, 180, 182, 185, 192, 197, 200, 202, 213–216, 218, 219, 221, 223, 226, 229, 234, 249, 260, 263, 265, 270
willingness, 13, 279
wisdom, 151
woman, 253
work, 1, 3, 5, 6, 16, 18, 25, 26, 29, 30, 33, 34, 41, 44, 47–51, 63, 75, 81, 102, 127, 146, 156, 164–166, 169, 195, 202, 204–207, 253, 254, 256–260, 267, 269, 270, 276, 277, 279
workforce, 16, 155, 157–160, 165, 201, 236
workplace, 164, 166, 182
world, 1–3, 5–7, 9, 10, 12–14, 16, 22, 27, 29, 36, 39, 42, 46, 47, 52, 54, 57, 64, 79, 83, 86, 87, 101, 108, 111, 125, 137, 140, 142, 145, 160, 168, 169, 172, 184, 185, 194, 200–203, 221, 236–239, 246, 249, 252, 254, 255, 257, 258, 267, 269, 270, 275, 276, 278
worldview, 6

yield, 150

Milton Keynes UK
Ingram Content Group UK Ltd.
UKHW020100271124
451585UK00012B/1334